D1121595

The Temper of Shakespeare's Thought

The Temper of Shakespeare's Thought

W. Gordon Zeeveld

Yale University Press, New Haven and London

1974

Published with assistance from the
Kingsley Trust Association Publication Fund
established by the Scroll and Key Society of Yale College.

Copyright © 1974 by Yale University.
All rights reserved. This book may not be
reproduced, in whole or in part, in any form
(except by reviewers for the public press),
without written permission from the publishers.
Library of Congress catalog card number: 74-75869
International standard book number: 0-300-01705-7 (cloth)

Designed by John O. C. McCrillis
and set in Baskerville type.
Printed in the United States of America by
The Colonial Press Inc., Clinton, Massachusetts.

Published in Great Britain, Europe, and Africa by
Yale University Press, Ltd., London.
Distributed in Latin America by Kaiman & Polon,
Inc., New York City; in Australasia and Southeast
Asia by John Wiley & Sons Australasia Pty. Ltd.,
Sydney; in India by UBS Publishers' Distributors Pvt.,
Ltd., Delhi; in Japan by John Weatherhill, Inc., Tokyo.

822,3
XD₂

TO MARGARET

with affection and no small gratitude

Mills College Library
Withdrawn

MILLS COLLEGE
LIBRARY

CONTENTS

ACKNOWLEDGMENTS

This book gathers together the thoughts of a decade in a common meeting place. Portions of it have been read at the Shakespeare Conference at the University of Miami, at a meeting of the Modern Language Association, in a lecture delivered at Merton College, Oxford University, at the Twelfth International Shakespeare Conference at Stratford-upon-Avon, and at the World Shakespeare Congress in Vancouver in 1971. Parts of the chapter on commonwealth appeared in an earlier version in the *Shakespeare Quarterly* and in *Modern Language Review*.

Grants from the Research Board at the University of Maryland have given that most valuable of all commodities, time; and I am particularly indebted to Professor James G. McManaway for his painstaking reading of the text before it was submitted to the publisher, and to Miss Nancy Paxton, Manuscript Editor, who groomed the horse for the track.

Deep Meadow   W.G.Z.
Woodbine, Maryland
June, 1973

PROLOGUE

I propose to speak in this book about the basic texture of Shakespeare's thought as stimulated by the intellectual milieu in which he lived. It has been the fashion in recent Shakespearian criticism to take a more abstract view of the plays, this in spite of the fact that of all the forms of art, the drama—and especially the popular drama—least lends itself to abstraction, and that Shakespeare frequently mirrored "the very body of the time his form and pressure." What follows is also predicated on what to some will seem like a far less tenable assumption: that Shakespeare's intellectual purview is ascertainable in a medium which is by its nature oblique. Every age, it is argued, has created its own Shakespeare consciously or unconsciously in its own image, and in so doing has found the image its forebears have created no longer acceptable. Restiveness is the condition of criticism and often its sole excuse; but what if we are merely looking through a mirror of our own? I do not therefore propose *the* meaning of the plays so much as *a* meaning consistent with Shakespeare's temperament and with that of the audience for which he wrote. In both of these respects, we are not without evidence. As for the man, his contemporaries confirm his gentleness and his facility; as for his intention, though it may continually elude us, we cannot ignore it or pretend that it isn't there.

Yet this negative view has had broad acceptance and in net result has isolated the plays in a literary limbo, as if Shakespeare had not lived in time (1564–1616) or space (London and Stratford). Indiscriminate pursuit of image patterns without regard either to their dramatic function or to their temporal and spacial context have not only disembodied the man but over-sophisticated his art. The essential condition of popular drama is an audience, and a popular audience would find slender subsistence in the orchid diet of an expanded image. Not that the

ensuing pages will neglect the continuing and various use
Shakespeare puts to the image in projecting the idea of the play.
In my opinion, he began to be aware of its effectiveness as a
theatrical device as early as *Richard II*; and throughout the
succeeding decade, he continued to explore and exploit its
capabilities on the stage. But modern imagistic criticism has little
to do with theatrical values. Use, in fact, is not at all what
Traversi has in mind when he asserts that in *The Tempest*
"symbolic function" finally administered a coup de grace to both
character and situation.[1] Art can hardly have accomplished such
a victory in the theatre, where the image pattern is no more than
a device. As symbol, it can only function there in directing us, just
as the characters in situ also direct us, to the core of meaning—
meaning in Shakespeare's time and Shakespeare's space.

Even among the historical critics, there has been a correlative
tendency to flatten Shakespeare's individuality as a dramatist. E.
M. W. Tillyard—to take a critic in high respect—after describing
the ideological background of the English history plays, comes to
the drab conclusion that Shakespeare held "normal" views. Such
a generalization is hardly a satisfying description of the man who
unknowingly wrote as much for all time as for his age.

Apparently, it does not satisfy Mr. Tillyard either, for the book
ends on a note of misgiving:

> There is no danger that very great poets such as Shakespeare
> and Milton should ever be found dull and undifferentiated.
> To deplore the discovery that they are more normal than was
> thought is to wish them to be freaks. Such a wish, it cannot
> be doubted, common opinion will firmly repudiate, rejoicing
> that our two foremost poets should show themselves, not
> more private, but more normal and at the same time more
> comprehensive than had once been supposed.[2]

The truth is that normality is meagre fare in the theatre. For to
be normal is to be undifferentiated, and to be undifferentiated is

---

1. *Shakespeare: The Last Phase* (1954), p. 193.
2. *Shakespeare's History Plays* (1946), p. 322.

to be dull, and *dull* is a damning word for a dramatist. An audience is a rigorous taskmaster, and we may be perfectly certain that the law of audience tolerance operated as inexorably in the Globe Theatre as in our own. Unlike Jonson and Webster, Shakespeare submitted to that law and wrote as the audience liked it.

> Like, or find fault; do as your pleasures are:
> Now good or bad, 'tis but the chance of war.
> [*Troilus and Cressida*, prol. 30–31]

There is a quiet confidence in this direct address to his audience as he lays himself open to their judgment. His pulse as theirs temperately kept time and made as healthful music, but he could not have achieved his immense theatrical success merely by keeping time in a healthy fashion along with the rest of mankind. We shall do Shakespeare something less than justice to allow that he was merely "comprehensive" or "normal" in Tillyard's meaning. There have been poets and playwrights who have written serenely oblivious of the world about them, and there have been critics, like Matthew Arnold, who thought that Shakespeare did so. But the popularity of the plays forbids such an impression of aloofness. Their very texture proclaims their historical relevance. It is inconceivable that Shakespeare should not have written with the same acute awareness of the issues of the day which his audience brought into the theatre with them. His living depended upon his proximity to their daily experience. We shall not anesthetize him from his environment, nor disengage him from the issues which aroused such heat and spilled so much printer's ink in contemporary London. As a Londoner, he shared the news of the day with his audience; as a playwright, he exploited it for the stage. Shakespeare enjoyed ribbing those poetasters who in a fine frenzy rolling gave to airy nothing a local habitation and a name; but in the practical business of writing for the stage, Shakespeare's poetic frenzy will be found again and again in the following pages to be firmly based in intellectual habitats instantly recognizable by his London public.

Yet not always by us. Words, phrases, freighted with meaning in the current language of controversy no longer wield the same power, the circumstances which called them into being having been forgotten. Place them in their immediate historical context and the contemporary dynamism of the plays is set in motion. If Shakespeare, in holding the mirror up to nature, expected his audience to see there the very age and body of the time, we who stand four centuries from that mirror might yet find it to our advantage to foreshorten the distance.

Basic in Shakespeare's representation of real life, because it was basic in his temperament, was a sense for order, tradition, decorum, stimulated in large part by the forces of disorder that were being felt in court, in parliament, in the courts of law, within the established church and outside it. Tillyard's postulate of an Elizabethan world picture of order and an orderly universe as characteristic of the age has been widely accepted. But was it Shakespeare's? The disruptive forces, though doubtless inevitable in a consciously flexible society, were persistent and palpable. Let us say with Tillyard that Shakespeare held contemporary ortho-dox views; more specifically, that he was a royalist and an Anglican, that he admitted to no power in England superior to law. But let us remember also that during the period when he was writing the plays, each of these principles was being subjected to overt attack: royalism by the increasingly evident encroachments of popular power in areas hitherto restricted to the royal prerogative, Anglicanism by the hard-core intransigence of the Catholic minority on the right and the highly vocal Puritan minority on the left, the rule of law by the rule of personal power. Consistently in Shakespeare's plays, these elements of change, no matter what the verbal context, are balanced by the value of historic tradition, an elemental gravitational pull, operating often with ironic crosscurrents against the centrifugal forces inherent in the rise of Puritanism, in the increasing presumptiveness of the common law and the common lawyers, in the new voices speaking for the people in the House of Commons, in the vistas of social utopias opening in the New World—all matters of common talk in Paul's Walk. No London audience, in daily contact with these forces in the late years of Elizabeth and the early years of James would have failed to recognize these tensions in Shakespeare's plays.

In asking, therefore, that the plays be returned once again to their historical perspective, I am doing so on the assumption that Shakespeare was neither immune to nor insulated from the same currents of opinion that occupied the minds and talents of his contemporaries, and that although as artist he did not make the plays vehicles of religious or political controversy, as dramatist he was sensitive to the fact that to his audience the stage of the Globe Theatre was a world of living men removed from reality on occasion by the thinnest of theatrical gauze.

It scarcely needs to be said that the aspects of Shakespeare's thought here dealt with are indicative, not definitive. My sole aim has been to trace the design in the fabric. For errors escaped, I borrow Borachio's words, "The poison of that lies in you to temper."

1

CEREMONY

The Effusion of English Blood

Shakespeare's deep-seated sense for tradition may well have determined his interest at the outset of his dramatic career in the civil wars of the fifteenth century. It was an interest that did not cease until he had dramatized the entire period of political disorder from its beginning in the dethronement of Richard II by Henry Bolingbroke in 1399 to its close in the accession of Henry Tudor in 1485, the event fixed in the minds of Elizabethans as terminating the wars and inaugurating the long period of domestic peace for which the new dynasty took credit. Not however without equivocation. It was an uncomfortable but none the less unavoidable fact that both Henrys had committed the greatest of political sins in taking the throne by force, and both had implicitly acknowledged their guilt in claiming it by parliamentary grant rather than by heredity. But Tudor historians astutely exonerated the seventh Henry from the stigma of usurpation by lauding his marriage to the heir of the opposing house. Henry IV was not so fortunate. To the historian Edward Hall, creator of the Tudor epic theme, whose narrative was silently copied by his successors, the fourth Henry was "the first author of this division"—he does not refer to him as usurper—the later Henry was restorer of unity. From his point of view, not the victory at Bosworth but the marriage to the daughter of Yorkist Edward IV was the climactic moment of the Tudor ascendancy:

> For as kyng henry the fourthe was the beginnyng and rote of the great discord and deuision: so was the godly matrimony, the final ende of all discencions, titles and debates.[1]

1. Edward Hall, *The Union of the Two Noble and Illustre Families of Lancaster and York* (1548), sig. Aii^v. Hereinafter referred to as *The Union*.

His title, *The Union of the Two Noble and Illustre Families of Lancaster and York*, epitomized the Tudor pattern he imposed on fifteenth-century history: its lesson, usurpation breeds civil dissensions, its theme, the long struggle and the loss of life on both sides—all brought to a glorious climax in the marriage of the first Tudor.

Writing in the triumphant reign of his son, Henry VIII, "the indubitate heir of both the said lineages," Hall could picture the future under his precocious heir, Prince Edward, as still all golden. It still seemed so when Elizabeth came to the throne. In her passage through London the day before her coronation, the first pageant presented for her inspection was entitled "The uniting of the two houses of Lancastre and Yorke," and she listened with particular attention as a child undertook to explain its "whole meaning": Like as long war between the two houses ended by the marriage of Henry VII to Elizabeth, so since that the queen's majesty's name was Elizabeth, first occasion of concord, "another Elizabeth might maintaine the same among her subiectes, so that vnitie was the ende whereat the whole deuise shotte, as the Queenes maiesties names moued the firste grounde." The child then broke into verse:

> Therfore as ciuill warre, and shede of blood did cease
> When these two houses were united into one
> So now that iarre shall stint, and quietnes encrease,
> We trust, O noble Queene, thou wilt be cause alone.[2]

But though that happy condition had by God's will continued into the declining years of the last Tudor, the dynastic myth of peace seemed less obviously perpetual. The children of Henry VIII had been childless. Was it wholly inconceivable that with Elizabeth's death another usurper might precipitate another period of bloodshed over a vacated throne? Elizabeth herself seemed to suggest that possibility when she asked publicly,

2. *The Quenes maiesties passage through the Citie of London to Westminster the daye before her coronacion* (1558), sig. Bii.

"Know ye not that I am Richard II?" By her loyal subjects, this question remained tactfully unanswered. But the tragic loss of blood which followed the deposition of Richard in that earlier time was sufficient cause for popular apprehensiveness in this, England's present and perhaps limited state of grace.

Shakespeare's audience would therefore have viewed the dramatization of the civil wars of the fifteenth century in the pattern laid down by Edward Hall as a warning, in an age of peace a not too remote and jarring reminder that English hands could again ruddy England's green and pleasant land. They would have understood why Shakespeare chose first to dramatize the moment of England's gravest internal weakness, the divided reigns of Henry VI and Edward IV, when the effects of civil war were most evident, and why he reanimated Hall's tragic implications with a special sensitivity. It was a conflict, as Hall knew from his own family history, "in maner unnaturall, for in it the sonne fought against the father, the brother against the brother, the nephew against the uncle, and the tenaunt agaynst his lord," [3] while the crown itself changed hands between consanguine Henry and Edward. Shakespeare projects Hall's observation dramatically as a tableau in which a son unknowingly kills his father, a father his son—the image of bloody deeds on both sides. The young Clifford's grief over the body of his father slain by the Duke of York is matched by Warwick's desperate cry that his "brother's blood the thirsty earth hath drunk."

> Then let the earth be drunken with the blood!
> I'll kill my horse, because I will not fly.
> Why stand we like soft-hearted women here,
> Wailing our losses, whiles the foe doth rage,
> And look upon, as if the tragedy
> Were play'd in jest by counterfeiting actors?
>
> [*3 Henry VI*, 2.3.15, 23–28] [4]

Shakespeare's audience, for whom these events were recent

3. Edward Hall, *The Union*, sig. Gg vii.
4. All references to *The Complete Works of Shakespeare*, ed. G. L. Kittredge, 1936.

history, would not have found their reenactment a theatrical jest.
And they are an index to the temper of the man who wrote them.
In the quick montage between stage and real life, these earliest of
Shakespeare's plays give continual surface evidence of his concern
over the possible recurrence of that vengeful carnage.

To Elizabethans, the reign of Richard of Gloucester epitomized
an age of blood. The editors of the 1563 edition of *A Mirror for
Magistrates* consigned him with Dives to the deep pit of hell.
Shakespeare furthers the legend, but his Richard is more than the
familiar story of the diabolical acts of a usurper, the portrait
which More's genius had etched on the popular mind; it is quite
as much a prelude to the happy completion of the Tudor design.
The self-conscious rhetoric of Richmond's closing speech comes as
a broad coda, recollective but also prospective, sweeping in major
chords from the dissonances of an era of bloodshed to the glorious
harmonies of peace under the benign rule of Elizabeth:

> England hath long been mad and scarr'd herself
> The brother blindly shed the brother's blood;
> The father rashly slaughtered his own son;
> The son, compell'd, been butcher to the sire.
> All this divided York and Lancaster,
> Divided in their dire division.
> O, now let Richmond and Elizabeth,
> The true succeeders of each royal house,
> By God's fair ordinance conjoin together!
> And let their heirs (God, if thy will be so)
> Enrich the time to come with smooth-fac'd peace,
> With smiling plenty, and fair prosperous days!
> Abate the edge of traitors, gracious Lord,
> That would reduce these bloody days again
> And make poor England weep in streams of blood!
> Let them not live to taste this land's increase
> That would with treason wound this fair land's peace!
> Now civil wounds are stopp'd, peace lives again:
> That she may long live here, God say amen!

$$[5.5.23-41]$$

Yet now, in the reign of a later Elizabeth, the union of the two royal houses which had hitherto seemed so providential was approaching its term. Whether England would once again weep in streams of blood depended upon the slender longevity of an aging queen. Until the event of her death, which settled the crown on James, the young Henry's closing benediction would remain a pious hope.

It is this nagging uncertainty that occupied Shakespeare's mind after he had written *Richard III*. Had he chosen to forego English history there, his audience would have felt no sense of incompleteness in theme or subject matter. In fact, with the exception of *King John*, written outside the pattern set by Hall, his dramatic energy was seemingly diverted to less serious occupations for two, perhaps three years. Even in this interim, however, the strength of the image of those years of blood continued to be reincarnated in more remote contexts. In 1595, once again two families, "both alike in dignity," fight out their petty and ridiculous quarrels in the streets of Verona, and the flower of their age become the victims of their folly. Would Shakespeare's audience in 1595 have failed to identify the "two noble and illustre houses of Lancaster and York" with Capulet and Montague, whose "civil blood made civil hands unclean"? "Never"—well, hardly ever—"was a story of more woe. / Than this of Juliet and her Romeo." For unlike *The Tragedy of Richard III*, prelude to a "union of the one lineage and the other," *Romeo and Juliet* ends in the death of the principals, "poor sacrifices of our enmity" and the cutting off of family hopes, as the contrite Capulet says—echoing the familiar melody with contrapuntal grace. Even more lightly, perhaps in that same year, Shakespeare restates the theme of family disruption when he sets about the celebration of a wedding. What more appropriate contrast to the perfect union of Theseus and Hippolyta than the tragical mirth of Pyramus and Thisbe parted by the wall that parted their fathers? Though the events at Niny's tomb were hardly such as would unduly discomfit wedding guests disposed to mirth, they were nevertheless fleeting reminders of partition by civil war and its cost in bloodshed.

Nor was the theme played out when in 1596 he turned to the

beginning of the conflict, Henry IV's deposition of his legitimate prince. Sometimes in *Richard II* it is renewed with great dramatic intensity, as when the Duchess of Gloucester appears somewhat out of context to remind us of the double dealing among the sons of Edward III which brought about the death of her husband, "one of the seven vials full of Edward's sacred blood" (*Richard II*, 1.2.11–19), and again when the Bishop of Carlisle brings down the heavy censorship of the church against the shedding of blood that will follow the desecration of the crown:

> And if you crown him, let me prophesy,
> The blood of English shall manure the ground
> And future ages groan for this foul act:
> Peace shall go sleep with Turks and infidels,
> And in this seat of peace tumultuous wars
> Shall kin with kin and kind with kind confound;
> Disorder, horror, fear, and mutiny
> Shall here inhabit, and this land be call'd
> The field of Golgotha and dead men's skulls.
> O, if you raise this house against this house
> It will the wofullest division prove
> That ever fell upon this cursed earth.
> Prevent it, resist it, let it not be so,
> Lest child, child's children cry against you woe.
>
> [4.1.136–49]

Such moments were ovbious reminders of the civil war which preceded the Tudor peace. In *1 Henry IV*, however, Shakespeare not only universalizes the theme but carries it to its highest degree of sophistication. For in this play, unlike the *Henry VI–Richard III* sequence where the chronicle of blood is merely sequential and cumulative, the tragedy in the shedding of English blood is the very nub upon which the entire action converges, the trick of it suddenly revealed in a single potent image at its organic center. By contrast with the discursive, amorphous Henry VI plays, Shakespeare here invested it with a new structural unity.

Written for a single afternoon's entertainment in the theatre,

Henry IV is a dramatic integer, simple and symmetrical.[5] Hal is the pivot of the action, and the dramatic statement implied in that action is reinforced by the complementary and opposing comment of Hotspur on the one hand and Falstaff on the other. These are the three chief characters in the play, the foci of attention. The spring and direction of the action is toward a vindication of the honor of Hal, which must be made to exceed that of Hotspur in spite of his habitual association with Falstaff, who openly belies honor in its formal sense and expressly will have none of it. The end result is a clarification of a wholly new kind of honor as exemplified in Hal. This, I take it, is the essential pattern of *Part 1*, a pattern in which history has been boldly subordinated to artistic convenience.

Hotspur's unrealistic conception of honor according to the code book has never caused the critics any trouble. He is a character drawn on simple lines. Convinced of the rightness of his brother-in-law's claim to the throne by his uncle, who sees an opportunity in Hotspur's enthusiasms over a wronged man's cause to serve his own ends, he is an appealing dramatic figure, and his sacrifice in the end because of his uncle's dishonesty and cowardice is capable of inspiring a high degree of human sympathy. But his limitations are clear. It becomes apparent as the action unfolds that his espousal of his brother-in-law's right has become ancillary to his ambition for personal glory, and that Hal, by overcoming him in personal combat at Shrewsbury, has deprived him of all. For others, except as they contribute to his personal ambition, he has little thought. His honesty of conduct is his most winning trait, and he recognizes forthright bravery and loyalty of the clannish sort in his followers, to whom he serves as an inspiring example— "the king of honor," in Douglas's view. But in pursuing his personal ends, he has no more thought for the value of other men's lives than he has for his own. He will ride pell-mell against

5. The play continued to be printed as *The History of Henry IV* until it was necessary to distinguish it from the second part in the First Folio. An entry in the *Stationers' Register*, 1603, is the earliest reference to "the first parte." E. K. Chambers, *William Shakespeare*, 2 vols. (1950) 1 : 376.

increasingly chilly and hopeless odds, but he never gives a thought
to the men, the common soldiers, whose personal loyalty will lead
them without glory—"honor" in Hotspur's vocabulary—to their
deaths.

In this respect, Hal easily and triumphantly exceeds Hotspur.
In the impending engagement, he proposes single combat with his
glittering adversary—precisely what Hotspur would have wel-
comed with a soldier's embrace had he known of it—not to crop
all the budding honors on Hotspur's crest, though this was
essential to his victory, but "to save the blood on either side."
Hal's part in the suppression of rebellion is an overt restatement
of the theme of the earlier historical sequence. But his offer before
the battle is more. Beyond the conventional Tudor theme
Shakespeare here makes explicit a broader ideal that underlay it.
Hal's honor is not plucked from the pale-faced moon or the
bottom of the deep. It is not to be won at the expense of life, least
of all of that brittle, brilliant life for which presently two paces of
the vilest earth will be room enough. It is beyond all else an
awareness that a definition of honor might more properly be
modest and earthbound, and above all, humane.

Within this larger concept of honor, Falstaff plays a more
complicated and more sophisticated role, a role which Hal finds it
impossible not to tolerate. Like all great comedians, Falstaff
makes himself the type of human frailty, simultaneously actor and
detached observer on the field of battle, where his opposite,
Hotspur, is so deeply drawn into the vortex of his own idealism
that death itself is a virtue, to be embraced rather than avoided.
"Doomsday is near; die all, die merrily," is Hotspur's response to
the news of the perilously reduced ranks with which he must face
the King's forces. It is a recourse to desperation to which a brave
soldier can make a soldier's answer:

> Talk not of dying; I am out of fear
> Of death or death's hand for this one-half year.
>
> [4.1.135–36]

Falstaff, on the other hand, coming upon the dead body of an equally brave soldier, Sir Walter Blunt, shows marked distaste for such grinning honor. "Give me life," he insists reasonably enough, "which if I can save, so; if not, honor comes unlooked for, and there's an end" (5.3.162–65). Like Hal (and how unlike Hotspur!) he would save blood on the battlefield, albeit his own, a judgment which Hal later confirms: "I could have better spar'd a better man." As for the foot soldiers whom he has pressed into service, they are expendable, as he confides to Hal; and Hal gives no sign of shock or moral outrage at Falstaff's bland opinion of such pitiful rascals: "Tut, tut; good enough to toss; food for powder, food for powder; they'll fill a pit as well as better: tush, man, mortal men, mortal men" (4.2.71–74).

Obviously, it would be beside the point to argue callous indifference to the effusion of blood in either Hal or the man who would presently put his own life at such a high rate of exchange. The comedian depends wholly on the collaboration of his straight man to uphold his story. Earlier, Falstaff's "Dost thou hear me, Hal?" and Hal's pointed retort, "Ay, and mark thee too, Jack," have already established the comic rapport between these two. Now their knowing exchange confirms the jest, while at the same time it serves as dramatic counterpoint to Hotspur's display of bravery. And the reason that Hal is not outraged lies in his awareness that Falstaff from his solipsistic premise has arrived at the same conclusion as the indulgent prince. Both see war for the inhuman business that it is. When E. M. W. Tillyard, seeking to force the play into the frame of a morality, finds in Falstaff the figure of dishonor, he gravely misrepresents the sophisticated un-honor of the fictive coward. For Shakespeare has placed in the mouth of the old master of evasion the frankest, most honest statement in the play on the ceremonious tin soldiery of war: "Can honor set to a leg? . . . or an arm? . . . or take away the grief of a wound?" (5.1.128–44). Honor, in the sense in which Hotspur takes it, is air, and Falstaff with reason will have none of it. It is also the trifle of killing me some six or seven Scots at a breakfast with a "fie upon this quiet life! I want work," and Hal, with reason, will have none of that. Not for the moment, at least.

Presently, however, he will redeem time by exposing the deficiency of Falstaff's reasoning and the excess of Hotspur's mindless enthusiasm.

Meanwhile, Hotspur, no more than Falstaff, can be passed off with witticisms. If the extravagance of his personal loyalty is offset by Falstaff's protest at an early payment of his debt of death, his stoutness in defending his convictions is wholly admirable. Like his prototype, Mercutio, he will be the surprised and humiliated victim of the brawls of two noble families. Mercutio, like a meteor, burns out all too quickly. But in *Henry IV*, Shakespeare exercises the height of tactical skill by introducing Hotspur's tragic victimization at precisely the moment to reveal the limits of Falstaff's logic. Furthermore, he exhibits a new sense for the ironic potential in stage montage. Even as Falstaff's formal conclusion that honor is a mere escutcheon sounds in the ears of his audience, the voice of Hotspur's uncle, "O, no, my nephew must not know the liberal and kind offer of the King" (5.2.1-2) confirms the open and substantial perfidy which makes of Hotspur the unknowing exemplar of honor misdirected.[6]

In the larger strategy of the play, it becomes evident that Hal must publicly redeem his honor by exceeding both Falstaff and Hotspur on the field of battle. There, where Shakespeare brings all three characters on stage together for the first time, Hal's more dextrous swordplay will easily expose both the vacuity of Hot-

6. I do not note in any previous play such consistent use of the theatrical capabilities of scene on scene. Thus, there is irony in juxtaposing the king's postponement of his pilgrimage to Jerusalem and Falstaff's time-wasting opening line, "Now, Hal, what time of day is it, lad?" (1.1-2); in Blunt's "Let's away. / Advantage feeds him fat while men delay" and Falstaff's "Bardolph, am I not fall'n away vilely since this last action?" (3.2-3). The irony is reversed in Falstaff's, "Well, / To the latter end of a fray and the beginning of a feast / Fits a dull fighter and a keen guest" followed by Hotspur's tight-lipped announcement, "We'll fight with him tonight" (4.2-3).

Perhaps this new technique suggested itself in the course of developing Falstaff's comic role. However it may have occurred, it is significant that Professor Nevill Coghill, in a stage-sensitive analysis of Shakespeare's juxtaposition of scenes, finds his most suitable illustration in *Henry IV*. *Shakespeare's Professional Skills* (1964), pp. 61-77.

spur's honor and the limitations of Falstaff's facile dismissal of it. Against the background of these inadequacies, Hal takes his place at the dramatic center of the play. The time has come for him to satisfy his obligation to honor. That Shakespeare carefully postponed the due date of the meeting of all three principals until Shrewsbury is sufficiently obvious. That the debt of each to the concept of honor should in some way be called is also clear. But it is a demonstration of his extraordinary sense of form that the final correction of focus should not be made until the moment of Hal's victory, and that the stamp of humanity by which he defines honor should only then be fixed indelibly in a metaphor.

The defeated Hotspur feels the cold hand of death on his tongue. Time, that takes survey of all the world, must have a stop, and now he, too, like Falstaff's starveling soldiers, like Sir Walter Blunt, has become food for powder. He for whom a kingdom was too small a bound will now find room enough—a feat the oily rascal could not match—in two paces of its vilest earth. Falstaff's jesting but proleptic "food for powder" flicks into the mind as Hotspur's dying lips form the metaphor—"Food for . . ." which Hal completes by turning it trenchantly earthward—"for worms, brave Percy" (5.4.85–86)—thus in a phrase uniting in the common fate of death the foot soldier and the gentleman. The irrefutable logic of war has left both Hotspur's gallantry and Falstaff's soliloquy-debate curiously empty. How irrational Hotspur's attitude toward honor, how rational Falstaff's, yet how inadequate they both are when they are measured against the unprovable proposition of Hal's challenge to single combat, the humane offer "to save the blood on either side."

Henry IV thus gives new depth to the theme of the *Henry VI–Richard III* sequence. So long as senselessness of bloodletting was mainly presented as ancillary comment on a continuing action in the style of the chronicles, it offered little more than color to the accepted Tudor pattern of history as it mounted to a climax in the "fair conjunction" of the two noble families at the close of *Richard III*. Now, some two years later, the desultory chronological apparatus of the Henry VI plays, measured out by the two-hours' traffic of his stage, has given place to a new and adroit cohesiveness, uncompelled by historic convention. The simple declaration of the earlier plays is no longer enough. Hal's farewell to Hotspur gives perspective to his perilously comic farewell immediately thereafter to the fallen (though not dead) Falstaff; both are delicately poised in the young prince's consciousness that on the battlefield of Shrewsbury the blood of Englishmen of whatever party or rank is held dear; and the whole action is raised to a higher dimension—the wry whimsy that food for powder will in any event presently be food for worms. For this, *Henry IV* is only the opening statement which the kaleidoscope of Shakespeare's thought could turn at will to comic or tragic uses. How innocent it would sound when very shortly after he wrote *Much Ado About Nothing*:

> *Leonato.* How many gentlemen have you lost in this action?
> *Messenger.* But few of any sort, and none of name.
> *Leonato.* A victory is twice itself when the achiever brings home full numbers.
>
> [*Much Ado About Nothing*, 1.1.5–8]

How heavily weighted when presently Shakespeare evokes that "certain convocation of politic worms" which busied themselves in Hamlet's brain, distinguishing neither the emperor's diet nor the maggots who diet on the emperor: "Your fat king and your lean beggar is but variable service, two dishes, but to one table." Can it not be allowed that Hal and Leonato and Hamlet are in the same regions of Shakespeare's mind?—that, in another setting, he is really telling the same story of the same prince?

I have argued that *Henry IV* is a sophisticated summation of the theme of effusion of English blood which runs through the early English history plays; but at the same time, I should say that these tonalities in the first series are in the second noticeably broadened. Shakespeare's decision to return to the beginning of the dissension would in itself have necessitated a fresh start, if only because the bloodletting, by historical convention, did not begin until the choosing of roses in the Temple Garden, half a century after Richard was dethroned. Shakespeare's *Richard II* is in fact a play in which the field is won without a battle, and the same can be said for 2 *Henry IV*. In *Henry V*, "civil swords and native fire" are diverted to foreign wars. Before the walls of Harfleur, the shedding of English blood is averted by sheer bluff; at Agincourt, thanks to clever tactics, the bloodletting is largely on the French side.

Plainly, we must look deeper for Shakespeare's primary incentive in opening the chronicles of fifteenth-century history once again. The cause for the costly struggle, "the beginning and root of the great discord," as Hall saw it, was the dethronement of Richard as well as the shedding of royal blood. To Shakespeare, writing a half century later, that act was more than political. It represented a violation of ceremony, a subject to which Shakespeare's audience was highly sensitive. In the English church, ceremony had been a cause of contention since its codification under Henry VIII; it was still so under Elizabeth. But inevitably, reformation in the church beyond the establishment posed a threat to political stability, and to that greatest of all earthly ceremonies, the crown. This was the danger which made the hollow crown bereft of its attendant ceremonies a peculiarly evocative symbol in the entire series of plays from *Richard II* to *Henry V*.

It is a commonplace of criticism to regard the later history plays as a comment on the responsibilities of kingship; more particularly, that they represent Prince Hal's growth in responsibility from the wayward prince to the commander at Agincourt. While I should in no way disagree that responsibility of the prince is a fundamental concern in the plays of the second series, the idea of growth is unsupported by the text. The fact is, there is nothing in the action to substantiate the frequently enunciated view that Shakespeare was depicting the education of a prince.[7] The only education Hal gets is in the tavern. However incredible the story,

7. Note particularly M. M. Reese, *The Cease of Majesty* (1961), p. 292, whose statement to this effect is immediately followed by reference to the sudden conversion from prodigal prince to responsible king, popularized in the chronicles and the *Famous Victories of Henry V*. E. M. W. Tilyard, on the other hand, frankly faces the fact that in *Henry V* Shakespeare "jettisoned the character he had created," *Shakespeare's History Plays* (1946), p. 306.

Shakespeare was sticking to his text in the opening scene of *Henry V* where we hear that the young king has astounded his learned advisors by the sudden and unaccountable depth of his learning in all the kingly arts. Though we need not jump to the conclusion that Athena has sprung full grown from the forehead of an earthly Zeus, our first news of him comes from that paragon of self-esteem, Hotspur, who far too eagerly volunteers the information to the father of the wayward prince that his son is in the stews. (*Richard II*, 5.3.16). It is an early intimation of what the audience expected of him, as deduced from the slender account in the histories. What is particular about Shakespeare's dramatization of the prince—and we have the assurance from his first appearance on the stage—is that he is never without a consciousness of the responsibilities of kingship, nor what is more fundamental in Shakespeare's thought, the personal restriction of the ceremonies incident to and indeed indissociable from it. He has simply put ceremony aside until there is need of it. This outward indifference does not please his father, who sees in Hotspur the model of an ideal son, but it does give a pleasing and secret sense of anticipation to the audience. His concealment of his true character, we learn from his first soliloquy, is a conscious policy to dramatize a calculated reformation, which when it comes will come "in a flood, a heady currance scouring faults" (*Henry V*, 1.1.34–35). What has led his critics to accuse him of Machiavellianism is in matter of fact no more than an assurance to the audience that Hal values and always has valued the appurtenances of the kingly office, but that this awareness is concealed as long as he is prince, only to make more dramatic his payment in due course of the debt he never promised. To his confidant, Poins, he confesses, "Thus we play the fools with the time, and the spirits of the wise sit in the clouds and mock us" (*2 Henry IV*, 2.2.154–56). But meanwhile we can enjoy his frivolities, knowing that when the occasion arises, he will confound the world, and in Saint Paul's words, "walk circumspectly, not as fools, but as wise, redeeming time, because the days are evil" (Eph. 5 : 15–16; *1 Henry IV*, 1.2.241). Of his instructor in vice, Falstaff, he will ask the same reformation. Falstaff, too, is loath to pay before his day.

The Boar's Head is his stage, its habitués his audience. Yet though he too promises to purge, and leave sack, and live cleanly, as a nobleman should do, we have good cause to doubt his newly donned cloak of sanctity; and his success in evading the debt offers the proper dramatic contrast to Hal's solemn assumption of the ceremonies of kingly office. Hal's eventual acquiescence to the demands of ceremony will stand as the outward evidence of his reformation—and incidentally of his father's lost opinion (*1 Henry IV*, 5.4.48).

For Shakespeare's audience, as I have suggested, the observance of ceremony was no idle gesture. In the London of 1595, ceremony had become a word of extraordinary emotive power with verbal and conceptual values instantly resonant in the theatre. Referable to an immediate day-to-day context, it was also capable of eliciting responses as far back as Shakespeare could remember, as old as the memory of any of his audience. Bound up in it was an intuitive—almost congenital—acceptance of tradition, essential to an inward sense for order. But corrosive to these instinctive patterns were living voices, ever more strident, ever more menacing avowedly committed to its destruction. In this charged atmosphere, Richard Hooker was moved to write his defense of the Church of England, and Shakespeare, stimulated by the same respect for tradition, but perhaps more immediately by Hooker's defense, turned once more to the civil wars of the fifteenth century to find in Richard II a political image of ceremony violated. Like Hooker's *Of the Laws of Ecclesiastical Polity*, Shakespeare's second series of English history plays speaks to an auditory who had lived through the controversy centering in ceremony, the history of which is a necessary prelude to consideration of its importance in the plays themselves.

The Desecration of Tradition

Before the establishment of the English church, the emotional impact of *ceremony* was ecclesiastical, not political. More's Utopians found in it a purely religious value:

> They burn incense and other fragrant substances and also offer a great number of candles. They are not unaware that

these things add nothing to the divine nature, any more than do human prayers, but they like this harmless kind of worship. Men feel that, by these sweet smells and lights, as well as by other ceremonies, they somehow are uplifted and rise with livelier devotion to the worship of God.[8]

But after the Reformation, ceremony became above all an inducement to political order. To Elizabeth, it was a condition of rule. This semantic shift might be expected in the reign of a monarch among whose many virtues a deep religious feeling cannot be numbered. Her reaction to the candles at her coronation, "Away with those lights," should not be interpreted as a desire to do away with ceremonies. Well she knew the value of tradition. When the state assumed pastoral care in her father's time, ecclesiastical rites and ceremonies had automatically become a part of its responsibilities. An affair of state had become a state of affairs that would please neither the papists who would oppose any change nor the reformers who regarded ceremonies as emblematic vestiges of papalism and who would not be content with less than a clean sweep. The establishment of a middle way between these two extremes was a delicate though essential task, complicated by the fact that violation of the laws of a state church could be logically interpreted as treason.

It was apparent from the first that a successful formula for ceremony in the English church was bound to have political overtones. To Henry VIII in 1536, Cranmer sounded the pitch:

[Ceremonies] ought neither to be rejected nor despised, nor yet to be observed with this opinion, that they of themselves make men holy or that they remit sin . . . nor the laws and ceremonies of the church at their first making were ordained for that intent, but for a common commodity, and for a good order and quietness to be observed among your subjects.[9]

8. St. Thomas More, *Utopia, Complete Works of St. Thomas More*, vol. 4, eds. Edward Surtz, S. J., and J. H. Hexter (1964), p. 144.

9. Letter CLXXVII, *Miscellaneous Writings and Letters of Thomas Cranmer* (Parker Society, 1846), pp. 326–27; John Strype's *Cranmer*, 2 vols. (1812), 1 : 42. All references to Strype's works are to the Oxford edition, 1812–1828, in 27 volumes.

Not all the English reformers would take such a frankly and exclusively utilitarian view, but in Cranmer's words it is possible to measure the distance from Rome to Canterbury. Since ceremonies are man-made, it is reasonable that they should be controlled by the civil authority. Here, value lay unexceptionably in their political usefulness. In the course of the long debate, milder counsels would prevail; but the concept of ceremonies as a "commodity . . . for a good order and quietness" had been established permanently in English policy.

What Cranmer's statement passed over, however, is quite as significant as what it includes. Surely he did not mean all the laws and ceremonies of the church. Certain ceremonies were instituted by Christ himself. And even among those "ordained for a common commodity," Cranmer makes no distinction of the relative values between one ceremony and another. Until such a distinction was made, any secularization of the regulatory powers of the church might lead to civil strife rather than good order and quietness. Plainly, the philosophic groundwork of ceremony needed to be laid, and this was primarily the achievement of Thomas Starkey. His distinction between God's law, essential to faith and immutable short of divine intervention, and man's law, not essential to faith (i.e., indifferent) and subject to such changes as might be expedient in the conduct of human affairs, religious or secular, became official policy.[10]

There was danger, however, that ceremonies unessential to faith, by being called "indifferent," might thereby lose dignity and value. Even the *Bishops' Book* (1537) seems to encourage such interpretation in describing ceremonies as "of themselves but mean and indifferent things." Whereas More had seen men as "somehow uplifted" by them,[11] there were many who degraded the Mass "as a thing of little or small value, and the ceremonies of the same for a mocking and a mumming, calling them also dumb

10. *An exhortation to the people instructynge theym to unitie and obedience* (1535–36). For the dating and political significance of this document, see my *Foundations of Tudor Policy* (1948), pp. 147–49.

11. More, *Utopia*, eds. Surtz and Hexter, p. 234: "nescio quomodo sese sentiunt homines erigi."

ceremonies." "They are not dumb," the *Portiforium secundum Sarum* retorted. "By such signs and ceremonies, they that be present thereat, may the better be admonished and reduced into the memory of the same." [12] But the ridicule continued, and from ridicule to a demand for their elimination was an easy step. From a safe haven abroad, William Turner under the alias "William Wraghton" declared that if the Jews needed no ceremonies but the law of Moses, Christians need no other law than the law of the gospel.[13] And John Bale followed up Turner's declaration with a direct attack on Edmund Bonner, Bishop of London, author of "the late Declaratyon of the Pope's olde faythe": "Wyll he make us Iewes again? Will he make us bond servants, and Christ hath made us free children? . . . Your own laws and doctrines besides the scripture granteth abrogation of the laws ceremonial." [14]

When Stephen Gardiner, Bishop of Winchester, answered [15] that the reformers would have us neither see, smell, nor taste in memory of Christ, and that "all the gates of our senses and ways to man's understanding should be shut up saving the ear alone," Turner retorted roguishly:

> What Jewish and dull Pharisees are these that either will not or cannot be content with the holy word of Christ and his Sacraments to bring Christ to their memories that they may think on him except they smell something to remember him and taste something also to remember him thereby?

> [With] unprofitable & leeworde ceremonies . . . you have made your traditional and ceremonial pale to keep the deer within it that they may not go forth to get themselves good meat abroad . . . If your pompous pale be made to holde out ye have wel obteyned your purpose, for withe your ceremonies and manne's inventiones whiche ye grant that the pope

12. Jeremy Collier, *An Ecclesiastical History of Great Britain*, 9 vols. (1840), 5 : 112.
13. *The Hunting and Fyndyng Out of the Romish Foxe* (1543), sig. Cii^v-Ciii.
14. *Yet a Course at the Romyshe Foxe* (1543), sig. Kvi. Gal. 4 : 3.
15. *The Rescuynge of the Romishe fox other wise called the examination of the hunter.* The book is not extant; its contents are known only through Turner's reply.

> hathe made ye hold out the worde of god which shuld only
> be the meat of all the dear of thys parke.[16]

He denied Gardiner's accusation that he was making "a tumult &
a clamor": "I never in all my book wrote agaynst one polytike
law. . . . I answer you as Eli answered Ahab. I trouble not
England but thou & thy father's house" (sig. Bv; Bii^v). But he
held firmly on the main point: "the ceremonies & traditions that
ye defend did the heavenly father never order, . . . they must be
pulled up by the roots & cast away" (sig. Div^v). Their use could
be only for confinement, like deer in a park. As significations, as
symbols of a time-honored tradition, as "gates of our senses," they
meant nothing to him. This insensitivity would continue to
characterize the Puritan movement during the youth of Shakespeare. Eventually, it would show the way to the Anglican
answer, the reaffirmation, both ecclesiastical and political, of
ceremony as symbol.

By the time of the publication of the first Prayer-Book, 1549,
ceremony had become a subject of public controversy. Issues had
been raised and sides taken. What had begun as an ecclesiastical
question had almost at once developed political considerations in
precisely the area where the Tudors were most sensitive, the
necessity for order and obedience. Policy dictated that ceremonies
remain adiaphoristic, that is, not essential articles of faith and
therefore under governmental control; at the same time, though
they were unessential, "indifferent" in the usage of the time, their
value in assisting the faith must be maintained. The balance was
delicate, and so far, it had met strong opposition at home and
suspicion abroad. To extremists like Turner and Bale, ceremonies
retained and sanctioned by the church were symbols, not of faith,
but of idolatry, vestiges of papistry which must be wholly
dispensed with, and there can be no question of the popular
strength of their position. A sympathetic Londoner, writing in
May 1547, reported the high temper in the city: "There hath

16. *The seconde course of the hunter at the romishe fox & hys sworne patrone steuen gardiner
doctor & defender of the pope's canon law and hys ungodly ceremonies* (1545), sig. Giiii; sig.
Avi–Avi^v.

nothing else been preached at the Spital these last sermons, but that almost [i.e., faith alone doth justify], and Down with Ceremonies, Down with Ceremonies of the Bishops of Rome." [17] Protestants abroad were likewise suspicious that under the "specious name" of adiaphora, many changes were being made to bring the papacy back again.[18]

In the face of such popular tensions, it is understandable that the authors of the Prayer-Book felt constrained to conclude it with an apologia on ceremonies entitled: "Why some be abolished, and some reteined." [19] Here, compendiously, the whole case for the Establishment was stated as it would remain essentially throughout Shakespeare's lifetime. Its major premises were political, its manner conciliatory. Primarily, ceremonies were conceived as subserving order. They should edify; but—following Cranmer's earlier expressions—they were "devised . . . for a decent ordre in the churche." Keeping or omitting a ceremony is in itself of small importance—except as it breaks "common ordre and discipline." Then it is "no smal offense before God." Between the two ecclesiastical factions, the Prayer-Book mediated with extraordinary astuteness and dexterity. As a gesture to the Puritans, it held that some ceremonies were "worthy to be cut awaie, and clene reiected"; to mollify the Romanists, it insisted that others were just as necessary to retain. As between those on the one hand who "thinke it a greate matter of conscience to depart from a pece of the least of their Ceremonies (thei be so addicted to their old customes)," and those on the other hand "so newe fangle, that thei would innouate all thyng, and so do despise the old that nothyng can like them but that is newe," the Prayer-Book chose neither, preferring rather "to please God, & profit them both." Answering the argument of those who feared being brought into bondage to a new Jewish law, it stressed the value of ceremony: "Christes Gospell is not a Ceremoniall lawe (as muche of Moses

17. Barbara Winchester, *Tudor Family Portrait* (1955), pp. 50–51.
18. *An Epistle from the Consistory at Hamburgh to Philip Melanchthon, with his answer concerning the Adiaphora*, 1549, in *Corpus Reformatorum*, eds. C. G. Bretschneider and H. E. Bindsell (1834–60), vol. 7, pp. 366–86.
19. *Booke of Common Prayer* (1549), sig. Tiiiᵛ–Tvi.

lawe was) but it is a Religion to serue God, not in bondage of the
figure or shadowe, but in the fredome of the spirite." It would
retain only such ceremonies "as be apt to stirre up the dull mynd
of man, to the remembraunce of his duetie to God, by some
notable and speciall significacion, whereby he might be edefied."
For those who scored ceremonies as "dark" or "dumb," they
would be "set furth that euery man maie understand." And
whatever the cause for apprehension, it should be remembered
that ceremonies were not irrevocable. They were, after all, man's
law, not God's, and therefore "upon iust causes" alterable.
Indeed, alteration and elimination might from time to time be
expected, "as in mennes ordinaunces it often chaunceth, diversly
in diverse countreis." Finally, the Prayer-Book appealed to
national instincts: it was English and merely English: "Wee
condempne no other nacions, nor prescribe any thyng, but to our
awne people onely. For wee thynke it Convenient that euery
countrey should use suche ceremonies, as thei shall thynke best to
the settyng furthe of Goddes honor and glory." While avoiding
allusion to any contemporary events, the Prayer-Book seems to be
particularly responsive to the recent executions under the Act of
Six Articles. It is significant that, of the six executed, three were
convicted of treason, three of heresy. But traitor or heretic, one's
attitude toward ceremony was incriminative; its method of
observance had become vital government policy.

As might be expected, the statement in the Prayer-Book, in
spite of its moderation, did not settle the dispute. During the
reigns of Edward and Mary, rumblings of discontent continued to
arise, rehearsing the same issues in the familiar language. Yet
occasionally, in the labyrinth of theological invective, one phrase,
like a leveled forefinger, arrests and directs the eye. Such a one is
Cranmer's "apparel of bread and wine" struck off in debate with
Stephen Gardiner. The Prayer-Book had countered the Puritan
attempt to reduce the Sacrament to a mere remembrance by
asserting "some notable and special significations" resident in
ceremonies. It was clever raillery to profess to catch the conservative Gardiner in retreat from the same Puritan position: "And
now I am glad, that here your selfe have found out a warrant for

the apparel of bread and wyne, that thei shal not goe altogither naked, and be nude and bare tokens, but have promises of effectual signification." [20] Gardiner's testy retort, "Albeit this auctor would not have them bare tokens, yet, and they be onely tokens, they have no warrant signed by scripture for any apparel at all," [21] is of less interest than his clothing the Sacrament in the language of cope and surplice. To think of ceremony as apparel is to anticipate the Vestiarian Controversy of the 60s; and this, in turn, anticipates Shakespeare's evaluation of the vestments of kingship in the English history plays.

When Elizabeth came to the throne, the ceremony of vestments became a matter of quandary to the exiled bishops, whose contact with continental Protestantism had instilled in them a determination not to be "burdened with unprofitable ceremonies." [22] Shortly enough, however, they discovered that their sentiments were not shared by the Queen. Ensued anxious letters to spiritual advisors in Zurich. Should they desert their ministry "for some rites, that were but a few and not evil in themselves," were indeed indifferent? Perhaps the controversial "costumes," "habits of the stage" in Jewel's phrase,[23] might be worn if enjoined by royal authority as a means for procuring good order in the church.[24] Matthew Parker thought so, and in the end, the approval of parliament and the allure of a bishopric salved conscience. Jewel of Salisbury struck an attitude against such ceremonies as were "unfit for men that had their right wits, of which sort of ceremonies there be at this day in the Papacy an infinite number

20. *An Answer . . . unto a craft and sophisticall cavillation devised by S. Gardiner . . . byshop of Winchester* (1551), sig. Dvi^v.

21. *An explication and assertion of the true Catholique fayth* (1551), sig. Biiii.

22. Stated in a formal resolution as a condition of their return, 3 January 1559. They could find support for their position abroad in St. Augustine's frequently cited letters to Januarius (Epistles 118, 119) advising him that while he lived abroad he should conform in matters of doctrinal indifference to the customs of the people among whom he had taken up residence. But his authority could hardly be invoked in the present circumstances.

23. *Zurich Letters*, ed. Hastings Robinson, 2 vols. (Parker Society, 1842–45) 1 : 134; Daniel Neal, *The History of the Puritans*, 5 vols. (1822), 1 : 159.

24. Strype, *Parker*, 1 : 322–45.

. . . because we would not have the right worship of God any
longer defiled with such foolishness." But he put on the garments,
nevertheless, "because we would have all things done in the holy
assembly, according as S. Paul commandeth, comely and in
order." [25] As a matter of fact, once the new bishops were
established in England, they found the ceremonies of the English
church not only endurable but defensible: "Every particuler and
nationall Churche, hath authoritie to ordayne, chaunge, and
abolyshe ceremonies or rites of the Churche ordeyned onlye by
mans aucthorite, so that all thinges be done to edifiying." [26] As
Archbishop Parker put it, they offered "decency, distinction, and
order for the time," [27] thus reaffirming the position of the English
church, judicious as a statement of policy but firmly grounded in
pragmatic values.

As in the Prayer-Book, the sense of official pronouncements was
to think of ceremony in terms of political order. More than any
other factor, this secularization of ceremonies served as a rallying
point for conservative opinion; but it could scarcely be expected
to dampen the inflamed opposition of those who, like John Field
and Thomas Wilcox (*Admonition to the Parliament*, 1572), would
presently seek to "abandon all popish remnants both in ceremonies and regiment." Against such intransigence, the Establishment hardened its stand. Tradition must be preserved in the
interests of state as well as church. Public good must outweigh
private judgment.

On these principles, the government attempted to stand firm
throughout the Vestiarian Controversy. But weaknesses in its
facade were being searched out with perspicacity and no small
effect. The Puritan point of attack centered on the argument that
vestments were not an indifferent matter; they were in fact badges

25. John Jewel, *An Apologie, or aunswer in defence of the Church of England* (1562),
sig. Div^v–Ei.

26. Church of England, *Articles whereupon it was agreed by the Archbishoppes and
Bishoppes of both provinces and the whole cleargie* (1562), sig. Cii^v–Ciii.

27. Matthew Parker, *Advertisements partly for due order in the publique administration of
common prayers and usinge the holy Sacramentes, and partly for the apparrell of all persons
ecclesiasticall* (1564), sig. Aii^v.

of popery and could not therefore be justified in the name of
tradition or public policy. The basic assumption of the Prayer-
Book was that ceremonies edify. But did they? "Wee graunt," said
Robert Crowley in his anonymous tract, *A briefe discourse against the
outwarde apparell and Ministring garmentes of the popishe church* (1566),
"that of themselues, they be things indifferent, and may be used
or not used, as occasion shall serue: but when the use of them will
destroy, or not edifie, then ceasse they to be so indifferent.[28] If, as
the *Advertisements* hold, apparel is used only for decency and
comely order, uniformity, and obedience to our prince, is the
refusal of it therefore an encouragement to disobedience, as
alleged? Crowley's answer put a shrewd test to the validity of the
principle of indifference: Let us admit that the ceremonies refused
are adiaphora, as the church maintains. In that case, "princes
have no authority either to command or forbid them." We are
subject to the prince, "but this subjection is not to do at the
Prince's commandment whatsoever the Prince shall for pleasure
command." Consequently, if we are commanded to do what does
not edify but destroy, "we must then refuse to do the thing
commanded by the Prince, and humbly submit ourselves to suffer
the penalty, but in any case not consent to enfringe the Christian
liberty which is to use things indifferent, to edification and not to
destruction" (sig. Av–Biii). Like Bale earlier, Crowley took Saint
Paul for his authority in defining Christian liberty as freedom not
merely from "the thralldom of sin, the curse of the law," but
also—with some liberty of his own—from "the ceremonies of the
same" (sig. Bii^v).[29] But Crowley was addressing Elizabeth herself,
not the Bishop of London; and in the name of "Christian liberty"
or any other, a challenge to a prince's authority had a frosty
sound.

Lacking Crowley's forensic skill, Archbishop Parker's answer is

28. Sig. Aiiii–Aiiii^v. Cf. Robert Crowley, *An Answer for the tyme, to the examination
put in print, without the authors name, pretending to mayntayne the apparrel prescribed against
the declaration of the ministers of London* (1566), sig. Biv^v.

29. Gal. 3 : 13: "Christ hath redeemed us from the curse the law, having
become a curse for us." Gal. 5 : 1: "With freedom did Christ set us free: stand fast
therefore and be not entangled again in a yoke of bondage."

little more than admonitory. It behooves a godly man to moderate his liberty in charity toward his neighbor and obedience to his prince; "forasmuch as garments are among things indifferent we may easily know how they are free as pertaining to our conscience, and yet notwithstanding we may be obedient to laws without impairing of Christian liberty." [30] From the Puritan point of view, this would be living with one's conscience and not acting upon it. "To binde a man to doe agaynst his conscience," Anthony Gilby would retort, "is against Christian libertie." [31] As to the fundamental question of who would determine indifference, *A briefe examination* is pontifical and arbitrary. For the individual priest "to admit no orders which may not manifestly appear unto them that they do edify" would reject the biblical injunction that "kings shall be thy nurse-fathers and queens thy nurses." Subjects cannot know as much as king and council, and must obey, even if they do not see why, so long as the order is not contrary to God's law. Individual judgment can only lead to rebellion, and rebellion is far worse than the use of the vestments (sig. Bii^v–Biii; Cv).

A briefe examination left very little room for either Christian liberty or charity as the Puritans quickly pointed out. Kings and queens should indeed be nurses of the church, but not lords of it nor of conscience.[32] Yet *An Answere* admitted a degree of flexibility. Ceremonies are not merely the smelling dung which Calvin had called them. They "might speak or as it were preach some part of godliness"; they might even have "their good significations." [33] To admit their value was an important concession, even though *An Answere* went on to insist that it detested them, not for their signification, but for their superstition. "Superstitious ceremonies are the chains whereby we were tied to popish religion" (sig. Hii^v; Iv^v).

A flurry of Puritan tracts followed *An Answere*, certainly less articulate in form and substance than the Pauline epistles which

30. *A briefe examination for the tyme*, sig. **** 4^v–***** 1.

31. *A Pleasaunt Dialogue*, sig. R6^v. See n. 34.

32. Crowley, *An Answere for the tyme*, sig. Fii.

33. Sig. Fiiii, citing Jean Calvin, *Institutes of the Christian Religion* (1536), 13 : 3.

they imitated, but zealous to comfort the brothers in adversity.[34]
In sum, they are the testimony of a grumbling, inchoate
discontent over "the popish and idolatrous garments," and as
such are indistinguishable from their predecessors. What is new,
however, is the violence of their attack on policy as a sufficient
reason for the use of vestments. Once again it puts the church on
the defensive as arbitrary and politically oriented; and it stems as
well from deep-seated social resentments. The author of *To my
lovynge brethren* speaks with the perennial scorn of the plain-spoken
country parson for the pretensions of the courtier-prelate:

> They say it is for policy. . . . There is less care for religion
> than for policy. . . . These garments were the show of their
> blasphemous priesthood. Herein they did sing & say their
> superstitious & idolatrous service. What policy can it be then
> to wear this gear but a superstitious wicked and popish
> policy; they do it for policy. [sig. Bi^v–Bii^v]

To my faythfull Brethren sounds a similar apostolic warning against
"pope-like garments . . . avouched & set forth under the visure
and countenance of policy" (sig. Aiiii–Aiiii^v). To Anthony Gilby,
bishops are "politic gentlemen," "our English Gospellers," who
have learned "Courtly Divinitie, to grounde all uppon pollicie."
He recalls that Gardiner and Bonner once fought "against us";
but even Gardiner "maketh the substance of popish religion to
stand upon Garments & such other popish inventions." Cross and
candlesticks stand on the Queen's altar for one knows not what
policy; fair and costly garments are commanded by the Queen for
policy. The best policy would be to root it all out.[35]

Do not ceremonies bring "a comelie order"? asks Gilby's
chaplain; to which the soldier, who carries the weight of the

34. *To my lovynge brethren that is troublyd about the popish apparrel* (1566); *To my
faythfull Brethren now afflycted* (1566); Anthony Gilby, *A Pleasaunt Dialogue betweene a
Souldior of Barwicke, and an English Chaplaine, wherein are largely handled & laide open,
such reasons as are broughte in for maintenaunce of popishe Traditions in our English Church*
(1581; but published first in an expurgated edition in *To my lovynge Brethren*, 1566).
See M. M. Knappen, *Tudor Puritanism* (1939), p. 203.

35. *A Pleasaunt Dialogue*, sig. A3^v; D7^v; D8.

argument responds like Bassanio in *The Merchant of Venice*: "Decencie and order is not outward, in pompe, in garmentes, and in outwarde shewes"; its comeliness rather "standeth in the renouncing of al the garish shewes, of the vain world, & in an inward holines of the mind." [36] Eleven years later, Gilby was still complaining to Cartwright of that same "outward hypocriticall shewe, onely for custome and policy. . . . So in the steade of the olde beaste popery that is wounded to death by God's worde, we rayse up this seconde beaste policye to do all that the other beaste dyde before." [37] Defenders of church policy were here caught in a dilemma of their own making. A word used to remove the habits from controversy had unexpectedly become a symbol of "popery." Never thereafter was it to be dissociated from its pejorative meaning; and as time would give proof, its further and political association with the name of Machiavelli would complete its semantic degeneration.

At this juncture in the controversy, Puritan attack, although far more effective than official rebuttal, had taken no direct action. In 1572, however, with the appearance of *An Admonition to the Parliament*, it initiated a potentially militant program. The authors, Field and Wilcox, proposed no less than a complete platform of a reformed church and the abandonment of "all popish remnants both in ceremonies and regiment . . . placing in God's church those things only which the Lord himself in his word commandeth" (sig. Aii). Apparel must go. For whereas apparel is commanded for order and decency, "there is neither order, nor comeliness, nor obedience in usinge it" (sig. Bviii; Ciii^v). Moreover, "all disordered ceremonies used in place of prayer" must be reexamined, and those abolished which are found "evil or unprofitable" (sig. Fiii^v). Those that remain should be few and edifying and free from the taint of popery, but by whose authority these reforms should be executed was not clear. There are occasional evidences that the crown might be called on for the purpose. But in one respect there was no question: decisions

36. Sig. G6–G6^v; *The Merchant of Venice*, 3.2.73–80.
37. *The Seconde Part of a Register*, ed. Albert Peel, 2 vols. (1915), 1 : 140.

would no longer be made within the episcopal framework appointed by the queen. Their kingdom is tyrannous and must be overthrown, hold they never so hard.

Such a thoroughgoing threat to the order established called for immediate defense. Since the main positions of the ecclesiastical settlement were already in print in Jewel's *Apology*, its defenders during the ensuing campaign mainly resorted to tactical sorties against their resourceful and dedicated opponents. Measured in mere bulk of printed pages, their successes appear minor. Yet the continual probing of weaknesses in the bastion had the effect of building up its strength. Against the cry in *An Admonition* for liberty from ceremony, John Whitgift, then vicechancellor of Cambridge University, maintained "the true libertie of the christian religion in externe rytes and ceremonies." [38] Against the strict requirement of a Biblical provenance for ceremony, he argued that if no ceremony, order, discipline or kind of government were allowed within the authority of the church unless expressly commanded of God, it could be argued conversely that all the commandments of God are needful for salvation, and hence we should be reasonably bound, on necessity of salvation, to observe the whole Jewish ceremonial law.[39] Against the abrogation of ceremony as no longer "profitable," Whitgift held that "even that change of Custom which helpeth through profit, doth trouble through novelty." And in such a case, he had no more to offer to the Bible-centered Puritan than Augustine's advice to observe the customs of the country one lives in, whenever the custom is not an essential of faith:

A private man may not breake the lawfull and good orders of the Churche, thoughe they be not expressed in the worde of God; yet maye suche as God hathe gyuen that authorite unto in hys Churche, alter and chaunge them as be most expedient. [sig. Iii^v–Iiii] [40]

38. *An Answere to a certen Libel* (1572), sig. [Aiiii].

39. *The Defense of the Aunswere to the Admonition, against the Replie of T. C.* (1574), sig. Gvi; Ii^v.

40. Whitgift's reference is to Augustine's Epistle 118. See above, note 22.

There were Puritans who would have responded that the cost of order under these circumstances was too great.

Whitgift was not unsupported by lighter artillery aimed at the preservation of church tradition. Cartwright, said one observer slyly, can "sing our psalmes in meter without offence or grudge of conscience, without either warrant or commandment of scripture." [41] But for the most part, defenders of ceremony showed neither persuasive power nor originality. The exception was Thomas Cooper, Bishop of Lincoln. Less concerned with the utility of ceremonies than their value, he did much to reinstate them as symbols. There was a time, he wrote, perhaps recalling More, "when the whole state of religion was turned to an outward shewe of gestures, signes, and ceremonies." [42] The newer fashion is to treat them as "trifles, vaine Ceremonies, and mens devises, that you may use or not use at your pleasures, as you list." Rather, since Christ is "author of sacraments, and none other, . . . you ought to reverence them, as the ordinance of God, and to receive them, even as at Christs own hand." The outward sign is in each sacrament; but sacraments are not "bare signs and tokens."

> Spiritual effectes are as certainely wrought, by the holy ghost in the sacramentes, as we see that the externall elementes haue their operation in the course of nature. For the sacramentes are as the deedes and Seales of almighty god, whereby he doth in deede and verily, not only by signification, but effectually conveighe unto us, the possession of his spiritual blessinges. [sig. Qiii–Rii]

"The faithful together with the outward sign receive the inward thing," just as in civil life "everie matter of conveighance we see passeth by deede and seale" (sig. Riiii^v–Si). When Bishop Cooper's sober definition is compared with that of his adversaries, it would seem possible for bishops and separatists to agree: "Ceremonies be outwarde sensible signes, sanctified and applied

41. *A Defense of the Ecclesiasticall Regiment in Englande, defaced by T. C. in his Replie Agaynst D. Whitgifte* (1574), sig. Bvi^v.
42. *Certaine Sermons* (1580), sig. Biiii.

by the worde duelie preached, to be religious shewes of some
spirituall graces, which are meant thereby." [43]

Mild language, however, was not to be the order of the day. *The
Articles sent to the bishops and clergy* in the convocation house,
January 1581, accused the clergy of making themselves "execra-
ble and accursed in receivinge those popishe garmentes, worldlye
ordinances, and traditions of men," and announced summarily,
"We have no part nor fellowshippe with you, nor with your
haltynge religion and traditions." [44] Mere scurrility was the
convenient and more frequent weapon, especially when it involved the Pope, "that man of Sinne, with his cursed Canon Lawe
and filthy Ceremonies." [45]

Not that the larger issues were ever wholly obscured by such
loose talk. The crucial problem of lay jurisdiction within the area
of indifference remained always not far below the surface. Use of
ceremonies was a political issue by the very conditions of the
establishment of the English church, and settlement for religious
dissidents of whatever party could only mean capitulation to the
established area of indifference. John Bridges, in *A Defence of the
government established* (1587) took umbrage in the customary
argument that Christ had ordered the governing of his church in
regard only to "unitie in doctrine of fayth, and to holy conversation of life, and not to th' externall orders of the Church's
ecclesiasticàl government" (sig. Fi). Who should be judge?
retorted Walter Travers. If that area of indifferent things were to
be left solely to the judgment of "the Sovereign Magistrates,"
whatever they "choose to call indifferent, it must be so holden of
all men without further inquiry." [46] And it was all too clear in the
late 1580s that neither Puritans nor Papists did so hold.

43. *A Booke which sheweth the life and manners of all true Christians,* 1582, in *The
Writings of Robert Harrison and Robert Browne,* eds. Albert Peel and Leland H. Carlson
(1953), p. 287.

44. *The Seconde Parte of a Register,* 1 : 148.

45. Robert Cawdry, *The request of all true Christians to the moste honourable high court
of Parliament for the Succession and restoring of Christe to his full Regiment* (1586–87), in
The Seconde Parte of a Register, 2 : 208–09.

46. *A Defence of the Ecclesiastical Discipline ordayned of God to be used in his Church*
(1588), sig. Ti.

The Ornaments of Sovereignty

In such an impasse, would the Church of England vanish altogether? There were those in the church who, in Shakespeare's early years in London, dared to face that grim possibility. One, on whom the great task of reconciliation fell, began it in very nearly the spirit of a commemorative exercise:

> Though for no other cause, yet for this; that posterity may know we have not loosely through silence permitted things to pass away as in a dream, there shall be for men's information extant thus much concerning the present state of the Church of God established amongst us, and their careful endeavour which would have upheld the same.[47]

He was also modest, gentle. He talked about the same matters that had troubled the English church since its inception, but without trace of rancor. He won no battles, nor did he lose them. But he did find reason for conserving rather than destroying, for reestablishing the respect for tradition inherent in ceremony before the Reformation. Richard Hooker's *Of the Laws of Ecclesiastical Polity* is a defense, but it is a defense of the hardest kind, against "them that seek (as they term it) the reformation of the laws and orders ecclesiastical in the Church of England," those laws and orders being themselves a reformation of what had gone before. Hooker's success must therefore be measured quite as much in terms of those who in his own day sought to purify the English church as in terms of those who had rejected it.

For this reason as much as any, "judicious Hooker" is an apt phrase, but it should not carry with it any connotations of neutrality. The chief defender of the Establishment was in the field, not above it. We now know that the immediate inspiration

47. Richard Hooker, Preface to *Of the Laws of Ecclesiastical Polity*, Everyman Edition, ed. Christopher Morris, 2 vols. (1907, reprint ed. 1954), 1 : 77. Hereinafter cited as *LEP*.

Some foresaw a collapse in quite different mood. See J. E. Neale, *Elizabeth and her Parliaments, 1584–1601* (1957), p. 218.

of the *Laws* was Archbishop Whitgift, and the immediate circumstance, the passage of the Conventicle Act of 1593;[48] but if one detects in it little of the smoke of battle, that is because, as its title indicates, it was only secondarily a defense at all. That had already been done in Jewel's *Apology* and Whitgift's *Defense of the Answer*. Nor was it essentially doctrinal. The Book of Common Prayer, the Articles of Religion, and Jewel's *Apology* again had for the time fulfilled this need. Hooker's distinction was to give scope both in space and time to a merely English church: in space, by setting forth the position of the national establishment in the whole hierarchy of laws, and thus elevating policy to polity; in time, by associating the present ecclesiastical establishment with the long tradition since 1534, when Henry VIII began "to repair . . . the ruins of the house of God . . . which were become, not in his sight alone, but in the eyes of the whole world so exceeding great, that very superstition began even to feel itself too far grown." The long continuance of God's grace and favor since that time seemed to have taught the world that the Church of England had indeed been established by Him, was indeed "that glorious and sacred instrument whereby He worketh" (*LEP*, iv.xiv.7).

Hooker's method was to locate all laws of ecclesiastical polity within the province of human legislation, and thus to relegate intransigence in either Catholic or Puritan thought to *adiaphora*, or matters of credal indifference. This had been the position of the English church from its inception; it was for Hooker, however, to validate it in terms of historical change: "Laws, as all other things human are many times full of imperfection; and that which is supposed behoveful unto men, proveth oftentimes most pernicious. The wisdom which is learned by tract of time, findeth the laws that have been in former ages established, needful in later to be abrogated" (*LEP*, iv.xiv.1).

Hooker's firm grasp of a dynamic principle in human law was of the utmost importance in justifying the *via media*. Those who would oppose it appealed in each case to a static and inviolable

48. C. J. Sisson, *The Judicious Marriage of Mr. Hooker and the Birth of the Laws of Ecclesiastical Polity* (1940).

code—Catholics to the Canon Law, Puritans to the Scriptures.
But to Hooker, the body of law governing the English church had
demonstrated its viability as an instrument of human reason,
susceptible to and subject to such changes as would best
accommodate the needs of a society in healthy evolution. And as
specifically related to the present controversy, it allowed the
English church to stay the Reformation at whatever point and
time suited its convenience. But amendments either by elimination or creation must be cautious. Hooker was not the one to
underestimate the danger, even the folly, of abrogation. "Do we
not herein revoke our very own deed, and upbraid ourselves with
folly, yea, all that were makers of it with oversight and with
error?" Furthermore, if the law has been long in use, rescinding it
may cause men to doubt

> whether any thing be in itself by nature either good or evil,
> and not all things rather such as men at this or that time
> agree to account of them. . . . What have we to induce men
> unto the willing obedience and observation of law, but the
> weight of so many men's judgment as have with deliberate
> advice assented thereunto; the weight of that long experi-
> ence, which the world hath had thereof with consent and
> good liking? So that to change any such law must needs with
> the common sort impair and weaken the force of those
> grounds, whereby all laws are made effectual. [*LEP*, IV.xiv.1]

Notwithstanding, alteration of laws is sometimes necessary, the
English Reformation being the case in point, when certain laws
became "an hindrance unto piety and religious service of God"
(*LEP*, IV.xiv.1). And he was willing to carry the point to its
arguable extremity:

> For there is not any positive law of men, whether it be
> general or particular; received by formal express consent, as
> in councils, or by secret approbation, as in customs it cometh
> to pass; but the same may be taken away if occasion serve.
> [*LEP*, IV.xiv.5]

This delicate equilibrium in ecclesiastical polity, brought to bear on the crucial subject of ceremony, could be maintained by throwing weight on either side of the fulcrum. A custom, however long in use, might become inconvenient and eventually more honored in the breach than the observance—that would be for the papists to whom the English church was a splinter. On the other side, strict traditionalism would dictate the return to Jewish ceremonial law—an inconvenience to which the stoutest scripturalist among Puritans would hesitate to submit. Thus by the strategy of weight adjustment, the central position remained secure: moderate and gradual reform of ceremonies, "cutting off such things as might . . . be extinguished without danger, leaving the rest to be abolished by disusage through tract of time" (*LEP*, iv.xiv.5). Catholic sentiment would not accept any of the changes; Puritans demanded the abandonment of "all popish remnants both in ceremonies and regiment." Both views were as familiar as daylight long before Hooker confronted them; but while the recent alarms over Jesuits had served as a reminder of Catholic intransigence, the daily and open truculence of the Puritan outcry against "your haltynge religion and traditions," "your filthy ceremonies," unquestionably gave direction to Hooker's thought as he turned in book iv, the final book in the first edition of the *Laws*, to the crucial question, how great use ceremonies have in the church:

> Those rites and ceremonies of the Church therefore, which are the selfsame now that they were when holy and virtuous men maintained them against profane and deriding adversaries, her own children have at this day in derision. Whether justly or no, it shall then appear, when all things are heard which they have to allege against the outward received order of this church. Which inasmuch as themselves do compare unto "mint and cummin," granting them to be no part of those things which in the matter of polity are weightier, we hope that for small things their strife will neither be earnest nor long. [*LEP*, iv.i.i]

The razor-edge of this reasoning proceeds from the Puritan admission (in this instance, Thomas Cartwright's) of ceremonies indifferent in church polity, a subject which Hooker had already treated at length in book II (*LEP*, II.iv.3–5). This agreed upon, he could assert his chief claim in opposition to the Puritans: ceremonies, indifferent as they are in matters of faith, have nevertheless their own value. Here he was on ground familiar since the statement on ceremonies in the Prayer-Book, and he uses similar language: "The end which is aimed at in setting down the outward form of all religious actions is the edification of the Church." Their appeal is to the mind and the heart, not merely by words but by other "sundry sensible means," especially to the eye, "the liveliest and the most apprehensive sense of all other." [49] Thus ceremonies have a value as symbols, a value which is evident in public as well as religious actions and extends to all nations, whereby it may be surmised that they must have "some ground of reason even in nature." It would therefore be unwise to condemn ceremonies "as follies and toys," merely because we are ignorant of their significance (*LEP*, IV.i.3).[50]

According to Puritan opinion, the English church must abolish all ceremonies retained from the pre-Reformation period. Says Hooker: We will retain them since "we judge them to be profitable, and to be such that others instead of them would be worse" (*LEP*, IV.iv.2). Furthermore, ceremonies so long held for good need no further proof of their convenience. "They which have stood up as yesterday to challenge it of defect, must prove their challenge." For Hooker, tradition and custom were instinctive. "We have the selfsame interest in them which our fathers before us had, from whom the same are descended unto us" (*LEP*,

49. Words, in fact, move less than visible signs, since they are "for the most part but slightly heard." *LEP*, IV.i.3. Richard Morison makes the same point in *A Discourse touching the reformation of the laws of England* addressed to Henry VIII: "Things sooner enter by the eyes, than by the ears, remembering more better that they see than that they hear," Brit. Mus. Ms. Ps. 21050 Roy 18 A L, fol. 19.

50. Hooker courses widely over history to illustrate his point, touching interestingly, in view of what Shakespeare will say later, on the symbolic use of hands.

IV.ix.I). Hooker cannot resist indulging in a gentle ribbing of the followers of Calvin:

> They must and will I doubt not find out some other good means to cheer up themselves. Amongst which means the example of Geneva may serve for one. Have not they the old popish custom of using godfathers and godmothers in Baptism? the old popish custom of administering the blessed sacrament of the holy Eucharist with wafer-cakes? These things the godly there can digest. Wherefore should not the godly here learn to do the like both in them and in the rest of the like nature. [*LEP*, IV.x.I]

But he is altogether serious in his closing advocacy of a moderate reformation. Short of a voice from heaven or a clear sentence from men, it would be better "to bear a tolerable sore . . . than to venture on a dangerous remedy." To have gone farther would have been to alter unnecessarily "the ancient received custom of the whole Church, the universal practice of the people of God, and those very decrees of our fathers, which were not only set down by agreement of general councils, but had accordingly been put in ure and so continued in use till that very time present" (*LEP*, IV.xiv.4). He closes on the conciliatory note with which he began. "Suspense of judgment and exercise of charity," he concludes, are "safer and seemlier for Christian men, than the hot pursuit of these controversies, wherein they that are most fervent to dispute be not always the most able to determine" (*LEP*, IV.xiv.6).

There can be no question that for Hooker as for his predecessors, ceremony was the crux of the English settlement. In the very fact that the ceremonies to which the Puritans most objected were to Hooker unessential matters of faith lay the weakness of their exorbitant threat of disorder to be rid of them. They, crying liberty, would take these laws into their own hands. Hooker, readily admitting that the laws of man must "abridge men's liberty," insisted nevertheless that laws must be maintained, "or else overturn the world and make every man his own commander." [51] To Hooker, the maintenance of order in society, indeed the stability of the entire social structure, depends on the observance of ceremony.

Whether within or beyond the arena of religious controversy, ceremonies have always possessed symbolic value. "Destitute of signification, [they are] no better than the idle gestures of men whose broken wits are not masters of what they do" (*LEP*, v.lxv.5). Puritans had disparaged "dumb ceremonies" as no more than "shadows of things to come" which the advent of Christ had rendered useless. Hooker retorted: "As the usual dumb ceremonies of common life are in request or dislike according to what they import, even so religion having likewise her silent rites, the chiefest rule whereby to judge of their quality, is that which they mean or betoken" (*LEP*, v.lxv.5). Clerical attire, though it is "indifferent," is no idle gesture. It is an unspreading token, observed without conscious thought, yet serving none the less its own function of comeliness like other objects of beauty in common use.

In this context, Hooker's words are reminiscent of Cranmer's phrase, "apparel of bread and wine." He sees no necessity for "stripping sacraments out of all such attire of ceremonies as man's wisdom hath at any time clothed them withal. . . . Ceremonies have more in weight than in sight; they work by commonness of use much, although in the several acts of their usage we scarcely discern any good they do" (*LEP*, v.lxv.3–4). [52] The "silent rites" of religion, as Hooker phrases it, are the signs and tokens that

51. *LEP*, v.lxxi.4.

52. *LEP*, vii.xx.3 is worth quoting in this connection, though it is unlikely that Shakespeare read it: "Something there is even in the ornaments of honour. . . . The robes of a judge do not add to his virtue; the chiefest ornament of kings is justice; holiness and purity of conversation do much more adorn a bishop, than his peculiar form of clothing. Notwithstanding, both judges, through the garments of judicial authority, and through the ornaments of sovereignty, princes; yea bishops through the very attire of bishops, are made blessed, that is to say, marked and manifested they are to be such as God hath poured his blessing upon, by advancing them above others, and placing them where they may do him principal good service."

Thomas More found in the smell of the frankincense and the sight of the candles by which men are "uplifted to the worship of God." We remember them as we turn to Shakespeare's Henry V weighing the value of ceremony in his moment of crisis at Agincourt. Across the years, More shares the same instincts as Hooker and Shakespeare, perhaps for the same reasons. From the depths of consciousness, More in 1516 and Hooker and Shakespeare in the 1590s felt the groundswell of change, and while they recognized its inevitability were nevertheless not without misgiving. In 1516, the church universal was fracturing, the traditions of a thousand years were being violated, and More found himself temperamentally apprehensive that those traditions could be longer preserved. In 1593, the Church of England seemed to be threatened with the same danger, and Hooker recoiled in precisely the same way. One is therefore not left wholly to an accident of publication to account for the fact that Shakespeare's historical plays written after 1593 reflect so markedly the same predisposition.

It is not my purpose to trace Shakespeare's indebtedness to Hooker. As a matter of fact, nothing that has been said on this subject can be adduced as proof that Shakespeare read Hooker at all. Ulyssus' speech on disorder in *Troilus and Cressida*, often quoted as derivative from the disorder passage in the *Laws* (*LEP*, i.iii.2), has usually been sufficient to satisfy most critics that the indebtedness exists. There are few who have ventured further, and almost none beyond book i. It is just as well. Shakespeare did not use Hooker as occasionally he did Holinshed, Plutarch, and Montaigne—with the book open before him. Yet not merely in the English history plays, and not merely in book i of the *Laws*, the affinity of the two writers is demonstrable, and nothing more particularly or more persistently than in their insistence on the values inherent in customary observances of tradition whether ecclesiastical or political. In 1597, Hooker found it natural to put the present dilemma of the English church in a political context. "To solemn actions of royalty and justice their suitable ornaments are a beauty. Are they only in religion a stain?" (*LEP*, v.xxix.1). For Shakespeare as a man of the theatre, such a question was just as easily reversible. What he found in the post-Reformation absorption with the use and abuse of ceremonies was a reservoir of theatrical emotive power readily applicable to political uses. If suitable ornaments were a beauty in religion, would not the use and abuse of the ornaments of throne and crown exert a like profound effect on an audience in the theatre? In the person of Richard II "solemn actions of royalty and justice" are irreverently stained by misuse; in both parts of *Henry IV*, Hal takes them up as a necessary burden of the office of king.

Twin-born with Greatness

Whether Richard Hooker was the catalytic agent or not, it is apparent that when Shakespeare turned once again to English fifteenth-century history in late 1595 or early 1596, his center of interest had noticeably broadened from the costly shedding of the blood of two noble families to the currently provocative public issue of the value of ceremony. To this theme, the deposition of Richard II was singularly appropriate; for it could be argued that for quite different reasons Richard in yielding the throne, and Henry, by supplanting him, were both guilty of the primal political fault of desecrating the crown—a correspondence highly congenial to the stage. Shakespeare found warrant for it in the equivocal position taken by Hall and the later Tudor historians, who found it necessary to deplore the deposition of a legitimate king and at the same time justify what was also a sensitive point, the seizure of the throne by a man whose blood flowed in the veins of the first Tudor. Hall was far from holding Richard guiltless of the crime of civil war. By seizing "without ryght or title" the possessions of Henry's father, John of Gaunt, and thus defrauding him of his lawful inheritance, he had broken "all lawes, all iustice and equite" (*The Union*, sig. Aiiii). Further, "by his slouth and negligence" he had suffered his realm to lose its "auncient fame and pristinate renoume" (sig. Aii); and even though he yielded it "frankly and frely of his own mere motion" (Aviii^v) so that "the publike welth of this realme maie be holpen and auaunced" (sig. Bi), his very lack of action was culpable. On the other hand, Hall does not palliate Henry's perfidy in ridding himself of the inconvenience of the living Richard once the crown was in his hands, nor does he conceal Henry's fumbling attempt to establish a legal title to the throne. In summing up his reign, he speaks, albeit circumspectly as one might expect him to do, of the first Lancastrian king: "After that he had apeased al ciuile discencions he shewed hym selfe so gently to all men that he gatt him more loue of the nobles in his latter daies then he had malice and ill will of them in the begynnynge (sig. Evi). But his later "gentleness" did not expiate his fault.

Hall's even-handed judgments are not surprising in view of his ancestry. Sir Davy Hall, his great-great-grandfather was captain of Caen under the regency of Richard, Duke of York. He remained close to him as his chief counsellor after York returned from France, and died with him on the field of battle at Wakefield. Hall's express purpose in writing *The Union* was to save from cankered oblivion the noble and illustrious dead on both sides. Fifty years after the event, he could see the tragedy of the original act in its proper perspective: "What noble man liueth at this day, or what gentleman of any auncient stocks or progeni . . . whose linage hath not ben infested and plaged with this vnnaturall deuision?" (sig. Ai). This is precisely the position that Shakespeare's Hal takes before the battle of Shrewsbury: "to save the blood on either side." From this vantage point Shakespeare views the tragic double fault of Richard and Henry. Amplified and refined, it becomes the core of *Richard II*. The central symbol of the play is the crown, which Henry approaches, but deviously, and Richard yields just as deviously. The whole action resembles a pirouette, the deadly seriousness of which almost escapes at times into comedy. For much of the play, Henry chooses a waiting game, while Richard attenuates his ignominious, unmuscular, though highly self-conscious ritual surrender of the ceremonies that belong to a king, their value to him no more than the tinsel garments of an actor especially privileged by their mere possession to give them away. Thus Richard and Henry, both violating the ceremonies of the kingly office, are drawn into a pageant royal, each in his own way playing out his own privately conceived public role. As a consequence, *Richard II* becomes a travesty on the ceremonies owing to royalty.

The pattern thus set in *Richard II*, from an artistic point of view stated negatively, antimasque before masque, is developed affirmatively though diversely in the two parts of *Henry IV*. Finally, and most explicitly, Henry V's acceptance of the burden of ceremony as an outward expression of inward responsibility becomes the necessary prelude for clearing the national conscience of his father's guilt before the brassy crescendo of Agincourt drowns out all else in a fanfare of patriotic glory. In that larger context, his soul-searching monologue on the meaning of ceremony is a definitive statement of the overriding theme which gives the second series of English history plays their distinctive quality. Much as Hall—and therefore the later Tudor historians—may be said to have conspired in Shakespeare's purposes, the main impact of the plays from *Richard II* to *Henry V* is generated in the same current tensions that produced Hooker's *Laws*. In the same nonpartisan fashion with which Hooker approached the topic of daily debate in the world outside the theatre, Shakespeare voiced within the theatre what the bishops sought to sustain, and what the Puritan "Down with ceremonies!" sought to destroy.

From the point of view of stage impact, how serious was the threat in 1595 when Shakespeare wrote *Richard II*? Sir John Neale believes that the battle in parliament had already been won, despite the fact that as late as 1593 the Puritans were showing signs of once again rallying to the attack. A petition against the received ceremonies presented in the Parliament of 1589 had used no more than the language of moderate reform, "not in any substance of doctrine, but only in some ceremonies and indifferent things, whereto the Apostle teacheth us that every man's conscience is not to be forced." [53] This as I have shown had been the collective sense of the English church since Cranmer had etched it into the public consciousness in the Prayer-Book. But it is far from clear that in the Parliament of 1593 the Puritan organization had suffered a collapse, even though the Separatists had apparently

53. J. E. Neale, *Elizabeth I and her Parliaments, 1584–1601* (1957), p. 237.

been silenced with the execution of Henry Barrow and John Penry. It certainly did not seem so to Hooker, the first four books of the *Laws* having just been readied for the press and licensed by Archbishop Whitgift in time to support the act enforcing conformity.[54] "With us," Hooker wrote, "contentions are now at their highest float" (*LEP*, pref.ix.4). To him, the English position gained after so long debate was in dire jeopardy.

Two years later, Shakespeare made dramatic capital of those same apprehensions in a deliberate and vivid political parallel of ceremony outraged by a legitimate king. How strong an impact the key deposition scene in *Richard II* made on his audience is indicated by its omission from print as long as Elizabeth lived. It is possible that Elizabeth's Master of the Revels, Edmund Tilney, sensing the public response to such a production, did not allow it; and indeed an uncritical audience probably would not have noticed the omission, in spite of the awkward jointure in the quartos printed before 1603.[55] In any case, popular interest in the debate on ceremony, not the indecorous and possibly dangerous association of the names of Richard and Elizabeth at court, is far more likely to account for the new surge of dramatic energy with which Shakespeare decided to dramatize the beginning of the great contention.

The almost complete absence of any substantive use of the theme of ceremony in the earlier plays is a further indicator that before 1595, Shakespeare's mind had not yet kindled to the theatrical potential of the controversy. Even in *Richard III*, a much grosser violation of the crown, it would be straining things to find in Buckingham's dismissal of the Cardinal's scruples at breaking the laws of sanctuary more than an accidental reference:

> You are too senseless-obstinate, my lord,
> Too ceremonious and traditional.
>
> [*Richard III*, 3.1.44–45]

54. Sisson, *Judicious Marriage*, pp. 61–62; Neale, *Elizabeth I and her Parliaments*, p. 284.

55. Chambers, *Shakespeare*, 1 : 355.

Little more could be made of Aaron's derisive accusation that
Lucius is religious and possesses a conscience:

> With twenty popish tricks and ceremonies
> I have seen thee careful to observe.
>
> [*Titus Andronicus*, 5.1.74-77]

And if the pleasant ritual of Portia's accusation of infidelity at the
moment when she has rendered her new husband defenseless at
the point of her knifelike wit, had measurable weight, it is the
weight of a feather:

> What man is there so much unreasonable,
> If you had pleas'd to have defended it
> With any terms of zeal, wanted the modesty
> To urge the thing held as a ceremony?
>
> [*The Merchant of Venice*, 5.1.203-06]

In *Richard II*, it is another matter. What has hitherto appeared
as a casual reference is here a major consideration, dramatically
functional in both plot and character. The galvanism of the play
is primarily generated by the stage contrast between the enormity
of Richard's repudiation of the kingdom and Henry's passive
acceptance of it, between Richard's brilliant but insufferable
histrionics and Henry's taciturn restraint. "I thought you had
been willing to resign," and "Are you contented to resign the
crown" are no more than terse, frustrated interruptions of
Richard's flow of rhetorical exuberance. The effect on stage is to
slow the exchange to the point where ceremony comes close to
being more ridiculous than tragic. Henry, lacking a title, must
whistle to the air until Richard is ready to undo himself.

The confrontation, their first since Henry's banishment, is
skillfully prepared for by establishing their difference in temperament. Up to the moment when Henry "in God's name" ascends
the regal throne, he has never been openly the aggressor. Both by
report and stage action he has covered his intentions by flattery.
He is politically astute. His unctuous "Thanks, my country-men,
my loving friends" (1.4.34), and "I count myself in nothing else so
happy / As in a soul remem'bring my good friends" (2.3.146-47)

seem little more than the time-honored promises of a rising politician. He complicates this carefully nurtured visibility with an equally calculated policy to keep out of sight until popular curiosity has been sufficiently whetted. Thus he wholly succeeds in creating a public image without betraying more than his legitimate intentions. From the first, Richard suspects his aim but superciliously brushes it aside: "As were our England in reversion his, / And he our subjects' next degree in hope." His ridicule is ironic. From the moment Henry cuts short his banishment and returns to England, he publicly disavows any further purpose than reclaiming his dukedom. Yet each shrewd move brings him closer to the crown he gapes for. He kneels to his uncle, the Duke of York and protector of the realm, forcing him into a position of neutrality, then uses his presence to lend authority to the execution of Richard's unpopular favorites as "caterpillars of the commonwealth" whom he has sworn "to weed and pluck away" (2.3.163–67). It is a sop to the popular favor he has so assiduously cultivated (3.2.112–20), but now so widespread that it has become the gossip of even the queen's own gardeners.[56] He makes a show of armed force at Flint Castle, but he is again kneeling when the king appears above him in all the ceremonies of his office. Even after he ascends the throne, his public demeanor conceals his private craft. By indirections he will continue to find directions out, so that his accomplishment of Richard's death without commanding it, a detail Shakespeare derived from Hall via Holinshed (*The Union*, sig. Bvi^v), only confirms a pattern of behavior long established. Henry's violation of ceremony would make for an uneasy reign, as the audience knew. Hall describes it as an "unquiet time," and Shakespeare later remembered the phrase (*2 Henry IV*, 1.2.170). Relying on this common knowledge, he chooses to make Henry in the closing lines of *Richard II* a conscience-stricken man, who reaches out his guilty hand for a Jerusalem that in the later plays will always elude him. He is

56. 3.4.33–53. "King Richard's men" still persisted as a catchword in Shakespeare's day. See John Strype's *Life of Grindal* (ed. 1821), p. 354, and references in Chambers, *Shakespeare*, 1 : 353.

destined to live privately but restively with the fact that he has
killed a king; and the irony of his passive acceptance of the
kingship is that, like Macbeth, his conscience will never allow him
to draw the vestments of royalty about him. In the eyes of the
spectators, he is as much a violator of an office he did not openly
seek as the king who had made such an exquisite public
performance in surrendering it.

Shakespeare seems quite consciously to have avoided the idea
of usurpation in *Richard II.* The Henry of the later plays,
ruminating on the events leading to his ascending the throne,
prefers to regard the event as inevitable. "I and greatness were
compelled to kiss." And in the hatch and breed of time,
succeeding events have persuaded him to a belief in determinism:
"Are these things then necessities? / Then let us meet them like
necessities" (*2 Henry IV*, 3.1.74, 86, 92–93). Only on his deathbed
when he confesses to his son the "by-paths and indirect crook'd
ways" by which he "met" the crown does he admit that he
"snatch'd" it "with boist'rous hand" (4.5.185–86, 192). Of this
long struggle with conscience, there is no hint in Shakespeare's
sources. Hall and Holinshed both affirm that Henry "never
thereof thought or yet dreamed." Shakespeare's Henry, like his
Richard, created his own fiction of what had happened. For him,
someone had to occupy the vacuum left by Richard's abdication;
it was fate that the kingship lay in his way and he found it.

This passive violation of the ceremony of the crown serves
Shakespeare as dramatic counterpoint to Richard's stagy misuse
of it—the crux of the play—and it constitutes Shakespeare's
contribution to the legend of Richard's fall. Richard is a
legitimate king, and therefore all the perquisites of office, however
vaguely defined, are his by right of his "estate," historically that
"mass of traditions, attributes, rites, powers—and perhaps duties
also—which were deemed to center in the monarch." [57] He exerts

57. S. B. Chrimes, *English Constitutional Ideas in the Fifteenth Century* (1966), p. 3.
Chrimes cites *Rotuli Parliamentorum* (1767–1777), vol. 3, p. 424, for Richard's use of
the word in reference to his regality, estate, and royal liberty; and his deprivation
in 1399 of the "Astate of Kyng" and of all the lordship, dignity, worship, and
administration belonging thereto.

them arbitrarily, quixotically, making the throne a convenience for the exercise of personal whim. The grossly unfair decision against Mowbray in the tourney which opens the play reveals his volatile nature; and his offense to Bolingbroke, and as a consequence to the estate of a king, is clear from York's reproof:

> Take Hereford's rights away, and take from Time
> His charters and his customary rights;
> Let not to-morrow then ensue to-day;
> Be not thyself—for how art thou a king
> But by fair sequence and succession?

[2.1.195–99]

His cold jest on hearing of Gaunt's grave illness is likewise a sudden shocking revelation of his self-centered, gaudy caprice (1.4.59–64). In spite of his inheritance, he is a playacting king. He knows all the forms and ceremonies of the part; but he chooses to act the role from the opposite side of the cloth, reveling in all the familiar rituals of kingship even as he violates them for the sake of the histrionic gesture. He has been crowned, enthroned, and anointed in the time-honored tradition of English kings, each station instinct with its own value: "the crown," in Hooker's words, "a sign of military; the throne, of sedentary or judicial; the oil, of religious or sacred power" (*LEP*, VIII.ii.13). Yet Richard deliberately desecrates the crown by yielding it, the throne by stepping down from it, the oil by washing it away. The relinquishing of each of his symbols of his royal estate becomes his unique opportunity to take the center of the stage.

From the early scenes of the play to the dethronement, references to these royal investitures continually recur. Gaunt reminds us of the coronation ceremonies that confirm Richard's royal power as "God's substitute / His deputy anointed in his sight" (1.2.37–38). But Richard has committed his "anointed body" to the care of flatterers, put "this royal throne of kings, this scept'red isle" in pawn, and so misused his powers that his royal ancestor, Edward III, had he known of it, would have taken them away,

> Deposing thee before thou wert possess'd
> Which art possess'd now to depose thyself.
>
> [2.1.107–08]

In the same vein, York speaks accusingly of Bolingbroke's disloyalty to the "anointed King" (2.3.97). But far more than any of his subjects, Richard misuses ceremony in his self-appointed role as tragic hero. He possesses the symbols of royal power; yet by his refusal to use them, they have become, in Hooker's words, "idle gestures, destitute of signification." While the substantial powers of Bolingbroke grow strong, Richard withdraws from reality, unwilling to rally the forces still loyal to him. The stage has become a substitute for real life. He lives in a world of illusion, and like an actor, he becomes enamored of the words in his script. After Gaunt's loving reference to England as "this earth of majesty, this seat of Mars," Richard's iteration of "dear earth," "my earth," "my gentle earth," which he salutes with "my hand," "my royal hands," is mawkish irony. Enough to be defended by spiders, toads, nettles, adders, or an army of God's glorious angels. If these fail him,

> This earth shall have a feeling, and these stones
> Prove armed soldiers ere her native king
> Shall falter under foul rebellion's arms.
>
> [3.1.24–26]

His soldier-audience cannot conceal their scorn of his performance, and both the Bishop of Carlisle and Aumerle dare to suggest the necessity for action in the face of real threat. But Richard feels an inward compulsion to play out his part, investing himself in the protective ceremonies of crown, throne, and oil, while he ignores the responsibilities of kingship which those ceremonies symbolize:

> Not all the water in the rough rude sea
> Can wash the balm off from an anointed king.

> The breath of worldly men cannot depose
> The deputy elected by the Lord.

$$[3.2.54-57]^{58}$$

The Book of Common Prayer was the readiest reminder to Shakespeare's audience that ceremony should edify; for Richard, ceremony has become the edifice itself, debased to the position of prop to his vanity.

Hard bright steel now covers the land, but Richard has become ensnared in the role of a martyr king. The histrionics of deposition fixed in his mind, his fancy is titillated by numbering himself anachronistically among the tragic kings of the *Mirror for Magistrates*. In self-pity he will tell sad stories of the death of kings, whose hollow crowns house Death (as for Gaunt they housed flatterers), allowing them a little scene to monarchize before their final farewell. Precisely because the crown has been reduced to a stage property, Richard as actor can ask why ceremony should be observed toward kings.

> Cover your heads, and mock not flesh and blood
> With solemn reverence. Throw away respect,
> Tradition, form, and ceremonious duty;
> For you have but mistook me all this while.
> I live with bread like you, feel want, taste grief,
> Need friends. Subjected thus
> How can you say to me I am a king?

$$[3.2.171-77]$$

How indeed? For it is Richard, not his subjects, who has made ceremony so hollow that it is no more than an actor's convenience. And when its value is so diminished, he has already deposed himself. Richard will presently descend from his throne, and a usurper, a king of smiles who can kneel to a brace of draymen or doff his hat to an oyster-wench, will take up the royal

---

58. P. E. Schramm, *The History of the English Coronation* (1937), p. 137: "Shakespeare has reproduced this conception with historic truth. But however dogmatically correct it may have been, it broke down in the political struggle for power. Nevertheless it was a reproach to the house of Lancaster that it had dethroned an anointed king."

responsibilities. Ironically, it is the lowly gardener who makes the proper comment several scenes later:

> Why should we, in the compass of a pale,
> Keep law and form and due proportion?
>
> [3.4.40–41]

For Elizabethans, the gardener's innocent image echoes the voices of the dissidents to ecclesiastical ceremony from William Turner to John Penry, for whom "the traditional and ceremonial pale" represented nothing short of tyranny in the clerical hierarchy.[59]

The infamous act of deposition has now become by dramatic necessity inevitable; infamous, because it violates all the ceremonials of the coronation, inevitable because both Richard and Henry feel trapped in roles from which, however indefensible, they have no intent to withdraw. Richard will presently acknowledge his on his way to the Tower: "I am sworn brother, sweet, / To grim necessity," just as Henry too will come to feel, long after the event, that he would not have claimed the crown were it not "that necessity so bow'd the state." There is no hint of such a rationalization, however, at the crucial moment when Bolingbroke overtly steps to the throne. Shakespeare's relocation of the Bishop of Carlisle's lone voice of protest immediately thereafter instead of in the first year of his reign, as in the chronicles, in itself gives dramatic intensity to Henry's violence to ceremony. But Shakespeare has further heightened it by adding specific reference to the coronation symbols. Compare the bishop's speech as reported in Hall:

> For I thynke ther is none of you worthy or mete to geue iudgemente on so noble a Prince as kyng Richard is, whom we haue taken for our souereigne and liege lorde by the space of xxii yeres, and I assure you, ther is not so ranke a traytor, nor so arrante a thiefe, nor so cruell a murderer, whiche is apprehended and deteigned in prisone for his offence, but he shall bee brought before the iustice to heare his iudgemente, and yet you will proceade to the iudgmente of an anoynted

59. See above, n. 16.

kyng, and here nother his answere nor excuse. [*The Union*, sig. Bii]

and Shakespeare's reworking of it:

> What subject can give sentence on his king?
> And who sits here that is not Richard's subject?
> Thieves are not judg'd but they are by to hear,
> Although apparent guilt be seen in them;
> And shall the figure of God's majesty
> His captain, steward, deputy elect,
> Anointed, crowned, planted many years,
> Be judg'd by subject and inferior breath,
> And he himself not present?
>
> [*Richard II*, 4.1.121–29] [60]

Here explicitly set forth, with all the weight of the church's authority, the nature of the king's vicegerency is defined; and three centuries of English law stand behind the words. The king was more than a person by virtue of the visual yet mystic symbols of enthronement, unction, and coronation, but his powers were nevertheless traditionally vicarious rather than sacerdotal. Bracton, to whom Thomas Cromwell referred, had described the king as "God's vicar" (*vicarius dei in terris* or *in terra*), Christ-like but never with powers of priesthood. [61] To Henry VIII, "it were *nimis absurdam* for us to be called *Caput Ecclesiae representans Corpus Christi mysticum*"; further, he was specifically reminded of his secularity by act of parliament: "your Grace being a lay man." [62] The common lawyers, intent on the protection of their own prerogatives, had followed the same lead, preferring the ancient and more

60. On the *character indelibilis*, see Ernst H. Kantorowicz, *The King's Two Bodies: A Study in Mediaeval Political Theology* (1957), p. 36, and especially n. 22, where he points out that historically there had always been "a lack of precision" concerning the sacramental character of the coronation. Chrimes (*Constitutional Ideas*, p. 7) points out, however, that its existence was never in doubt.

61. *Letters and Papers, Foreign and Domestic, of the Reign of Henry VIII, 1509–1547* (1862–1932), XII (i), no. 1038; hereinafter referred to as *L&P*. Fritz Schulz, "Bracton on Kingship," *EHR*, 60 (1945) : 149; Kantorowicz, *King's Two Bodies*, pp. 155–56.

62. *L&P*, v, appendix no. 9; *Statutes of the Realm*, 37 Henry VIII (1545), c. 17.

ambiguous phrase: "Rex est persona mixta cum sacerdote." [63]
And Article Thirty-seven of the Act of Supremacy at the
beginning of Elizabeth's reign, in granting the queen "chief
power," specifically excluded her from "the ministering either of
God's word or of the Sacraments." In Shakespeare's day, this
traditional unwillingness to grant sacerdotal powers to the king
was strengthened by Puritan sentiment; so much so, that Richard
Hooker felt it necessary to reject any priestly powers in the king
beyond the appointment of clerics as "a shift vain and needless,"
even though he was not unsympathetic with those "that will not
have kings be altogether of laity, but to participate that sanctified
power which God hath endued his clergy with, and that in such
respect they are anointed with oil" (*LEP*, VIII.vii.1).

So for Shakespeare's Richard, who was somewhat less the
martyr king Yorkist sympathizers had made of him. "God for his
Richard" might have "in heavenly pay / A glorious angel"; but
he had best listen to Aumerle's advice, "Remember who you are"
(3.2.60–61, 82). For Richard's powers, we might well infer from
the Bishop of Carlisle's words, partake in an executive sense only
of both God and man. He is "the figure"—some in Shakespeare's
audience would have said merely the figure—"of God's majesty";
but he is also a person whose powers derive in part from popular
consent. Richard would learn, as Claudius would later learn, that
the divinity that doth hedge a king has terrestrial limitations.[64]
The irony of Richard's sole reliance on the support of heaven rests
in his haughty disregard of the earthly support offered him by his
Yorkist followers. Unwilling in his role as actor-king to recognize
his political danger, he dallies with words while Henry busies
himself in the practical politics of power, and not without success

63. J. N. Figgis, *The Divine Right of Kings*, ed. G. R. Elton (1965), pp. 17–18.
64. G. R. Elton acutely summarizes the mystique of the king's dual derivation
of power in his introduction (1965) to Figgis's *Divine Right*, pp. xxxii–xxxviii. It
may be added, however, that when he defines it as "the rule of men's bodies and
the protection of their souls," he is using a language which Shakespeare would not
have understood. More agreeable to Elizabethans would be Henry V's response to
the misgivings of Michael Williams before Agincourt: "Every subject's duty is the
King's, but every subject's soul is his own."

(3.2.112–19). Enough for Richard that *rex* and *sacerdos* were in some long-forgotten way commingled; his stage conduct in no way conflicted with and indeed confirmed the dramatic power still resident in throne, oil, and crown as political symbols.

In this playacting context, the stage picture of Richard's entrance immediately thereafter assumes a special significance. Hall is more specific than Holinshed at this point:

> Kyng Richard appareled in vesture and robe royall the diademe on his head, and the scepter in his hand, came personally before the congregacion. [*The Union*, sig. Aviii[v]]

Shakespeare departs conspicuously from his source by giving Richard an uncrowned entrance, officers bearing the regalia. Of this stage business there can be no doubt even though it is not a part of the stage direction until Edward Capell (1767–68). All seventeenth-century quartos indicate merely "Enter king Richard," the folios, "Enter Richard and Yorke." However, Richard's "Give me the crown. Here, cousin, seize the crown. / Here, cousin"—with its deliberate short line to allow for the reluctance of Henry to take a part in the rite—"on this side my hand, and on that side yours," is clear warrant for Capell's expanded stage direction: "Re-enter YORK with RICHARD, and officers bearing the Regalia," thus bearing out Holinshed's account. There is every evidence that this crown-play, both by word and gesture, is for the king a *tableau animé* to dramatize his conscious abdication of public responsibility, as he first withholds his cares by Bolingbroke's leave, then gives them all away, one by one, with a "Now mark me how I will undo myself" to leave himself nothing:

> I give this heavy weight from off my head
> And this unwieldy sceptre from my hand
> The pride of kingly sway from out my heart.
> With mine own tears I wash away my balm,
> With mine own hands I give away my crown,
> With mine own tongue deny my sacred state,
> With mine own breath release all duty's rites.
>
> [4.1.204–10][65]

65. Gaines Post in *Studies in Medieval Legal Thought* (1964), pp. 369–70, quotes

Thus divested of all ceremonies, he finds his own soul an accomplice to the "traitors" who surround him:

> For I have given here my soul's consent
> To undeck the pompous body of a king.
>
> [4.1.249–50]

As Kantorowicz states it, the "king" has committed high treason against the "King" (*King's Two Bodies*, p. 39).

But all this is not enough. The enormity of his offense to Shakespeare's audience lies in his presumption to sanctity, the character no English king had been allowed. His ultimate theatrical gesture is to identify his deposition with that of Christ, King of the Jews, thus associating the reverse-ceremonial of royal divestment with the stripping off of the kingly robes before the Crucifixion (Matt. 27 : 28–31). It is a parallel of unexampled abhorrence since it springs from vanity utterly devoid of the essential nature of sacrifice. The regalia are thùs made a mockery, "dumb ceremonies" without meaning, which Hooker had so cogently defended against Puritan derision, the "silent rites" whose quality must be judged by "that which they mean or betoken." Richard has already labeled his supposedly defected favorites (they had, in fact, been murdered) as "three Judases, each one thrice worse than Judas!" (3.2.132). At his entrance to his "trial," his regalia borne behind him, he has faced his erstwhile supporters in the same role:

> Were they not mine?
> Did they not sometime cry "All hail!" to me?
> So Judas did to Christ; but he, in twelve,
> Found truth in all but one; I, in twelve thousand none.
>
> [4.1.168–71] [66]

Now, divested wholly of any appurtenances of kingship, he assumes once more the Christ-like role:

Kantorowicz's comments on *Richard II* with approval; but he overlooks Shakespeare's stress on the coronation balm, which above all the royal ceremonies proclaims Richard's sacred state. I cannot agree that "the royal 'sacred state' . . . was virtually the crown" (p. 370).

66. Matt. 26 : 47–50; 27 : 28. Luke 23 : 28, 36.

Nay, all of you that stand and look upon
Whilst that my wretchedness doth bait myself,
Though some of you, with Pilate, wash your hands,
Showing an outward pity, yet you Pilates
Have here deliver'd me to my sour cross,
And water cannot wash away your sin.

[4.1.237-42] [67]

Meeting his solicitous queen thus uncrowned, he insists that henceforth "our holy lives must win a new world's crown" (5.1.24). Incredibly, relinquishment of this world's crown never occurs to him as profanation.

Acting as both king and priest, Richard has thus brought the abominable rite of self-deposition to its close. Yet the great question remained. The ceremonies by which these kingly powers were assumed were sanctified by ages of emotionally weighted tradition. Could anyone other than Christ lay them by? Where were the rites to be found by which these rites might be reversed? Walter Pater was intuitively at the heart of the matter in pointing out that there was no counter-ceremony for the order of coronation. "No rite of 'degradation,' such as that by which an offending priest or bishop may be deprived. . . . It is as if Shakespeare had had in mind some such inverted rite . . . in the scene where Richard 'deposes' himself, as in some long, agonizing ceremony, reflectively drawn out." [68]

Long and agonizing may well have been the effect Shakespeare intended to induce, stretched out to the limits of emotional endurance. Small wonder if Elizabeth abhorred it. Richard had already "leased out" his kingdom; now, "bankrout of his majesty," in a ritual of his own devising, he shatters his mirrored glory. Following the words of the Statutes, "your Grace being a

67. For Bolingbroke's association with Pilate in *Chronique de la Traîson et Mort de Richard II*, and in Créton's *History of the Deposition of Richard II*, see Professor J. Dover Wilson's introduction to the play in his New Cambridge edition (1939), pp. xlv–xlvii. Professor Wilson feels that the play should be played throughout as ritual (p. xiii).

68. *Appreciations, with an Essay on Style* (1898), pp. 205–06.

lay man," he acts as a layman merely in a part not of his own choosing. Then in a swift reversal, Richard the layman becomes king again. Looked at retrospectively, it is artfully prepared for by the queen's first show of impatience at his pusillanimity as she recalls an earlier Richard in the roll of English kings:

> What, is my Richard both in shape and mind
> Transform'd and weak'ned? Hath Bolingbroke depos'd
> Thine intellect? Hath he been in thy heart?
> The lion dying thrusteth forth his paw
> And wounds the earth, if nothing else, with rage
> To be o'erpow'r'd; and wilt thou pupil-like
> Take thy correction, mildly kiss the rod,
> And fawn on rage with base humility,
> Which art a lion and the king of beasts?
>
> [5.1.26–34]

Hardly less effective in setting off Richard's high-handed misuse of the value of ceremony is the happy invention of the groom whose loyalty remains unaffected by Richard's failure to recognize the man who has handed him his horse daily. "What my tongue dares not, that my heart shall say" rebukes the man to whom the kingship has been a mere personal convenience. Now alone with his contentious still-breeding thoughts, Richard makes the prison a figure of the discontented world, himself a king yet no king but nothing. Thus Shakespeare attenuates the playactor's role to the very moment before he faces his murderers in fierce deadly strokes with a weapon wrested from one of them. And what a battle it is! The stage directions barely give it justice. We have to read it in Holinshed as Shakespeare must have read it, and take our cue there for his single-handed battle royal before he is overpowered. Without an audience at last, and wholly stripped of his ceremonies, he drops his actor's role and becomes the lion-hearted Richard thrusting forth his paw, by his unadorned manliness making the ceremonies of a king for the time superfluous. In that moment, one almost forgives the rest.

Formal Majesty

Wherein, then, lay the value of ceremony? During the period of writing the two parts of *Henry IV* and *Henry V*, Shakespeare contemplated the answer to that question. Hooker, analyzing the insufficiencies of the Puritan position, approached it negatively by requiring the value of ceremonies to be disproved; so Shakespeare, after the negative statement of *Richard II*, found his positive answer in the figure of Hal, as heir apparent and as king. Whether in religious or political context, the answer is central to both *The Laws of Ecclesiastical Polity* and the Henry plays. In terms of dramatic strategy, the spectacle of Richard's insouciant exploitation of ceremony is complemented in the two parts of *Henry IV* by an old king's remorse for his wrongful seizure of a power which could only turn to ashes with his touch. As a consequence, he is condemned to live within the shadow of his crime, a prime offense against royal blood never to be expiated by his long hoped for but unrealized pilgrimage to the Holy Land. Each will find his peculiar rendezvous with grim necessity, Richard relishing it with never a thought of the commonwealth: "He and I / Will keep a league till death," Henry quelling past sin and present conscience in a futile *cri de coeur*: "The body of our kingdom, / How foul it is; what rank diseases grow, / And with what danger near the heart of it." The disruption of the commonwealth which Richard has prophesied, Henry ruefully reflects on later, not knowing that in the necessity of event he will die in his own Jerusalem chamber, whereas his son Hal, in spite of his apparent dereliction from his expected role as prince, will in proper time take up his inheritance together with the responsibilities of kingship which alone give ceremony meaning.

Just as we are expected to accommodate ourselves to Hal's assertion that he revels now so as to make his later reform shine the brighter, so on a comic level we can expect him to accept Falstaff's ex post facto recognition of the true prince as a sufficient justification of his running away. Both are temporary indulgences. The ingenuity of escape from logic in egregious, irresponsible deception is a properly allowed humor when humor needs no excuse. Too soon, the time will come for another kind of logic. It is the loan of a bottle instead of a pistol that eventually draws Hal's righteous anger. Up to that time, Hal has been a party to Falstaff's burlesque of the ceremonies of royal office: "This chair shall be my state, this dagger my sceptre, and this cushion my crown." The prince's cue is to insist that they are indeed a joined stool, a leaden dagger, and—for the pun's sake—"a pitiful bald crown" (*1 Henry IV*, 2.4.415–20). Falstaff's prophetic "Depose me?" is the baldest impudency to the son of Richard's deposer. Yet even while duty in the person of the sheriff knocks at the door, Falstaff will—and knows he can—dare the consequences. Both the Prince of Purpool and the Prince of Wales have debts to pay in a responsible world; but while Falstaff's consumption of the purse is obviously incurable, and while Hal's consumption of time in the tavern far exceeds that in the council chamber, it will be a humorless world that will not agree that before the due date for payment of debt there is much to say in behalf of cakes and ale.

The very ephemerality of their sophistical exchanges makes them a commodity all the more precious. We know, as Hal knows, how beguilingly Falstaff pleads his case: "Banish plump Jack and banish all the world." And we know, as Hal knows, how inevitable and even regrettable is Hal's response. "I do, I will" is not a threat but a prognosis, a reluctant admission of the ineluctability of that idol, ceremony, to which as heir apparent he must pay deference all too soon.

The king, on the other hand, weighed down by his cardinal violation of ceremony, is humorless and aloof, his guilt forcing him into a formal role of occasional visibility. By the same pattern, he exhorts his son to make himself less common, so that when he does appear his person will seem "fresh and new . . . like a robe pontifical, / Ne'er seen but wond'red at" (3.2.55–57). Well did that subtle king know how to put ceremony to use to gain by humble courtesy the state that Richard discarded by mingling his royalty "with cap'ring fools." Hooker had described the visual appeal of ceremony, and he was thinking in political as well as religious terms:

> No nation under heaven either doth or ever did suffer public actions which are of weight, whether they be civil and

> temporal or else spiritual and sacred, to pass without some
> visible solemnity: the very strangeness whereof and difference
> from that which is common, doth cause popular eyes to
> observe and to mark the same. [*LEP*, iv.i.3]

So the elder Henry reflects on his own rise to power: "being
seldom seen, I could not stir / But, like a comet, I was wondered
at" (3.2.46–47). Seeing his son "so common-hackney'd in the eyes
of men" that "not an eye / But is aweary of thy common sight"
(3.2.40, 86–87), he fails to understand what the audience has been
aware of from the beginning, that the prince is in fact imitating
the policy of his father by permitting

> the base contagious clouds
> To smother up his beauty from the world,
> That, when he please again to be himself,
> Being wanted, he may be more wond'red at
> By breaking through the foul and ugly mists
> Of vapours that did seem to strangle him.
>
> [1.2.222–27] [69]

In his own time, Hal too will be publicly punctilious in visual
solemnity. That will be at his coronation. For the present on the
field of battle, he must "redeem" his personal honor even though
it be clad in a garment of English blood, staining his own
"favours" in that bloody mask (3.2.135–36), but that only after his
attempt to prevent the shedding of blood has failed. Over the
dead Hotspur, the ceremony he could not perform for the living,
he performs for the gallant dead: "Even in thy behalf, I'll thank
myself / For doing these fair rites of tenderness" (5.4.97–98).
What is "food for powder" in the shared jest is "food for worms"
when the jest is over.

In the meantime, Falstaff has become too valuable a stage
property not to be resurrected to fight again another day. For *2
Henry IV* may well be mainly the result of the resounding success
of the humors of Falstaff (*ecce signum*) which Shakespeare as a

---

69. Cf. Hotspur's contempt for "base and rotten policy" (1.3.108).

popular dramatist simply could not ignore. That, the title pages of both parts advertise.[70] Viewed as a dramatic action, *1 Henry IV* is a complete, self-sufficient action brought to its conclusion in the battle of Shrewsbury with the death of Hotspur, the "purge" of Falstaff, and the vindication of Hal's honor. Writing a sequel in response to popular demand involved therefore both historical and structural problems. Historically, Shrewsbury was the most important military engagement of a reign which Shakespeare remembered from Hall's description as "unquiet" (*2 Henry IV*, 1.2.170). Not certainly a propitious prospect for an historical play. From a structural point of view, the possibility of a sequel was bleak, not to be accomplished without unraveling ends already tied up in *Henry the Fourth*. Hotspur could be, and was, brought back to life—defying Falstaff's proposition that detraction will not suffer honor to live with the living—in the impassioned description of that "miracle" of men by his widow Kate. Falstaff must be, and was, unreformed again. With an effort, Hal could be continued as straight man to Falstaff's humors. But the theme of honor which bound them all together had been brilliantly concluded, and there lay the inescapable dilemma.

The virtue that Shakespeare made of this necessity is testimony of his flexibility as a dramatist. It will be observed that the one important innovation in the serious action of *2 Henry IV* is the Lord Chief Justice. For this character Shakespeare had set aside Holinshed for Stow and / or Elyot's *Governour*, with the result that the theme of royal responsibility which in a military sense had been fulfilled at Shrewsbury will now be fulfilled in a judicial sense by the rejection of Falstaff. The king's disappointment in his son continued to be exploited to great advantage in this structural context; and his death before the rejection allows for a narrower final tableau in which, precisely as in *1 Henry IV*, the three main

70. Until the editors of the First Folio found it necessary to distinguish the two plays (Quartos, 1–6), the first part was entitled *The History of Henrie the Fourth*. On the other hand, the humorous conceits of Sir John Falstaff were advertised on the title page of the first quarto (1598), and in all the succeeding quartos printed in Shakespeare's lifetime, as well as in the two quartos of the second part.

characters are for the first time in the action brought together, the Lord Chief Justice in effect substituting for Hotspur.

This final disposition of characters is prepared for very early in the action. As soon as act one, scene two, the stage opposition of Falstaff and the Lord Chief Justice has established the image of lawlessness in the one and authority in the other, between which Hal must at the last exhibit his choice; it is renewed in act two, scene one; and finally in the crucial scenes which conclude the action, image and symbol are combined as essential instruments in dramatizing the relation of a king to law. Again, as in the earlier plays, the royal regalia are theatrically exploited. The king's crown becomes for the newly reflective prince an object of his new concern: "a troublesome bedfellow," "a polish'd perturbation," "a golden care," which as visual symbol he removes and places on his own head, figuratively deposing his father. With that removal, he transforms the sleeplessness of a king's care to the sleep of a king's death. On the other hand, the king too, who just previously has described the prince as "the noble image of my youth," now sees that image as unhappily confirmed by Hal's "theft" of the crown. As in *Richard II*, Shakespeare likewise associates the coronation ceremonies of crown, oil, and state to give ironic weight to the king's present care. Ceremonies which he himself had snatched from Richard seem now to have been snatched from him, despairing prefigurations, as he thinks, of his too eagerly hoped for death:

> Then get thee gone and dig my grave thyself
> And bid the merry bells ring to thine ear,
> That thou art crowned, not that I am dead.
> Let all the tears that should bedew my hearse
> Be drops of balm to sanctify thy head.
> Only compound me with forgotten dust;
> Give that which gave thee life unto the worms.
> Pluck down my officers, break my decrees;
> For now a time is come to mock at form.
> Harry the Fifth is crown'd. Up, vanity!
> Down, royal state! All you sage counsellors, hence!

[4.5.111–21]

Now, ceremony discarded, England may expect a new regime of those who

> will swear, drink, dance,
> Revel the night, rob, murder, and commit
> The oldest sins the newest kind of ways.
>
> [4.5.125–27]

Precisely this image of Falstaff was presented in Hooker's description of those who believe that in government "the fullest bellies are happiest":

> Therefore the greatest felicity they wish to the common-wealth wherein they live is that it may but abound and stand, that they which are riotous may have to pour out without stint, that the poor may sleep and the rich feed them, that nothing unpleasant may be commanded, nothing for-bidden men which themselves have a lust to follow, that kings may provide for the ease of their subjects and not be too curious about their manners, that wantonness, excess, and lewdness of life may be left free, and that no fault may be capital besides dislike of things settled in so good terms.
> [*LEP*, v.lxxvi.4] [71]

The dying king can foresee only a reign of lawlessness:

> When that my care could not withhold thy riots,
> What wilt thou do when riot is thy care?
>
> [4.5.135–36]

Unfortunately, he will not live to see the Fifth Harry cast aside the vanities of his youth and confirm the reign of law in the person of the Lord Chief Justice, nor to hear his public affirmation of the ceremonials of state:

> The tide of blood in me
> Hath proudly flow'd in vanity till now.
> Now it doth turn and ebb back to the sea,

71. Published in 1597, the same year in which Shakespeare was probably writing 2 *Henry IV*.

> Where it shall mingle with the state of floods
> And flow henceforth in formal majesty.
>
> [5.2.129–33]

This choice in matter of fact had already made itself felt in Hal's recognition of the crown as a value symbol. His excuse for taking the crown, as he explained to his father, was to upbraid it "as having sense" (4.5.158). And his father quite properly had accepted this earnest of Hal's change of mood. All that remained was to make the image of authority explicit and public. And this is the reason for the so-called rejection scene, which might more properly be called an induction scene. The image of royalty is operative on various levels. There is first "this new and gorgeous garment," authority's visual presence. But what sort of authority? From Aristotle to Hooker, the answer lay in the father-child relationship of monarch and subject,[72] which Shakespeare extends to brother and brother. The new king, uneasy at his brothers' misgiving over his past conduct, assures them that henceforth he will remain both father and brother to them (5.2.57). But Shakespeare significantly reverses the Hooker relationship of father-son in defining the nature of the king's authority. Hitherto, Hal has appeared to reject "the rusty curb of old father antic the law" (*1 Henry IV*, 1.2.68–69), making Falstaff his "father," and jestingly changing roles with him. Now that he is himself the king-father, he deposes himself, not as Richard did to please his histrionic temperament, nor yet in any personal sense to elevate the Lord Chief Justice, who like Hal's brothers, has cause to fear, but rather to erect the office as a symbol of the law to which a king, like his subjects, must bow. It is precisely this point that the Lord Chief Justice is at pains to make:

> I then did use the person of your father;
> The image of his power lay then in me;
> And in th' administration of his law,

72. *LEP*, I.x.4. "It is no improbable opinion therefore which the arch-philosopher was of, that as the chiefest person in every household was as it were a king, so when numbers of households joined themselves in civil society together, kings were the first kind of governors amongst them. Which is also (as it seemeth) the reason why the name of Father continued still in them, who of fathers were made rulers."

Whiles I was busy for the commonwealth,
Your highness pleased to forget my place,
The majesty and power of law and justice,
The image of the King whom I presented,
And struck me in my very seat of judgment.

[5.2.73–80]

"Be now the father," he urges, "and, as you are a king, speak in your state." To which injunction Hal wholly concedes: "You shall be as a father to my youth," thereby relinquishing arbitrary rule for government in which Lex supersedes Rex.

In the ceremony of Hal's induction to formal majesty, Falstaff's rejection as father of Hal's riots is a necessary if joyless corollary. "Choose what office thou wilt in the land, 'tis thine . . . the laws of England are at my commandment," was far from jest to the ambitious Justice Shallow; a bribe of a thousand pounds hung on Falstaff's influence at court. And the arrest of the ale-logged Quickly and Doll Tearsheet as they protest "that right should thus overcome might!" points to the lawless extremities to which Falstaff's fatherhood would lead. In this context, his appellation, "my sweet boy," is a vain appeal to an irrevocable past (5.3.128–29, 141–42; 5.4.27–28; 5.5.47). From the moment of Hal's acceptance of kingship, the image of disorder has given place to the image of authority. Behind the ceremonies of coronation, behind the new and gorgeous garment of majesty is responsibility. The young King Henry has chosen law, and thus refuted his father's grave prophecy:

For the Fifth Harry from curb'd license plucks
The muzzle of restraint, and the wild dog
Shall flesh his tooth on every innocent.

[4.5.131–33]

The fact is that

The breath no sooner left his father's body
But that his wildness, mortified in him
Seem'd to die too.

[*Henry V*, 1.1.25–27]

Years later, we hear an echo of Henry IV's despair in the cry of another disillusioned royal father: "Behold the great image of authority: a dog's obey'd in office." But Lear was in his madness.

What is affirmed in the Henry IV plays becomes explicit in *Henry V*, the focal point of which trains on the young king's conscience in office. Shakespeare states the value of ceremony first on a comic level in the person of the Welshman, Fluellen, whose valuation of ceremony is limited to the laws of war as practiced by the ancients:

> It is the greatest admiration in the universal world, when the true and ancient prerogatifes and laws of the wars is not kept. If you would take the pains but to examine the wars of Pompey the Great, you shall find, I warrant you that there is no tiddle taddle nor pibble pabble in Pompey's camp. I warrant you, you shall find the ceremonies of the wars, and the cares of it, and the forms of it, and the sobriety of it, and the modesty of it, to be otherwise. [4.1.66–75]

Ceremony, care, form, sobriety, modesty—these are the qualities of the kingly office as Henry presently demonstrates when in disguise he walks among his soldiers on the eve of the battle. Like most soldiers in imminent danger, they are utterly frank in their analysis of their position. The king's identity concealed, he too speaks frankly, but insists that his fears should not be revealed to the "king." To the audience, who are party to the secret of the king's identity, his statement constitutes Shakespeare's reaffirmation of the essential humanity that underlies royal ceremony.

> For though I speak it to you, I think the King is but a man, as I am. The violet smells to him as it doth to me; the element shows to him as it doth to me; all his senses have but human conditions. His ceremonies laid by, in his nakedness he appears but a man; and though his affections are higher mounted than ours, yet, when they stoop, they stoop with the like wing. Therefore, when he sees reason of fears, as we do, his fears, out of doubt, be of the same relish as ours are. Yet,

in reason, no man should possess him with any appearance of
fear, lest he, by showing it, should dishearten his army.
[4.1.104–117]

Shakespeare may have been reminded of a passage from Machiavelli's *Florentine History* in which the garments a king wears are
made the only distinction between him and any other man.[73] But
Machiavelli put the argument in the mouth of a demagogue to
incite the populace of Florence to insurrection. Whatever the
source, Henry's words instantly recall the outrageousness of
Richard II's earlier claim to ceremonious duty on precisely the
same human conditions. Richard's histrionic "I live with bread
like you, feel want, taste grief, / Need friends" (*Richard II*,
3.2.175–77), is the felt need of both kings, despite the polarity of
their responses to kingship. In the larger pattern of Shakespeare's
thought, Richard had defaced ceremony by surrendering royal
responsibility; Henry V, by taking up his royal responsibility for
the lives of his soldiers, restores its value.

It is within this larger framework that Henry's soliloquy on
ceremony takes a central place. Ideologically, it reveals in a stage
moment the dynamic behind the second great series of historical
plays. It may be safely taken as Shakespeare's maturest definition
of the relation of king and subject. Simply spoken, ceremony is an
outward symbol of a king's responsibility to his subjects, willingly
assumed, and resident as much in the silent rites as in the spoken
words of the coronation. To the searching questions of the
common soldiers, he outlines the limits of that responsibility. In *1
Henry IV*, he had offered as prince to engage himself in single fight
with Hotspur "to save the blood on either side"; at Agincourt, the
impersonality of disguise sets aside ceremony to unite him with his
"brothers" in arms. But even though responsibility on the field of
battle must be shared, for both king and subject their souls'
fortunes remain their own. Only after the soldiers have gone, the
king alone must face the crucial fact that the coroneted king is
both man and symbol:

> Upon the King! Let us our lives, our souls,
> Our debts, our careful wives,

73. *Florentine History*, ed. W. K. Marriott (1909), p. 118.

Our children and our sins, lay on the King!
We must bear all. O hard condition,
Twin-born with greatness, subject to the breath
Of every fool, whose sense no more can feel
But his own wringing! What infinite heart's-ease
Must kings neglect that private men enjoy!

[4.1.247-54]

The sole difference between king and subject lies in ceremony:

And what art thou, thou idol Ceremony?
What kind of god art thou, that suffer'st more
Of mortal griefs than do thy worshippers?
What are thy rents? What are thy comings-in?
O Ceremony, show me but thy worth!
What is thy soul of adoration?
Art thou aught else but place, degree, and form,
Creating awe and fear in other men?
Wherein thou art less happy being fear'd
Than they in fearing.

[4.1.257-66]

The coronation symbols will neither cure sickness nor allow a
king repose:

I am a king that find thee; and I know
'Tis not the balm, the sceptre, and the ball,
The sword, the mace, the crown imperial,
The intertissued robe of gold and pearl,
The farced title running fore the king,
The throne he sits on, nor the tide of pomp
That beats upon the high shore of this world—
No, not all these, thrice-gorgeous ceremony,
Not all these, laid in bed majestical, ,
Can sleep so soundly as the wretched slave,
Who, with a body fill'd and vacant mind,
Gets him to rest, cramm'd with distressful bread;
. . . .
And but for ceremony, such a wretch,

Winding up days with toil and nights with sleep
Had the forehand and vantage of a king.

[4.1.276–97]

Ultimately, the answer to the question "What is the value of ceremony?" is also the answer to the question "What is a king?"

It is significant that this crowning soliloquy to the historical plays does not appear in print in Shakespeare's lifetime. Like the deposition scene of *Richard II*, one can conjecture practical political reasons for its omission. But there can be no doubt that it is Shakespeare's explicit superscription on the nature of kingship.

As the king concludes his soliloquy, urgent and immediate responsibility in the person of the good old knight Erpingham, intrudes on his thought. Morning will bring the battle; yet before it is joined, one private duty, still hidden *in scrinio pectoris*, needs to be performed, its broader implications analyzed. What of that double violation of the ceremony of kingship for which neither Richard nor Henry could disclaim responsibility? And in what sort did his father's original sin against majesty descend on his head? What now appears is that the expiation of that guilt has long troubled the conscience of the young king, that in fact he has kept "five hundred poor in fee" to pardon Richard's blood and built two chantries where priests may sing for Richard's soul. War, he has told his brothers in arms, "is [God's] beadle, war is his vengeance; so that here men are punish'd for before-breach of the King's laws in now the King's quarrel" [4.1.178–81]. But now the outcome of the battle may depend on God's willingness to forgive his father's original breach of ceremony, and his prayer is an exposure of his conscience in the matter:

Not to-day, O Lord,
O, not today, think not upon the fault
My father made in compassing the crown.

[4.1.309–11]

Thus having sought absolution, his royal responsibilities squarely on his shoulders, he proceeds to the immediate business of battle with clear conscience. A prince whose youthful spirits disinclined him to the observance of ceremony as long as he was prince has now as king made amends for his father's wanton disregard of it. For Shakespeare, ceremony and the misuse of it is the binding factor of the plays from *Richard II* through *Henry V*.

The bridge between contemporary religious controversy and the historical plays was easy of access to Shakespeare's audience. What garments a priest should wear, what ceremonies should be followed, were in themselves matters of credal indifference. But precisely as they were matters of indifference, they came within the purview of man's law. As outward symbols, their acceptance was essential to order in either church or state. On this ground, Richard's laying off of the garments of state and Henry V's taking them up were exact correspondences in Shakespeare's thought. But observance of ceremony means clearly a loss of liberty. As Hooker pointed out, the laws of man abridge men's liberty; we must either maintain them or else overturn the world and make every man his own commander. To Falstaff, with the news of the old king's death and Hal's accession ringing in his ears, a future of lawlessness without restraint immediately expands before him. "The laws of England are at my commandment!" is an unconscious exposure of error of which even his formal banishment by the king fails to convince him. Not until the Lord Chief Justice's public censure does it become apparent to the old reprobate that he is not superior to law. But, as the Lord Chief Justice argues, and as Hal has always known, neither is the king free. Sooner or later, both king and subject, in church or state, must acquiesce to the self-imposed proprieties of conscience, silken threads of ceremony, which to the libertine seem so easily broken, to the conscientious, binding—yet if society is to be sustained, binding on all alike with a perdurable toughness.

The pattern of ceremony so strongly woven into fifteenth-century history continues to reappear as a minor motif in the history and quasi-history plays of Shakespeare's late career. Hamlet's inky cloak has personal, not political, signification; and though we are given glimpses of that happier life before Claudius popp'd in between the election and his hopes, the prince of Denmark's perturbation arises as much from the killing of his father and mother as from the usurpation of his place as heir apparent. How can he assert that he lacks advancement if, as Rosencrantz claims, Claudius has assured him of the succession? (3.2.354–57). The heart of his mystery will continue to elude us as it does Rosencrantz and Guildenstern. But of one thing we may be sure: the ceremonies of his position as prince do not greatly concern him; and it is significant of his reaching out for human contact that his warmest greeting is to the common players. Not merely because of his rank, he is contemptuous of "that which passeth show" and appealingly eager to break through the outward forms that conceal the dishonesty of the Danish court and make a prison of it, or, as with Osric, a fetish. Montaigne, "crawling on the face of the earth," admires "even into the clouds, the inimitable height of some heroicke minds." [74] Hamlet, likewise "crawling between earth and heaven," in awe of the capabilities of that piece of work that is a man, yet finds "our beggars bodies, and our monarchs and outstretch'd heroes the beggars' shadows." Characteristically, he identifies himself with the unheroic level of mankind. "We are arrant knaves all; believe none of us," he tells Ophelia; but his words, here as elsewhere, are in the first person plural, like the General Confession in the Prayer-Book. Hamlet, the person, by extension has become the figure of all men, Ophelia by the same reasoning, of all women. Ceremony in such circumstances is an impertinence.

In *King Lear* and *Macbeth*, Shakespeare still pursues the idea of kingship in terms of a garment to be divested or put on. Lear, having unkinged himself by dividing his kingdom, discovers that he has lost "that ceremonious affection" to which he was accustomed. Thrust out of doors, he finds pity for the "loop'd and window'd raggedness" of other victims of the storm, and feverishly throws off the garments of royalty ("Off, off, you lendings! Come, unbutton here"). While robes and furred gowns hide the poverty of spirit of Lear's unspeakable daughters, he pulls off his boots, last vestiges of his royal clothing. As Henry V had put it, "his

74. *Essays*, "Of Cato the Younger," Everyman Edition, 3 vols. (1910, reprint ed. 1946), I : 243.

ceremonies laid by, in his nakedness he appears but a man." But
coincident with the end of the storm the ministrations of the
doctor must return him to sanity, precarious but indubitable.
"The great rage . . . is kill'd in him"; and with his recovery he
has arrived at a new self-knowledge: "I am a very foolish fond old
man."

Cordelia has played a different but no less important part in
Lear's recovery, and it is apparent as soon as he appears on stage
after his long ordeal. "Is he arrayed?" she asks of an unnamed
gentleman attending on him, and his response, "Ay, madam. In
the heaviness of sleep. / We put fresh garments on him" explains
what the eyes of the audience confirm: Cordelia in her solicitude
has restored him to his kingdom and ordered that he be reinvested
in his royal robes, symbols of his restitution. Viewed so, there is a
particular and poignant irony in his uncertainty of his present
condition.

> Methinks I should know you, and know this man;
> Yet I am doubtful; for I am mainly ignorant
> What place this is; and all the skill I have
> Remembers not these garments.
>
> [*King Lear*, 4.7.64–67]

It is generally accepted that in this play, Shakespeare deliberately departs from his sources to contrive a tragic ending. But the
turn to tragedy is held off until Lear has been reinstated in
the kingship. It is crucial that when he appears on stage with the
dead Cordelia in his arms he be invested. The shock is the
stronger inasmuch as Shakespeare seems up to this point to be
following the familiar story in Holinshed and Spenser. It was so
devastating that Nahum Tate may have been answering a felt
need in restoring the traditional happy ending; its domination of
the stage for a century and a half thereafter reinforces the point.
In Shakespeare's theatre, much of the effect derives from the
helplessness of a once powerful king to prevent a death for which
heaven's vault should crack yet does not. In staging that moment,
Shakespeare may well have reverted to lines written some ten
years earlier for a star-cross'd lover:

> Heaven is here
> Where Juliet lives; and every cat and dog
> And little mouse, every unworthy thing,
> Live here in heaven and may look on her;
> But Romeo may not.
>
> [*Romeo and Juliet*, 3.3.29–33]

Edgar is willing to believe in his innocence that "the gods are just, and of our pleasant vices / Make instruments to plague us." But to a foolish, fond old man, unkinged and kinged again, heaven's laws are as inexplicable as the world's law was to Romeo:

> And my poor fool is hang'd! No, no, no life!
> Why should a dog, a horse, a rat, have life,
> And thou no breath at all? Thou'lt come no more,
> Never, never, never, never, never!
>
> [*King Lear*, 5.3.305–08]

In such a situation, "Pray you, undo this button," reminding us at the last of the ceremonies of a king, seems to place the action outside the whole hierarchy of Hooker's laws.

The pervasive image of Macbeth's ill-fitting garments in the office of a king has long been a staple of criticism. What has not been noted is its extension of the vocabulary of royal ceremony. It is a sharp reminder of Henry Bolingbroke's violation of the English crown and its cost in English blood. In the context of the Scottish succession, it was obviously designed to please the new king of a united England and Scotland; but especially to Shakespeare's English audience, it brought to mind that earlier union that settled the crown on the house of Tudor. Francis Bacon in dedicating the second book of his *Advancement of Learning* to James shortly before Shakespeare wrote *Macbeth* proposed as "perfect history" the story of the two kingdoms now happily combined:

> And if it shall seem that the greatness of this work may make it less exactly performed, there is an excellent period of a much smaller compass of time, as to the story of England;

that is to say, from the uniting of the Roses to the uniting of
the kingdoms.[75]

Plainly, Bacon took Hall's *The Union* as a model in suggesting a
beginning and terminal point for its successor.

Shakespeare held the same point of view in writing *Macbeth*.
Macduff, with the tyrant's dripping head in his hand, predicts the
future:

> The time is free.
> I see thee compass'd with thy kingdom's pearl,
> That speak my salutation in their minds.
>
> [*Macbeth*, 5.8.55–57]

Yet from the first it has been clear that conscience would not be
dressed in borrowed robes, "strange garments" which "cleave not
to their mould / But with the aid of use." It remains a farce even
when Lady Macbeth goads him with the same image, "Was the
hope drunk / Wherein you dress'd yourself?" Macduff sees old
robes sitting easier than our new, and Macbeth's associates
observe that his kingly title hangs loose about him, "like a giant's
robe / Upon a dwarfish thief." But he must bear out the unlikely
part, nevertheless, knowing, as Lady Macbeth well knows, that
"the sauce to meat is ceremony; / Meeting were bare without it."
But the ceremonies alone will not do, and Macbeth like Henry IV
discovers that they will not allay the prick of conscience. The
irony of that burden for Henry was a pilgrimage unfulfilled; for
Macbeth, it is the death of his dearest partner of greatness.
Without her, the killing of a king is a meaningless act, "a
tale / Told by an idiot, full of sound and fury, / Signifying
nothing." Suddenly and quite devastatingly, Macbeth has discovered that the chiefest rule whereby to judge of the quality of the
ceremonies of royalty is, in Hooker's phrase, "that which they
mean or betoken." Ceremonies, even royal ceremonies, have lost
their signification.

The value of ceremony in the daily acts of life reverberates

75. *The Advancement of Learning*, ed. William Aldis Wright (1920), book 2,
Dedication to the King, sec. 8, p. 93.

throughout the plays. Shakespeare writes it into Portia's imperious foolery, into Ophelia's return of Hamlet's love tokens: "Their
perfume lost, / Take these again." It becomes significant as a
national symbol in Hector's valuation of Helen, measured against
the nine-years' siege of Troy which has long since ossified in
meaningless ceremony:

> But value dwells not in particular will:
> It holds his estimate and dignity
> As well wherein 'tis precious of itself
> As in the prizer.
>
> [*Troilus and Cressida*, 2.2.53–56]

It forges a link between Henry IV's entrapped conscience and
Macbeth's, identifying at first and last in Shakespeare's thought
that most shocking of public violations, the killing of a king. The
worse, in Hamlet's eyes, when Gertrude has compounded it by
marrying the murderer.

2

COMMONWEALTH

Rome as Political Exemplum

Shakespeare had not completed the last of the English history
plays before his mind was busy with Roman history, and
particularly with the fall of Julius Caesar. It is not surprising. In
the summer of 1599, the Earl of Essex at the head of the English
army in Ireland must have seemed as much as any living person
like the Roman conqueror of Britain. He was a soldier in the
moment of his greatest popular expectation, and Shakespeare in
comparing him with Henry V saw in him also a loving if lower
likeness to the antique Roman (*Henry V*, 5, chorus, 22–34). The
similarity of the political situation in fifteenth-century England
and in the First and Second Triumvirate invited further comparison. *Julius Caesar* like *Richard II* describes the removal of the head
of state, and then in a miniature of fifteenth-century English
history courses over its bloody and disruptive consequences. Here
again is the theme of civil war with its train of justifications and
recriminations. The tragic structure, epitomized, is the same.
Even the characters—without stretching the comparison—are
similarly patterned, the idealist Hotspur prefiguring Brutus, the
practical politician Worcester anticipating Cassius. As in the
English history plays, the idealisms engendered at the beginning
too soon evaporate; only the revenges go on.

But the differences exhibited in the Roman histories are quite
as conspicuous as the likenesses, and they arise in part from the
special disposition of Shakespeare's audience toward Roman
history. Bloody and protracted as were the civil wars following
Richard's death, Elizabethans could always view that past as
prologue to the marriage which inaugurated a rising age of

prosperity and domestic peace; in the fall of Caesar they professed
to see the beginning of the decline of an empire, the greatest the
world had known, and a critical moment in the most thoroughly
documented case history of the decline and fall of a great
civilization. Since history was expected to teach, existing civiliza-
tions might study the Roman debacle with profit, examine their
own past, and project their own future, knowing what excellences
to emulate, what pitfalls to avoid.

The meaning of history, however, is as elusive as the facts, and
for the central fact in Roman history, Tudor opinion depended on
one's politics. Viewed within the conventional morphological
concept of commonwealth with its neatly gradated duties from
king to lowliest subject, the assassination of Caesar was an
unmitigated disaster.[1] It was an observation indulged with no
little satisfaction by Elizabethans who could cite Roman political
misfortunes by comparison with their own felicity. William
Fulbecke expresses the common view in surveying the one
hundred years of factional quarrels before Augustus Caesar as an
illustration of "the mischiefes of discord and civill discention"
which followed the killing of the head of state, and he finds it an
appropriate occasion to thank God "for this sweete quiet and
serenitie of this flourishing estate, in which England now standeth."[2]

But by other less orthodox writers the killing of Caesar was
regarded as salutary for the common weal. To the republican
author of *The Tragedy of Caesar and Pompey or Caesar's Revenge* it was
a noble attempt to liberate Rome, purchased earlier by the
"ancient Brutus," now to be won again from a tyrant's yoke. The
tone is patriotic and public minded: "another Tarquin to be
expelled, / Another Brutus to act the deed,"[3] and the conspirators die with appropriate sentiments: Brutus, "dismayed in-

1. *The Boke named the Gouernour* (1531), ed. H. H. S. Croft (1883), bk. 1, ch. 2, p. 20.

2. *An historicall collection of the continuall factions, tumults, and massacres of the Romans and Italians during the space of one hundred and twentie yeares next before the peaceable Empire of Augustus Caesar*, sig. A2. Printed in 1601 but written in 1586.

3. Malone Society Reprints (1911), p. 11.

wardly" remembering that Caesar saved his life at Pharsalia;
Cato with the wish, "Help Rome in this extremity"; Titinius sure
that "this accurs'd and fatal day must end both our lives and
Roman liberty." Papists under Elizabeth likewise found the deed
politically excusable. To Robert Parsons, S. J., seeking justification for the removal of a despotic head of state, Rome was well
served by the assassination since it restored the principle of
consent and contract by which government was originally established. Kings hold their power by gift of the commonwealth, he
postulates; hence the commonwealth may dispossess them of it
again "if they fulfil not the lawes and condicions, by which and
for which, their dignity was given them." The conspiracy against
Caesar was consequently justifiable:

> When Iulius Caesar uppon particular ambition had broken
> al law both humane and divine, and taken al government in
> to his owne hands alone, he was in revenge hereof, slayne as
> the world knoweth, by senators in the senatehouse: and
> Octavius Augustus preferred in his roome, who proved
> afterwards the most famous Emperor that ever was.[4]

Tyrannicide, by this reasoning, was a benefit, since as Montaigne
argued, Caesar's ambition brought about "the ruine of his
country, and subversion of the mightiest state and most flourishing Common-wealth, that ever the world shall see."[5]

But whatever the alleged advantages in quelling Caesar's
ambition, republican associations surrounding the event were
tainted by the democratic heresy. *Res publica* was too easily
converted to *res plebeia*. John Hayward, in refuting Parsons,
maintains that the people have no power to remove the authority
of princes, and that the tragedy to commonwealth of the
protracted civil war was a direct consequence of the murder of
Caesar in the name of liberty. For to revenge his death,

4. Robert Parsons [R. Doleman], *A conference about the next succession to the crowne of Ingland* (1594), sig. E4.

5. *Essays*, "The History of Spurina," Everyman Edition, 3 vols. (1910, reprint ed. 1946), 2 : 462.

"Augustus, Antonius and Lepidus did first knit in armes by the name of Triumviri, . . . whereupon a long cruell and doubtfull warre was set up, which continued the space of xx. years; first, betweene these three, and the murtherers of Caesar; then, between Lepidus, and the other two; lastly betweene Augustus and Antonius. . . . "And this," Hayward comments dryly, "was the sweet successe of the murther of Caesar." [6] Thomas Craig is even more specific in his scorn of Parsons. After ticking off a long list of "the dreadful miseries" that followed the murder, he exclaims with even broader sarcasm:

> Finally, the Commonwealth was so distress'd and torn in pieces and so tired with its Liberty and Democracy, that all consented to have a Monarchy, which all the people formerly had in great abhorrence, and chose to rest there only, as in a safe and fortified harbour against all Storme, Seditions and Tumults of the people. These were the fruits of Democratic Government, these were the prosperous Successes after the killing of Caesar.[7]

It will be observed that semantic ambiguities were in fact endemic in the idea of commonwealth long before Shakespeare took up the subject in *Julius Caesar*. Elyot as lexicographer could identify commonwealth and res publica; but Elyot as landed knight of the shire felt constrained to add a caveat against "a few fantastic fools" who could mean by it that "everything should be to all men in common."

Shakespeare's audience would therefore have been of two minds about the assassination and its significance: Brutus as the figure of republicanism had become the classical object of praise for his private virtue but of condemnation for his public ineptitude. As Seneca observed in referring to Brutus's killing of Caesar: "Although in all other thinges he were a noble man: yet in this / cace mee thinkes he was farre ouershot, and behaued not

---

6. *An answer to the first part of a certaine conference concerning succession* (1603), sig. Ii.

7. *Concerning the right of succession to the kingdom of England* (1703), p. 173. Written in 1603, but unpublished during the century.

himself according to too [*sic*] the disciplyne of the Stoikes." Brutus
may, Seneca speculates, have feared the name of a king even
though "the best state of a cammon weale is under a ryghtful king
[*cum optimus civitatis status sub rege iuste sit*]. But how quyte had he
forgotten the nature of the world, or of his owne Countrie, whiche
beleeued that if one were dispatched, there were no mo of the
same mynde." [8] It is nothing strange that Shakespeare should
have responded in the same way to his school text. Indeed
Fulbecke had made the same qualified judgment of "the bloudie
exploit" while deploring the tragic blow to commonwealth that
resulted from it:

> I cannot give Brutus praise for this, but I rather thinke that
> he deserveth dispraise: for had the cause of quailing [Caesar]
> bene iust, yet the course and manner of killing him, doth
> apparently seeme unlawful. . . . Brutus was like to the
> Comet, who feeding upon vapours and vaine opinions, at
> length consumed and confounded himself: and thus were the
> two Bruti, I meane the first and the last, famous men of that
> honorable name, both fatall to the estate of the Romane
> Common weale: for the former of them did expell the last
> king of the Romanes, and the later did murder their first
> Emperour.[9]

It is this republican jeopardy to the traditionally structured
commonwealth which constitutes the political tragedy of Shakespeare's *Julius Caesar*. The irony of Shakespeare's Brutus is that he
should have become "fatal to the estate of the Roman common
weal" when his intentions were precisely of the opposite sort. In
contrast to the fortunate conclusion of civil dissension in the
English history plays, Shakespeare rejects Fulbecke's view of
Roman civil war as terminating in the glories of the Augustan
empire; but further, and quite deliberately, he places the fall of

8. *De Beneficiis*, trans. Arthur Golding (1578), sig. [Eiiii^v]–F1. Professor T. J. B.
Spencer cites the passage in Thomas Lodge's translation (1601). "Shakespeare and
the Elizabethan Romans," *Shakespeare Survey* 10 (1957) : 34.

9. *An historical collection*, sig. Z–Z².

Julius Caesar in the tragic perspective of a commonwealth deserted by its best spokesman. As a consequence, the death of Caesar has in no way bettered either the commons or the common weal.

When some seven years later he turns backward in time to the downfall of Coriolanus, the idea of commonwealth again dominates the action. Power politics among the members of the body politic has brought about an internal disruption which threatens to destroy it. But there is a difference. In *Julius Caesar*, the commons are pawns in a power struggle waged at the top of the social scale. Commonwealth as an ideal is not in question. But during the course of the struggle in *Coriolanus*, a revolutionary concept of the very nature of commonwealth has asserted itself. The hitherto nice gradation of mutually sustaining duties has been broken down by class claims of rights, and in the process the customary concept of the body politic as a royal estate has given way to the idea of state as a national entity, the preservation of which depends upon the accommodation of the ruling class to rival claims of authority. Coriolanus, wholly unsuited to such an accommodation, refuses to submit to the "right and strength o' th' commons," and in the ensuing struggle for sovereignty, the headless commonwealth is prostrated before a foreign power. The novelty of this confrontation of an intransigent patrician and a newly articulate populace would not have been lost on a Jacobean audience; indeed it is hard to conceive that such a play could have been written earlier. In the English history plays, the image of the realm is invariably an hereditary estate—even Jack Cade pretends to be a Mortimer. It is still an estate in *Julius Caesar*; Cassius matches the name of Brutus with the name of Caesar. But in *Coriolanus*, the rise of popular sovereignty insults this traditional sense of commonwealth, and in the resulting contention, the whole structure of society has become politicized.

Such a marked shift of attitude toward commonwealth from the conventional corporation of duties in *Julius Caesar* to a corporation of rights in *Coriolanus* is a reflection of germinal influence steadily at work in Tudor society affecting the concept of state. When Ralph Robinson in translating More's *Utopia* at mid-century

chose to describe it as "a frutefull pleasaunt, and wittie worke, of
the beste state of a publique weale," he could hardly have stated
the customary nonpolitical use of the words "state" and "commonwealth" more succinctly if he were a lexicographer. By
comparison with the political machinations of the first half of the
work, the second half traverses the whole range of ideal human
relationships which comprise a commonwealth as commonly
understood in the sixteenth century. Thomas Starkey in 1535
likewise defines commonwealth as "the prosperouse & most
perfayt state of a multytud [10] assemblyd togyddur in any cuntrey
cyty or towne gouernyd vertusely in cyuyle lyfe accordyng to the
nature & dygnyte of man," nearest perfection when it is healthy,
beautiful, and strong, nourished with abundance, and living
peaceably together, "ych one louyng other as partys of one body,
euery parte dowyng hys duty and offyce requyryd therto." [11]
Draft legislation of the same period proposes a new court of
"Justices or Conservators of the Common Weal" (Statutes of the
Realm, III, 132. "Common weal of the Realm" is the normal
phrase, "state" in a political sense a rarity.[12]

While it is safe to say that during the early Tudor period,
neither "state" nor "commonwealth" involved political overtones,
it was inevitable that the growth of nationalism on the continent
and the state-consciousness of a much earlier date in the Italian
city states, aided and accelerated by the republicanism of
Machiavelli,[13] should be reflected in English thinking at the same
time.[14] By the end of the century, it is well established in current

10. The word used for *res publica* in William Marshall's translation of Marsilius's
Defensor Pacis (1534).

11. PRO, MS. SP/1/90, p. 94. Edited by J. M. Cowper under the title *A
Dialogue between . . . Pole . . . and Lupset*, Early English Text Society, extra series,
no. 12 (1871). Subsequent references to this ms. are abbreviated *A Dialogue between
Pole and Lupset*.

12. T. F. T. Plucknett reprints this bill with comment in "Some Proposed
Legislation of Henry VIII," *TRHS*, 4th ser., 19, p. 119. F. W. Maitland calls "the
state" a late comer, little known before 1600 in his *Selected Essays* (1936), p. 113.

13. J. W. Hexter has demonstrated the semantic change in his study of *The
Prince: "Il Principe* and *lo stato*," *Studies in the Renaissance* 4 (1957) : 113–38.

14. See my *Foundations of Tudor Policy* (1948), pp. 184–89. For an excellent
appraisal of the whole span of Machiavelli's influence in England through the

usage. Thus, in *A Comparative Discourse of the Bodies Natural and Politique* (1606), Edward Forset speaks with ease of "the affayres of a state" (sig. ¶ iii^v), of "the stage of State," and "the States bodie" (sig. ¶ iiii^v), of "a State incorporat" (sig. A^v), of "state businesse" and of "the reuerend and sage Senators of the State" (sig. Oi^v).

Consequent to this political orientation of the idea of state, the members composing it think beyond their duties to the commonwealth; they become newly conscious of their political rights within it, quite distinct from the rights which had always been a condition of social life in the commonwealth of Tudor England. The rights of the sovereign were an accepted condition of rule; the jealously guarded privileges of parliament existed "of right" and not "of grace";[15] and in the daily administration of government, there were, of course, individual rights aplenty, fought out with bitter tenacity in the courts, and spilling over into legislation.[16] On a theoretical level, the concept of the contractual origin of society, stated authoritatively from Starkey to Hooker, was inadmissible without the assumption of rights growing from demands and agreements between politically polarized parties. Magna Carta, though far from being a dead letter, [17] was seldom a grounds for appeal. It was such practical exigencies as exile under Mary and Elizabeth that made it necessary for religious dissidents at both ends of the political spectrum to seek authority for the right of rebellion. The consequence was new semantic demands on the idea of commonwealth at the end of the century. They were clearly evident in Forset's *Comparative discourse of the bodies natural and politic*, "wherein out of the principles of Nature," he proposes to set forth "the true forme of a Commonweale, with the dutie of Subiects, and the right of the Soueraigne." On the

---

seventeenth century, see Felix Raab's *The English Face of Machiavelli: A Changing Interpretation, 1500–1700* (1964).

15. Sir Herbert Butterfield, *Magna Carta in the Historiography of the Sixteenth and Seventeenth Centuries* (1969), p. 11.

16. See Plucknett's article referred to in note 12 above. As he there reminds us, the common law was essentially a law of property (*meum* and *tuum*).

17. Butterfield, *Magna Carta*, pp. 15–18; Faith Thompson, *Magna Carta: Its Role in the Making of the English Constitution, 1300–1629* (1948), p. 139.

one hand, he insists on "the rights of souereigntie not to be far extended, nor too much restreyned" (sig. Ci^v); on the other, and more in accordance with the views of James, that "our Soueraigntie . . . hath still, and reteineth to it self certaine prerogatiue rights of most ample extensions, and most free exemptions" (sig. Diii).

Recent scholarship stressing the social and religious aspects of commonwealth, particularly in the 1950s, has tended to overlook its most important political implications,[18] and to conclude that for the Tudors before Elizabeth "no conception of political rights in the modern sense existed" [19] is simply at odds with the facts. It is clear that long before the first Stuart, the usual anthropological image of commonwealth had undergone modification, supplementing it rather than displacing it. The change can be well illustrated in Giovanni Florio's Italian–English dictionary. In 1598, he thinks of *stato* solely as "an estate, a dominion, or signorie of anybody, a mans whole wealth or stocke"; in 1611, he redefines it first as "a state," and it can be assumed that in 1603 when he translated Montaigne's description of Rome as "the mightiest state and most flourishing Common-wealth that ever the world shall see," he intended no verbal incompatibility for English readers.

The same semantic shift is observable in related words. "Statist" (Italian *statista*), a word with Machiavellian overtones, is not in use until the 1580s. Sir Philip Sidney writes in his *Defence of the Earl of Leicester*: "When he plais the Statist wringing very unlikkili some of Machiavels exiomes to serve his purpos then indeed then he tryumphes." It also occurs in an anonymous late Elizabethan manuscript, *A Brife discourse in praise of Kinge Richard the third*, and in John Marston's *Sophonisba*.[20] Shakespeare uses it

18. Arthur B. Ferguson, *The Articulate Citizen and the English Renaissance* (1965), p. 367. But Ferguson deals largely with the first half of the century.

19. Whitney R. D. Jones, *The Tudor Commonwealth, 1529–1559* (1970), p. 209.

20. Sidney, *Works*, ed. Albert Feuillerat, 4 vols. (1939), 3 : 64; Huntington Library MS 199. See my "A Tudor Defense of Richard III," *PMLA* 55 (1940) : 950, n. 12. I am indebted to J. W. Lever for the Marston reference. See his *The Tragedy of State* (1971), p. 5.

twice in his later career, both times with pejorative implication (*Hamlet*, 5.2.31–35; *Cymbeline*, 2.4.15–17).

"Statesman" is almost as rare a word until the end of the century. Ben Jonson specifically identifies it with Machiavelli;[21] Forset, on the other hand, with favorable connotations.[22] Shakespeare uses it twice in a favorable sense: Duke Vincentio refers to Angelo as "a scholar, a statesman, and a soldier" (*Measure for Measure*, 3.2.155), and Brabantio appeals for senatorial action against Othello from his "brothers of the state," for otherwise "bondslaves and pagans shall our statesmen be" (*Othello*, 1.2.95–99). In a third instance, Polyxenes' characterization of his child as "now my sworn friend, and then my enemy; / My parasite, my soldier, statesman—all" (*Winter's Tale*, 1.2.167–68) may also be passed off as loving understatement. The rarity of either "statist" or "statesman" in Shakespeare's usage is in itself of some significance in the establishment of a new political vocabulary.

Shakespeare's usage follows the pattern of his age. In his earliest Roman play, Rome is usually the body politic. Titus at first refuses because of his age to become "candidatus" for emperor, but presently is persuaded by the Tribunes to ask the voices of the Roman people in order to "help to set a head on headless Rome" (1.1.186, 218). It proves to be a futile gesture, though after the carnage is over, Marcus offers to teach the Romans "how to knit again / This scattered corn into one mutual sheaf, / These broken limbs again into one body" (5.3.70–72). In *The Merchant of Venice*, much is made of the inviolability of Venetian laws, and on two occasions, Venice is referred to as "the state" (4.1.354, 365), though again the context is legal, not political. Only in the last plays does "state" as a depersonalized political organism become common currency. As might be expected, res publica in the Roman history plays is as much social as political. But one fact is clear: In the dramatic representation

21. *Every Man Out of his Humor*, 2.6.166–68: "For that were to affirme, that a man writing of Nero, should meane all Emperours: or speaking of Machiavel, comprehend all States-men."

22. *A Comparative Discourse*, sig. Fii^v, as a marginal note: "The gifts of statesmen to be wel disposed of" and again in the text (sig. H) "their choicest statesmen."

84   THE TEMPER OF SHAKESPEARE'S THOUGHT

of the commons' revolt led by the tribunes in *Coriolanus*, Rome is
very clearly no man's "whole wealth or stock"; it is conceived as a
political entity over which the commons dare to assert sole
sovereignty.

In *Coriolanus*, Shakespeare reached his political maturity. It is
also his last direct focus on the idea of commonwealth. The Rome
of *Antony and Cleopatra* is not a commonwealth; it is an empire. But
it is worth remembering two occasions when nonethical statism
appears in the other later plays. Three characters are left on stage
at the end of *Lear*. Albany proposes to Kent and Edgar that they
"rule in this realm, and the gor'd state sustain." But there is no
state to sustain. In *The Tempest*, three characters: a jester, a butler,
and a savage and deformed slave, all drunk, contemplate the rule
of an island. "They say there's but five upon this isle. We are
three of them," says the besotted Trinculo. "If th' other two be
brain'd like us, the state totters" (3.2.6–8). But presently, there
will be no state. Only Caliban will remain. In *Lear*, the state has
suffered a calamity. In *The Tempest*, the state is a figment of a
drunken imagination. *Lear* presents the mask of political tragedy,
The Tempest the mask of political comedy. They are the two sides
of the coin. As for Gonzalo's commonwealth, is it any more than
the pipe dream of an old man, laughed at by the pragmatist-poli-
ticians of a new age? Let us look more closely at the idea first in
Julius Caesar.

Let Brutus Be Caesar

The political struggle in *Julius Caesar* is between members of a
common weal, whose duty to it is never in question. It is a body
composed of members unequal yet mutually dependent and
responsible collectively for the general good. It is in health when
each member executes his proper and vital function; it is disabled
or diseased when any member fails in his public duties or
encroaches on the functions of others. In this context, the most
conspicuous cause of Brutus's failure is not his politics but his lack
of political skill. His amputation of the head for the patriotic
purpose of benefiting the commonwealth actually deals it a
mortal blow, and his failure to anticipate, let alone control, the

subsequent paroxysm invites the operation of less scrupulous
surgeons. At the conclusion, he has earned a name as the noblest
Roman, but in terms of the common weal, nobility is not enough.

There is a special irony too, that in spite of his devotion to a
social ideal, Brutus plays a lonely and tragic role, not less lonely
because it is self-imposed. At the opening of the action, he has
convinced himself that the commonwealth is threatened by the
imperial designs of Caesar, and that it will be enslaved if he is
crowned. At whatever expense to friendship, he feels an enormous
sense of public duty to set it straight:

> If it be aught toward the general good,
> Set honour in one eye and death i' th' other,
> And I will look on both indifferently
> For let the gods so speed me as I love
> The name of honour more than I fear death.
>
> [1.2.85–89]

Such idealism proceeds with the greater effect from a patrician
with a proud republican ancestry; and it is sharpened quite as
much by Antony, whose suave and ruthless political dexterity
mocks the common good, as by Cassius, who as a practical
politician recognizes the political potential of Brutus, but is no
more capable of understanding Brutus's insusceptibility to political persuasion than he is of the idealism which prompts it. "What
you would work me to I have some aim" (1.2.162) is not, as
Antony publicly announces, the murder of a friend for personal
gain, nor yet, as Cassius would like to have it, Brutus's consent to
substitute his own image for Caesar's, but a reluctant admission,
since he does not envy Caesar, that Caesar's crescent power has
become a jeopardy to commonwealth, and that he must be the
necessary instrument to preserve it. When Cassius holds the
mirror up to Brutus, he is asking him to see what is not there to
see. For an image of a very different character is most certainly
taking shape in Brutus's mind as Cassius speaks. In the present
disposition of affairs, he begins to see himself, not as a rival to
Caesar, but as a "conservator of the common weal," as the *Statutes*
put it, acting in his ancestral role as defender of the liberties of

Rome against a potential tyrant. As patriot-idealist, he must implement his ideals with action—not an easy decision to make since he must weigh the too obvious personal cost (the death of his friend) against the gain to the common cause. "Poor Brutus, with himself at war," must choose between public and private loyalties, and the choice must be his alone.

The interim between the first motion and the dreadful act is like a phantasma or a hideous dream. His secret mind at this juncture is by his own confession a microcosm of commonwealth in crisis:

> The genius and the mortal instruments
> Are then in council, and the state of man,
> Like to a little kingdom suffers then
> The nature of an insurrection.

> [2.1.66–69]

Genius and mortal instruments are plainly the whole state of politic man acting in its deliberative capacity—a parliament in miniature. In the familiar words of Sir Thomas Smith:

> All that ever the people of Rome might do . . . the same may be done by the parliament of England, which representeth and hath the power of the whole realm both the head and the body. For every Englishman is intended to be there present . . . from the Prince to the lowest person. And the consent of the Parliament is taken to be every man's consent.[23]

Until policy and the means for executing it have been settled, however, the threat of Caesarism is real and inescapable. Brutus's internal debate, thus early made explicit, is the central image of the play. It is intensified by awful cosmic disturbances, which to Casca suggest "civil strife in heaven," and to Cassius, who professes scepticism of omens, "instruments of fear and warning/ Unto some monstrous state." Brutus is not a Jove any more than Caesar, yet he must poise the scales over the civil war in himself as if he were disinterested.

23. *De Republica Anglorum*, bk. 2, ch. 1.

In this lonely debate, Cassius exerts a decisive though partly
unsuspected influence. There is some small encouragement for
Brutus in his remark that many "of the best respect in Rome"
groan "underneath this age's yoke." But for the moment Brutus
prefers to wrap himself in Olympian silence. Studiously with-
standing Cassius's appeals to ambition, he presently falls an easy
victim to the spurious "popular" petitions thrown in at his
window. To Cassius, Brutus has proved not impervious to political
pressure, indeed he is three-fourths won. It is a mistake, of course;
but he has succeeded in his persuasions quite without knowing
why. For Brutus, convinced of popular support, has come to his
momentous decision independently and on pure principle:

> It must be by his death; and for my part,
> I know no personal cause to spurn at him,
> But for the general.
>
> [2.1.10–12]

Having made it, deliberation gives way to action; his course is
clear; and when he meets the conspirators immediately thereafter,
he has adopted a wholly impersonal attitude in committing
himself to an act of blood. He has transfigured the act into
sacrifice just as Richard II acts as priest and clerk in his own
deposition. Ceremony, for all its outward show, propels both men
to their tragic destiny.

The Priestlike Task

Not that Brutus's case bears any color of legal justification. It is
preventive murder, by which Caesar's ambition is punished for
what it might lead to; it is condemnation by hypothesis. But
Brutus steps easily over such niceties. Once his conscience is clear,
he is zealous to root out of others what in spite of Cassius he is
satisfied the mirror would not show in himself. For above all,
Brutus always sees himself as superior in moral principle to the
world about him. It is clear in his prejudgment of Caesar; if
anything, more conspicuous after the deed is done. He is
arrogantly contemptuous of Cassius's condonation of the practice
of bribery:

> By heaven, I had rather coin my heart
> And drop my blood for drachmas than to wring
> From the hard hands of peasants their vile trash
> By any indirection.
>
> [4.3.72-75]

And when he has driven Cassius to abject admission of his faults, he continues to stand vaingloriously on his honesty. He humiliates the poet who forces himself into their presence to stop their quarreling. Then, flushed with his moral victory, he goes on to demonstrate his Stoic fortitude in adversity by revealing that throughout his altercation with Cassius, he knew of the death of his wife and said nothing. "No man bears sorrow better," he asserts blandly; and as if this were not enough, receives the news over again with a final display of moral pyrotechnics:

> Why, farewell, Portia. We must die, Messala.
> With meditating that she must die once
> I have the patience to endure it now.
>
> [4.3.190-93] [24]

Thus he gains a double personal triumph: Messala's admiration of his moral control, and Cassius's admiration of his artistic performance. The victories in the microcosm will eventually seem to the dying Brutus far greater than the glories of the battlefield which Octavius and Antony by their "vile conquest" will attain to.

This pride in moral rectitude throughout the later action of the play is of a piece with the priestlike role which Brutus assumes once he has decided to enter the conspiracy. Knowing that the conspirators look to him for leadership—the kind of justification that the rebels in the English historical plays find in the clergy—he asks for their hands, "all over, one by one." In a manner of oath-taking reminiscent of the Bond of Association

24. I am not of the mind of those critics who see Brutus playing a dual role in the quarrel scene. To Professor Brents Stirling in *Shakespeare Quarterly* 10 (1959): 211, Brutus is "fraudulent and smug," an opinion unwarranted by the stage situation.

against Mary Queen of Scots,[25] he insists that the sole binding
ingredient should be the principle of "sufferance of our souls"
under "the time's abuse," not an oath sworn by "priests and
cowards and men cautelous." In short, he has asserted his
superiority as a man of virtue, entering into an enterprise wholly
without taint, a priest performing an impersonal sacrifice for the
benefit of an impersonal common weal. In this spirit, he vetoes the
killing of Antony as a course too bloody, hacking the limbs after
cutting the head off. "Let us be sacrificers, but not butchers, . . .
purgers, not murderers, . . . For he can do no more than Caesar's
arm / When Caesar's head is off" (2.1.162–83).[26]

The assassination of Caesar, an act of dismemberment of the
body politic, has thus become identified in Brutus's mind with the
ritual of sacrifice. Yet by his curious illogic the hands which will
perform the rite are consecrated, and now become the controlling
image of his conduct. In the action leading up to the stabbing,
Calpurnia dreams of the statue of Caesar spouting blood while
many lusty Romans come smiling and bathe their hands in it
(2.2.76–79). As the conspirators press about Caesar, Cinna
reminds Casca, "You are the first that rears your hand"; and
Brutus, conscious of his consecrated role, kisses Caesar's hand,
"but not in flattery." The moment of climax has arrived. With the
physical picture of the upraised hand of Casca over the head of
Caesar, image and symbol join: "Speak hands for me!"

The ritualistic character of this action is reinforced, as in
Richard II, by the religious associations familiar to Shakespeare's
audience. Again, his sense of the value of ceremony reveals itself,
the affinity between Hooker and Shakespeare extending beyond
thought to technique. In a passage already referred to, Hooker
emphasizes the importance of "certain sensible actions, the

25. J. E. Neale, *Elizabeth I and her Parliaments, 1584–1601* (1957), pp. 16–18.
26. F. W. Maitland, ahead of us as he so frequently is, in defining "the
corporation sole" quotes J. Fineux (1522): "A corporation is an aggregation of
head and body: not a head by itself, nor a body by itself." Elsewhere, he quotes
Willion vs. *Berkley* (1559) in Plowden's *Reports*: "The king and his subjects together
compose the corporation, and he is incorporated with them and they with him,
and he is the head and they are the members." *Selected Essays* (1936), pp. 79, 124.

memory whereof is far more easy and durable than the memory of speech can be." Among these sensible actions, Hooker particularly mentions the ceremonial use of hands as "a forcible signification" (*LEP*, iv.i.3–4). To Shakespeare's audience, Brutus's raised hand speaks for him—it does not for the other conspirators with less exalted motives—as the signification, the symbol, of sacrifice; and at the same time, anticipated by Calpurnia's dream, it bespeaks the enormity of the deed. Of this enormity, Brutus in his dedication to the commonwealth seems unaware. While the other conspirators excitedly proclaim the slogans of liberty, freedom, and enfranchisement, while "men, wives, and children stare, cry out, and run / As it were doomsday," he alone stands utterly unmoved. Ambition's debt has been paid; his sacrificial task is completed; and only the public ritual, confirmation of his inward peace, remains to be performed:

> Stoop, Romans, stoop,
> And let us bathe our hands in Caesar's blood
> Up to the elbows and besmear our swords.
> Then walk we forth, even to the market place,
> And waving our red weapons o'er our heads,
> Let's all cry "Peace, freedom, and liberty!"
>
> [3.1.105–10]

Brutus shows an almost naive confidence in the rightness of their deed, "or else were this a savage spectacle," as he rightly senses; and it is reinforced by the irony of Cassius's exultant prediction, "the knot of us" shall be called "the men that gave their country liberty" (3.1.116–18). But the stage moment is quickly over. Even as he speaks, Antony appears, their fortunes have turned, and the image of speaking hands undergoes the fateful change which anticipates the conspirators' ruin and the ruin of the commonwealth Brutus had stabbed to achieve.

Suddenly, by Antony's lethal verbal dexterity, the hands of Brutus are the hands of a murderer, not a priest, "purpled with the noblest blood of all this world." A sacrificial rite has become a butchery. Though Brutus insists that Antony sees only their bloody hands and not their hearts filled with pity for the general

wrong of Rome, the wily Antony persists in taking the bloody
hand of each of the conspirators in seeming token of friendship—
sharp visual reminder of Brutus's earlier clasp of those same
hands—and left alone, he utters the word that Brutus abhorred.
To Antony, they are indeed butchers, this is indeed a savage
spectacle, and where hands spoke for Brutus, now by transmutation the wounds the hands made, "like dumb mouths, do ope their
ruby lips / To beg the voice and utterance" of Antony's tongue
(3.2.260–61). And that tongue speaks revenge.

How under these circumstances will Brutus's ideal of commonwealth be attained by the killing of Caesar? How can his act now
seem more than an exercise in futility? It will be of little use for
him to argue that he set aside his love for Caesar for the love of
Rome, as long as Rome remains without a head, and as long as
the lesser members of the Roman commonwealth are innocent of
any political pretensions whatsoever. They respond emotionally
to Brutus as a person. They utter, though they do not comprehend
such abstractions as freedom and love of country. But they are not
at that point of political sophistication where they can approxi-
mate a practical realization of common weal. Impelled by lesser
motives, they look no farther than Brutus's leadership; but Brutus
is as politically ingenuous as they are, and having removed the
head of state, he has neither the intention nor the taste to supply a
new one. For him, as for Cassius, the world's great age has begun
anew:

> How many ages hence
> Shall this our lofty scene be acted over
> In states unborn and accents yet unknown!
>
> [3.1.114–16]

But their vision quickly dies down into recrimination. The
tragic irony of their inadequacy will soon be echoed in the
response of the commons to what Brutus obviously intended to be
his farewell to public life. Crowning Caesar is no outrage to
political principle when political principle is summed up in
personal loyalty. "Let him be Caesar . . . Caesar's better
parts / Shall be crown'd in Brutus." In such non-politics, one

reason for Brutus's failure as a public benefactor becomes explicit;
the other is the political adroitness of an Antony whose mind
never lends itself to commonwealth. He steps quickly into the
political vacuum and appropriates the commons' affections, his
first object to reestablish the Caesar image which Brutus had just
obliterated. He then bends his rhetorical talents to mold his
auditors into instruments of destruction. Like Marullus, the
tribune, who herds the demonstrators for Caesar off the streets in
the opening action, he knows how to control them, though his
methods are much more sensitive. Marullus exercises a rough,
jocular superiority:

> You blocks, you stones, you worse than senseless things!
> O you hard hearts, you cruel men of Rome!
>
> [1.1.40–41]

Antony, using the same image, manages to humor them, flatter
them, finally seduce them by appeals to their personal cupidity.
His gesture of showing Caesar's will, then withdrawing it, offers
the necessary incitement:

> Have patience, gentle friends; I must not read it.
> It is not meet you know how Caesar lov'd you.
> You are not wood, you are not stones, but men.
>
> [3.2.146–48]

But, of course, he doesn't show it; he shows the body of Caesar
instead, the mantle rent by daggers, the blood of Caesar. Then
comes his pretended restraint, his show of modesty. And as
collective emotions in his audience are raised to mutiny pitch, the
previously opposed images of speaking hands and speaking
wounds likewise converge and concatenate to force the action to a
heightened climax. Where at the moment of supposed realization
of commonweal, Casca's cry, "Speak, hands, for me," precipitated
the murder, now at the moment of doom of commonwealth,
Antony's impassioned declaration to his spellbound audience of
his intention to "show you sweet Caesar's wounds, poor poor
dumb mouths / And bid them speak for me" precipitates the total
destruction of Brutus's republican ideal. Cause and effect are

welded together in the ironic verbal echo. But even as Antony
puts a tongue in every wound of Caesar, his contempt for the
commons he has victimized complicates the image pattern.
Patronizingly, he has assured them they are not stones, but men;
now that they have become his creatures, he is ready to convert
the stones of Rome to his own mortal instruments to serve his
cynical incitement to mutiny. Now they will burn the house of
Brutus; they will pluck down benches, forms, windows, anything;
under his tutelage, these senseless stones, limbs of the commonwealth, will tear to pieces the innocent little poet, Cinna, because
his name is Cinna, while the perpetrator of his murder gloats over
the destruction:

> Now let it work. Mischief, thou art afoot,
> Take thou what course thou wilt.

> [3.2.265–66]

Men have ceased to be men, and the commonwealth that Brutus
had envisioned is mortally stricken.

I Am Brutus, I

The Antony of the latter half of the play remains conformable
to the image now established. Hardly have Brutus and Cassius
ridden like madmen through the gates of Rome than he is busy
exploiting his success. His private face, now exposed, is cold and
ruthless. In the back-room political settlements with Octavius and
Lepidus—an arm's length alliance of mistrust where stakes are
high—he joins without a qualm in the cold-blooded game of
condemning relatives to death; the will of Caesar having served
his purpose, he announces tersely that he will reduce the legacies
to manageable size; and he undercuts Lepidus, his fellow
triumvir, as soon as that unfortunate bearer of burdens is out of
hearing. These acts openly proclaim a man whose love for Caesar,
like everything else, has been turned to his personal advantage.
Human beings as human beings mean little or nothing to him;
and since hitherto we have not seen this side of his character the
shock is the greater.

Even so, his present ruthlessness is not inconsistent with what

MILLS COLLEGE
LIBRARY

we already know of the man. It is Brutus, particularly the later
Brutus, who has caused the critics much trouble, even to the
extent of earning him a place among Shakespeare's "problem"
characters. We are momentarily put off, of course, that after his
measured calm under the gravest of political exigencies, he should
seem so willfully testy. The erstwhile noble idealist is now
niggling, censorious, a petty tyrant to his closest associates. But
presently we discover that Shakespeare is playing the dramatic
game here, deliberately withholding the cause of Brutus's bad
humor until the quarrel with Cassius has descended to personal
abuse before revealing its cause in the news of Portia's death.
Only then does it fall into the pattern of humanitarian instincts
already demonstrated and presently to be exhibited again in his
solicitude for his servant Lucius asleep over his lute and for the
soldiers standing guard at his tent. In contrast to Antony's callous
opportunism, we are reassured that the human impulse beneath
his public face has been consistent throughout.

The real puzzle is the apparent disappearance of Brutus's
republican views as soon as his public defense is over. Of his ideal
of the common good, from this time forth, we hear nothing. It is
not enough to say that he is now a man without a cause. How
could he have so soon forgotten the Ides of March or the role he
then played? When he faced the people over the dead body of
Caesar, then was the moment of his greatest stature: "As I slew
my best lover for the good of Rome, I have the same dagger for
myself when it shall please my country to need my death"
(3.2.49–50). Now the murderer of Caesar has become a mere
relict, so removed is he from the deed and at times even from
accurate recollection of it. Was it for supporting robbers, he
accuses Cassius, that he "struck the foremost man of all this
world?" (4.1.22–23). Such recrimination over "base bribes" comes
with little grace from the man who would hold his personal honor
at no less a price than he did when he stabbed Caesar. The
splendid idealism of his appeal to the commons, "Who is here so
base that would be a bondman?" now seems utterly obliterated by
the scornful, almost peevish sarcasm of the aristocrat: "Go show
your slaves how choleric you are / And make your bondmen
tremble (4.3.43–44). It is as if he had outlived his great moment

unwittingly, with the consequence that when he meets his opponents before Philippi, he is no longer in a moral posture to withstand Antony's maliciously grotesque parody of the stabbing:

> Your vile daggers
> Hack'd one another in the sides of Caesar.
> You show'd your teeth like apes, and fawn'd like hounds
> And bow'd like bondmen, kissing Caesar's feet;
> Whilst damned Casca, like a cur, behind
> Struck Caesar on the neck.
>
> [5.1.39–44]

Somewhere in the rush of events, the freedom of a republican Rome has quite plainly been lost sight of; the dream of commonwealth remains only a dream.

If Shakespeare's Brutus is puzzling to the critics, it may be because he is puzzled about himself. Only in part because of Antony's cruel distortions is the failure of his public image reflected in his person. The conviction which compelled him to draw his dagger against Caesar seems so completely dissipated that he finds it difficult to identify with what he so recently was. There is poignant irony that at Philippi his perplexity comes close to a parody of his own ideal: "I am Brutus, Marcus Brutus I! / Brutus, my country's friend! Know me for Brutus" (5.4. 7–8).[27] But fighting is the order of the day; there is now no occasion for response to his inner need. It is this same necessity for reestablishment of his ego that in the face of military defeat moral victory is imperative:

> Countrymen,
> My heart doth joy that yet in all my life
> I found no man but he was true to me.
> I shall have glory by this losing day
> More than Octavius and Mark Antony
> By this vile conquest shall attain unto.
>
> [5.5. 33–38]

---

27. We may of course follow the Folio assignment of this speech to Lucilius, as many editors have done, but the impact of Brutus's bewilderment is the same.

His paradoxical discovery of glory in defeat goes uncompre-
hended by those still faithful to him, swept away in the swirl of
ignoble and meaningless battle—meaningless, measured against
the final handclasp, which like the first, has removed his
uncertainties and confirmed his resolve. True to his public
declaration of personal dedication, he is convinced that the time
has come "when it shall please my country to need my death."
True also to his private promise for the common good ("It must
be by his death"), an arch-traitor to his "best lover," he has made
his rendezvous at Philippi, his conscience now at rest.

Brutus has suffered a major political reverse; but he is most
certainly not morally bankrupt. Quite as important as his peace
with Caesar is the fact that he is once more at peace with his
political conscience. In fact, the Brutus of the second half of the
play by the Stoic principles he professes is no less republican in
outlook than he was before. In *The Myth of the State*, Ernest Cassirer
describes the later Stoicism of Cicero and Seneca as making no
distinction between the individual and the political sphere of
action:

> They were convinced that reality taken as a whole, physical
> reality as well as moral life, was one great 'republic.' . . . All
> rational beings are members of the same commonwealth.
> . . . The personal and the universal order are but different
> manifestations of a common underlying principle.[28]

Answering to this philosophic position, Brutus has not repudiated
his republicanism, nor given way to accidental evils; rather, he
has sequestered himself in a republic of the mind. G. L. Kittredge
feels that Brutus has chosen suicide because he is "unequal" to the
"disgrace" of being led in triumph through the streets of Rome,
basing his deduction perhaps on Lucilius's confident assertion to
Antony that Brutus is "safe enough":

> I dare assure thee that no enemy
> Shall ever take alive the noble Brutus.

28. Trans. C. W. Hendel (1946), pp. 101–03.

> The gods defend him from so great a shame!
> When you do find him, or alive or dead,
> He will be found like Brutus, like himself.
>
> [5.4.20–25]

But Brutus is not a mere preview of Cleopatra; still less is he in the Stoic sense, deserting his post. Rather, he is playing out the unfitting role of military strategist while he steels himself with Stoic aplomb to the successive evils of Portia's death and Caesar's ghost. In that context, what can the victory of Octavius and Mark Antony amount to but "vile conquest"? His criticism of Cato's suicide is precisely that Cato had "prevented the time of life," whereas for him, the ghost had prevented his. "Why, I will see thee at Philippi then," reaffirms his acceptance of accidental evils, his determination, having done all, to stand. Such is his self-sufficiency before the joining of battle: "But it sufficeth that the day will end, / And then the end is known." Thus armed, *integer vitae,* he enters the battle like a soldier, fully aware but resigned that his hour has come. Even as he kills himself, Strato's answer to Messala's question, "Where is thy master?" links the early and the later Brutus in Stoic propriety: "Free from the bondage you are in, Messala."

The fact remains that though he is still able to summon the Stoic fortitude by which he has hitherto exercised moral dominance over friends and foes alike, the occasion no longer seems to warrant high nobility. "Are yet two Romans living such as these?" he asks at news of the deaths of Titinius and Cassius. To him, they are "the last of all the Romans," though presumably he is not excluding himself from that select company. The stark truth is that when he would fall on his sword in the high Roman fashion, the cause of commonwealth which would make it a glorious act appears all but obliterated by partisan rather than patriotic motive. It is Caesar's hand as well as his own that turns the sword into his own proper entrails. Certainly the cruelest irony is that the noblest Roman of them all had outlived Rome's need for him. Could Antony have forgotten his elaborate public denigration of the honorable men who killed Caesar when from

the safe position of his military victory he spoke Brutus's brief
valedictory? Noblest Roman indeed! Antony from a position of
power could easily afford generosity. He could take smug
satisfaction that for all Brutus's nobleness, the ideal commonwealth was safely stowed. It was a cunning move for the slayer of
Caesar to kill himself and save his honor; but of the outward plan
of a republic little remained, and that alone makes public the
personal tragedy of the play.

Res Plebeia

Coriolanus also represents the disruption of common weal, but
the center of interest has markedly shifted. The essential fact in
Julius Caesar is that the head of state has been killed, and on this
point as I have said, the attitude of the audience, whatever the
personal tragedy of Brutus amounts to, will be divided. Even
presuming that it could be condoned—a debatable point—the
tragedy to commonwealth must be attributed to him as much as
to Antony. Structurally, insurrection in the little kingdom of
Brutus's mind prefigures the larger insurrection that signals the
dismemberment of the body politic. His failure to undertake the
responsibilities of headship is as much the cause of the larger
tragedy as Antony's deliberate encouragement of riot. In the later
action of the play, his mission in his own mind accomplished, he
exhibits no public concern for the common good. Honor remained
throughout his greatest care, res publica one means of main-
taining it—the more appealing since, as Cassius argues, it was in
the tradition of his republican ancestors. But at no time does he
show the slightest interest in the life of the forum, no inclination—
actually no need, to climb ambition's ladder. All of this, plus the
political acuity of other men, leaves commonwealth no nearer
achievement at the end of the play than it was at the beginning.

In this respect, *Julius Caesar* invites comparison with *Coriolanus.*
In both plays, the larger political tragedy arises from personal
inaptitude for politics, more generally, the failure of executive
power in a time of public crisis, though Brutus up to that time has
acted with resolute moral conviction, and Coriolanus in his own
opinion is more sinned against than sinning. In terms of

commonwealth, it is in not carrying out their assigned and organic function in the body politic that their ultimate public failure lies. When Brutus with all power in his hands surrenders his place to Antony, and when Coriolanus publicly renounces the willing electorate, each has arrived at a moment of personal crisis in which, while remaining true to his own nature, he has inadvertently become the instrument of chaos in the commonweal. In both plays the commonwealth is not served.

But here the similarity ends. *Julius Caesar* is based solely on the traditional sense of commonwealth as a regularly escalated calibration of duties. Authority, whether it be in the hands of a Brutus or an Antony, is always at the top, obedience on the part of the other members a necessary adjunct to government. The commons waver from one obedience to another, but they obey even as they substitute one idol for another. "Let [Brutus] be Caesar" is a measure of their political innocence. It will be the same in *Coriolanus*. But though in Coriolanus they are ready enough to admit inexpertise, they find themselves unexpectedly in a posture to challenge the power of the patricians. Newly sophisticated by this heady realization, they presently discover that the customary pattern of duties has broken down and is superseded by a wholly novel sense of popular rights. For the first time, they have become politically aware, and in the exhilaration of the moment they forget the real grievance which brought them together in the first place. Unlike the craftsmen in *Julius Caesar*, who are on a Roman holiday, they are hungry. They have vented their complaint against the patricians whom they hold responsible, and especially against Caius Marcius, who is in their eyes "chief enemy of the people." But now, under suggestion from the tribunes, their hunger has become political and their menace to commonwealth fatal. Viewed as images of the body politic, both plays are tragedies of social malfunction; but in *Julius Caesar* commonwealth dies from amputation, in *Coriolanus* from cancer.

For this reason, in spite of the considerable gap in time between the writing of the two plays, *Coriolanus* should be regarded as the political successor and supplement to *Julius Caesar*, though we should not ignore its social components in asking why after so many years, the busiest in his career, Shakespeare should have returned to the theme of commonwealth to restate it in such dramatic fashion. For there is no question that the opposition between head and limbs has been intensified by the towering contempt of Coriolanus for the "rank-scented meiny." While it becomes a means of inducing their political pretensions, at the same time it makes utterly remote any hope for the social equilibrium upon which a healthy commonwealth ideally depends. So scathing is Coriolanus's vituperation that in our age of the common man it has often been erroneously transferred to Shakespeare himself. Yet there is no reason for assuming that the character of the commons is different in any respect from what it was in Jack Cade's rebellion at the beginning of Shakespeare's playwriting career. Like their earlier counterparts, they are essentially well-meaning, good-humored, and likeable as individuals; they stand up well under Menenius's tolerant raillery; and they are willing to accept Coriolanus as consul despite his truculence. They are not without opinions; but since their opinions are east, west, north, and south, they both need and are susceptible to direction. By their own admission, they are a many-headed multitude, the very diversity of their opinions precluding any common purpose, without which the ideal of common weal cannot exist. But they are at one in their gratefulness to Coriolanus for his service to Rome, even as their thanks reduce political platitudes to broad comedy: "Ingratitude is monstrous; and for the multitude to be ingrateful were to make a monster of the multitude, of the which we being members, should bring ourselves to be monstrous members" (2.3.10–14).

Although Coriolanus hardly understands it himself, the major cause for his scorn is not their bad breath but their incapacity to rule. Not the people, but popular government, is insufferable. And this, to Tudor political theorists, was a commonplace, demonstrable from the instability of classical republicanism. We are again reminded of Thomas Elyot's acceptance of commonwealth as "a body lyuyng, compacte or made of sondry astates and degrees of men," but of his rejection of any implication

deriving from the Roman res publica that in a commonwealth
"euery thinge shulde be to all men in commune." [29] As for the
Greek republic, when the Athenians "abandoned kynges, and
concluded to lyue as it were in a communaltie, whiche abusifly
they called equalitie," and government was "only by theyr holle
consent," Greek democracy proved itself to be a "monstre with
many heedes nor never it was certeyne nor stable: and often tymes
they banyssed or slewe the beste citezins, whiche by their vertue
and wisedome had moste profited to the publike weale." (bk.2,
ch.2, pp. 9–10, 17–18), Sir Thomas Smith in *De Republica Anglorum*,
will allow minor offices to English tradesmen: they may sit on
inquests and juries, and act as churchwardens, constables, and the
like; but as for government, they may have "no voice nor
authoritie in our commonwealth, and no account is made of them
but onelie to be ruled, not to rule" (bk. 2, ch. 24). Thomas Floyd
is more caustic. He silently accepts Elyot's definition of commonwealth; but he wholly rejects "the pernicious state of Democra-
tie."

> The common people doe desire nothing more, then libertie to
> live at their plesure . . . There can no greater daunger
> ensure, or happen to a Common wealth then to tollerate the
> rude, and common sorte to rule, who (as their propertie is)
> are alwayes noted to be unconstant and wavering.[30]

At the end of Elizabeth's reign, William Fulbecke expresses the
same bias:

> Democracie I haue alwaies taken contrarie to the auncient
> diuision of Monarchie, aristocracie, etc. to be no forme of a
> commonweale, if it bee properly taken for the equal sway of
> the people without any superioritie. For the heele can not
> stand in place of the head, unlesse the bodie be destroyed and
> the anatomie monstrous. It is against the nature of the people

to bear rule; for they are as unfitte for regiment as a mad man to give counsaile.[31]

Like Elyot, Edward Forset feels constrained in *A Comparative Discourse of the Bodies Natural and Politique* (1606) to insist that a commonwealth does not imply that all the wealth should be common, but that "the whole wealth, wit, power and goodness whatsoever, of every particular person, must be conferred and reduced to the common good" (sig. [Giiiiᵛ]). In a true commonweal, subjects have duties; only the sovereign has right.

Menenius's familiar parable of the stomach and the members,[32] the central statement of the opening action in *Coriolanus*, was therefore axiomatic to his audience and to Shakespeare, a self-evident defense of commonwealth. The toe cannot stand in place of the head, else the anatomy is monstrous. No more can it stand without the stomach. Yet when the succeeding action is dominated by the threat of just such a monstrosity, and Menenius, the master politician of the right-hand file, finds it necessary to muster all his powers of raillery to dominate the "muniments and petty helps in this our fabric," it is mainly because a new and unstabling element has been introduced into the analogy as hitherto understood, an element which Menenius, with all his political astuteness, will be unable to control. The people have found a voice—or rather, twin voices, for their satirical value, like Rosencrantz and Guildenstern. Faced by famine—Shakespeare makes it more urgent than Plutarch—and by unheeding patri-

31. *The Pandectes of the Law of Nations* (1602), sig. H4ᵛ–11.

32. Besides North's Plutarch, ed. C. F. Tucker Brooke, 2 vols. (1909), 2 : 145–61, Shakespeare could have read the story in Holland's Livy, bk. 2, sec. 32; in Sidney's *Apology for Poetry*, ed. A. S. Cook, p. 25; in Bacon's *Advancement of Learning*, bk. 2, Dedication to the King, sec. 8, p. 78; in Camden's *Remaines*, sig. Gg4; and in Edward Forset's *A Comparative Discourse of the Bodies Natural and Politique*, sig. ¶iiii; though in Sidney and Bacon the moral is philosophical, not political. Machiavelli does not recount the fable in his *Discourses on Livy*, though he does make repeated reference to Coriolanus vs. the tribunes from a republican point of view, ed. Max Lerner (1940), pp. 116–32, 191, 208, 455. Shakespeare may have first encountered the story in a school text, *A booke called the Foundation of Rhetorike* (1563), sig. [Biᵛ].

The legend was already well established in fifteenth-century England. See S. B. Chrimes, *English Constitutional Ideas* (1966), p. 332.

cians, the commons have sought relief through representation, tribunes "to defend their vulgar wisdoms," as Coriolanus scornfully observes. He foresees immediately the revolutionary potential in the act: "It will in time / Win upon power and throw forth greater themes / For insurrection's arguing." And in a fine fury, he dismisses them as "fragments."

But they are no longer fragments. A syndicate of head, eye, heart, arm, leg, and tongue has risen to contest the authority of the ancient cupboarder of the viands. The tribunes are the syndics, speaking for the members. They are the one clear structural innovation in *Coriolanus*. For good or ill, in them is embodied a new power in the commonwealth, and a new threat to its traditional balance.

There was no such threat in the Coriolanus story as told by Plutarch and Livy. To them, the rise of the popular faction as a political power signalized a favourable event in Roman history. In Plutarch, the establishment of *tribuni plebis* came as a result of a popular revolt against violence and aggression,[33] and it was through the tribunes that the Roman people first obtained a "free voice" (vol. 2, p. 170–73). Livy's account of the story, particularly Machiavelli's version in the *Discourses*, which Shakespeare may have read, made much of the creation of tribunes as an important advantage to the state: "For besides giving the people a share in the public administration," they became "the most assured guardians of Roman liberty."[34] Machiavelli pressed the point in the following chapters in which Menenius submitted his cause to the judgment of the people. Arguing the value of public accusation for the maintenance of liberty, he described Coriolanus as Shakespeare's citizen does in the opening words of the play, "a declared enemy of the popular faction."[35]

The Tudors had a different view of the matter. When Elyot

33. *Shakespeare's Plutarch*, ed. Brooke, 2 : 145–46.
34. *Discourses*, ed. Lerner, bk. 1, ch. 4, p. 121.
35. Ibid., bk. 1, ch. 7, p. 131. When Coriolanus attempted to keep the people in a famished condition, he so excited them that "he would have been killed in a tumultuary manner, if the Tribunes had not summoned him to appear before them and defend his cause." See also bk. 1, ch. 29, p. 191.

read Plutarch on the establishment of tribunes, he saw it as the immediate cause of dissolution of a long monarchical tradition. After the expulsion of Tarquin and all his posterity from Rome,

> the communaltie more and more encroched a licence, and at the last compelled the Senate to suffre them to chose yerely amonge them gouernours of theyr owne astate and condition, whom they called Tribunes: under whom they resceyued suche audacitie and power that they finally optained the higheste authoritie in the publike weale, in so moche that often tymes they dyd repele the actes of the Senate, and to those Tribunes mought a man appele from the Senate or any other office or dignite.
>
> But what came therof in conclusion? Surely whan there was any difficulte warre immynent, than were they constrained to electe one soueraine and chiefe of all other, whom they named Dictator, as it were commander, from whom it was not laufull for any man to appele. But bicause there appered to be in hym the pristinate authorite and maiestie of a kyng, they wolde no longer suffere hym to continue in that dignite than by the space of vi. monethes, excepte he then resigned it, and by the consente of the people eftsones dyd resume it. Finally, untill Octauius Augustus had distroyed Anthony, and also Brutus, and finisshed all the Ciuile Warres . . . the cite of Rome was neuer longe quiete from factions or seditions amonge the people.

Elyot concludes that

> if the nobles of Rome had nat ben men of excellent lernynge, wisedome, and prowesse, and that the Senate, the moste noble counsaile in all the worlde, . . . had nat continued and with great difficultie retayned theyr authorite, I suppose verily that the citie of Rome had ben utterly desolate sone after the expellyng of Tarquine: and if it had bene eftsones renewed it shulde haue bene twentye tymes distroyed before the tyme that Augustus raigned: so moche discorde was euer in the citie for lacke of one gouernour. [*The Gouernour*, pp. 18–20]

Clearly, the period of Roman history spanned by Shakespeare's
Coriolanus and *Julius Caesar* represented an object lesson in the
hazards of popular government. Monarchy, declared Sir Thomas
Smith in *De Republica Anglorum* (bk. 1, ch. 2; bk. 2, ch. 4), has
always been natural in England, the prince being head, life, and
governor of this commonwealth, distributing his authority to the
rest of the members. How then could the tribunes in Sir Thomas
North's translation of Plutarch be other than "flatterers," "busy
prattlers," or in Coriolanus's opinion other than "people pleasers"
and "traitors to the nobility" (ed. Brooke, 2 : 164)? Fulbecke
expressed the sentiments of his Elizabethan readers towards
Roman history when he deplored the release "by plebiscite or
popular determination" of such a "convicted villain" as Verres,
and praised Coriolanus as a man "of rare vertues." [36]

Vox Populi, Vox Dei

The audience who listened to *Coriolanus*, however, was Jacobean, not Elizabethan. The point must be emphasized, for in the
brief years since the writing of *Julius Caesar*, the political climate
had undergone a perceptible change which affected radically the
customary idea of commonwealth. "Popular determination," the
Elizabethan equivalent for chaos, was in the early years of James
offering its first serious challenge to the royal prerogative.[37] Sir
John Neale has shown that the rise of parliament men was well
under way before James came to the throne. Only a few years
earlier, Justice Shallow, relying on the dubious influence of Sir
John Falstaff, was to get no closer to Westminster than Clement's
Inn. His successors would do much better. Like Justice Shallow,
they were men of substance, but they were also strongly conscious
of their responsibility in Commons as representative of a broadly
based, influential, and increasingly vocal squirearchy (Judson, p.
283). Peter Wentworth spoke for them when he rose to say: "I am

36. *Pandectes*, sig. I3–I3ᵛ.
37. Two studies, Margaret A. Judson, *The Crisis of the Constitution* (1949), and
George L. Mosse, *The Struggle for Sovereignty in England* (1950), deal primarily with
the 1620s. See also Louise F. Brown, "Ideas of Representation from Elizabeth to
Charles II," *J.M.H.* 11 (1939) : 39.

now no private Person. I am a publick, and a Councellor to the
whole State in that place where it is lawful for me to speak my
mind freely." [38] Christopher Yelverton plainly considered it
within his province as an M.P. to announce that "it was fit for
Princes to have their Prerogatives, but yet that same to be
straightened within reasonable limits." [39]

Elizabeth was well aware of this new mood in Commons, but
the wily old queen had always known when to be firm, when to
yield. By the time James came to the throne, the popular voice in
the House of Commons, hitherto disparate, had become politically articulate, skilled in the exercise of their suddenly ancient
prerogative. Had the king been a little less intransigent, a little
more diplomatic, popular grievances, many of which carried over
from Elizabeth's parliaments, might have been dealt with more
amicably. But his jealousy of royal power had the effect of
bringing these grievances to a head at the opening of his very first
parliament. The debate on purveyance, that is, the supply of the
royal household at values assessed by the purveyors, had been a
perennial and increasing source of contention between crown and
commons,[40] but its prompt renewal under James revealed the
existence of a well-organized opposition, led by men experienced
in the late Elizabethan parliaments and ready to seize the
initiative at the strategic moment.

Indicative of this political sophistication is the fact that the
London public instantly recognized these voices in the current
parliamentary debates as living counterparts of the Roman
tribunes. An intensely interested public followed the course of the
debates from day to day; and I think we may safely say that
Shakespeare was aware of them. Describing the situation, Wal-
lace Notestein slips unconsciously into theatrical metaphor: "In
the last years of Elizabeth and the first of James, the House of
Commons gained the center of the stage in London as never

38. Simonds D'Ewes, *The Journals of all the Parliaments during the Reign of Queen
Elizabeth* (1682), p. 241.

39. Ibid., p. 176.

40. Allegra Woodworth, "Purveyance for the Royal Household in the Reign of
Queen Elizabeth," *Trans. Amer. Hist. Soc.*, n.s. 35, pt. 1 (1945) : 1–89.

before"; in 1614, one courtier wrote that "Parliament business is the greatest entertainment that we have." [41] It is not a wholly unreasonable conjecture that while interest in the debate on purveyance was at its height, Shakespeare should have exploited the parallel in Plutarch's story of the rebellion of the discontented members against the smiling belly.

Public interest in purveyance is easy to understand since it touched the king's prerogative on the one hand and the purses and therefore the sentiments of many of the M.P.'s on the other. Hardly had parliament convened in 1604 before a committee was appointed to draw up a bill for the restraint of purveyors and cart-takers. It was to be composed of Sergeant Tanfield, John Hare, Lawrence Hyde, and Nicholas Fuller, or any three or two of them. Hare had been the author of the same bill in 1589 which had been vetoed by Elizabeth together with an expression of "especial dislike of certain young gentlemen who have been much busier—both in these bills and others—than they needed." [42] The current bill was drawn up by Hare with the assistance of Hyde and presented to the king a month later. When the king objected to the bill on the grounds that it constituted an invasion of his prerogative, the House defended itself in that remarkably outspoken document, *Apology of the House of Commons, made to the King, touching their Privileges*, in which they declaimed against "the general, extreme, unjust, and crying oppression" of cart-takers and purveyors, "who have rummaged and ransacked since your majesty's coming in, far more than under any of your royal progenitors." Conscious of the possible charge of trespass, the House asseverated its powers as a representative body: "Neither yet durst we impose it by law upon the people, without first acquainting them, and having their consents to it." [43] Many M.P.'s would have remembered the classical parallel cited in Elizabeth's last parliament when the Speaker's privilege to

41. *The Winning of the Initiative by the House of Commons*, Proc. British Academy, 11 (1926) : 4.

42. Neale, *Elizabeth I and her Parliaments*, pp. 187–88, 208–11.

43. William Cobbett, *Parliamentary History of England*, 36 vols. (1806), 1 : 1040.

determine the priority of bills had been questioned. The government had then argued that the consul in the Roman state had
exercised such powers in the Senate, and that the Speaker's place
was a consul's place. At which, an un-Roman House member
took sharp issue:

> I make great difference between the old Roman Consuls and
> him. Ours is a municipal Government, and we know our own
> Grievances better than Mr Speaker; and therefore 'tis fit,
> that every man Alternis vicibus should have those Acts to be
> called for, he conceives most fit.[44]

There is one striking piece of evidence in the peroration to the
Apology that the voice of the commons was assuming new
authority. The familiar axiom, *vox populi, vox Dei*, as commonly
understood, testified to the rightness of popular judgments.[45] In
1593 Richard Hooker was still voicing the phrase in its accepted
meaning:

> The general and perpetual voice of men is as the sentence of
> God himself. For that which all men have at all times
> learned, Nature herself must needs have taught; and God
> being the author of Nature, her voice is but his instrument.
> [*LEP*, I. viii. 3]

But even before Hooker, the phrase was used to opposite purpose.
To George Gascoigne, *vox populi* meant the voice of the many-
headed multitude, and he rejected it as politically incendiary.[46]

44. Williams M. Mitchell, *The Rise of the Revolutionary Party in the English House of
Commons, 1603–1629* (1959), pp. 22–23, quoting Townshend's *Historical Collections*
(1680), pp. 306–07.

45. The editors of the 1563 *Mirror for Magistrates* (ed. L. B. Campbell (1938), p.
359), suggest that Richard III and his councillors should have listened to the
popular voice: "Vox populi, vox dei, in this case is not so famous a proverbe as
true: The experyence of all times doth approve it."

For a history of the proverb since Alcuin, see George Boas, *Vox Populi: Essays in
the History of an Idea* (1969), pp. 3–38. S. A. Gallacher, "Vox Populi Vox Dei,"
Philological Quarterly 24 (1945) : 12–19, traces its origins in church history, A.D.
400–800, not in the classics.

46. *The Posies* (1575), ed. J. W. Cunliffe, p. 143.

By the time of the *Apology*, however, it was again being mustered (within limitations) to support the stand of the commons against the royal prerogative:

> Let your maj. be pleased to receive public information from your commons in parl. as to the civil estate and government; for private informations pass often by practice: the voice of the people, in the things of their knowledge, is said to be as the voice of God.[47]

Set in a fresh context, the traditional phrase had narrowed in meaning from the general voice of mankind to the particular voice of the commons; and so understood, it was resounding on the public stage that same season in the accents of Chapman's Bussy, who scorns Monsieur's reliance on the people's voice as the voice of God, in favour of law of his own making: "His greatness is the people's; mine's mine own." [48] To such popular lawlessness, James retorted: Beyond written law, "rex est lex loquens," [49] and the issue had been joined. The commonwealth had suffered a cleavage which neither king nor Commons could settle short of civil war.

It is with full consciousness of the new strength in the commons that the king in opening the second session on 18 November 1605, expressed open distaste of the new popular voice. "Diversities of spirits" were to be expected in parliament, he admitted wryly, some of them "more popular than profitable, either for that council or for the commonwealth." But particularly offensive were "some Tribunes of the people, whose mouths could not be stopped, either from the matters of the Puritans or of purveyance." Huffily, he declared that he would never make a separation of the people's will and the will of the king; but at the same time, he warned the House that subjects also were accountable, and that "if any such plebeian tribunes should incur

47. Cobbett, *Parliamentary History*, 1 : 1042.

48. *Bussy d'Ambois*, 3.2.25–27, 75.

49. *The Political Works of James I*, ed. C. H. McIlwain (1918), Speech to Parliament (1607), pp. 291, 299; Speech to Parliament (1609), p. 309.

any offense . . . [the Commons] would correct them for it."
Meanwhile, they should "judge themselves, as St Paul saith, that
they be not judged, and that the whole body receive not a wound
by one ill member thereof" (Cobbett, *Parliamentary History*,
1 : 1071–72). No one missed the significance of the Roman
reference. And the fact that it had been spoken by the king
himself made its circulation in London a certainty. James was a
self-conscious phrase maker, and a phrase invented is not easily
forgotten. In the ensuing debates, Hare and Hyde, the promulga-
tors of the bill for reformation of purveyance, were to become in
the public mind "tribunes," profitable or dangerous to the
commonwealth depending on one's political leaning.

The association was still fresh in the public mind when on 14
February 1606 Hare rose to speak for the Commons. His speech
was long and well composed, but as he warmed against the
wrongs endured by the people from purveyors, he boldly demanded no less than the "rooting out of theis wicked seed of the
divells which like the froggs in Pharoes tyme skippe in every mans
dishe." [50] Just as boldly, other voices, including Hyde's, were
raised to support his stand, one describing the Treasury as "a
royal cistern, wherein his Majesty's largesse to the Scots caused a
continued and remediless leak" (Bowen, p. 311). The whole
matter was shocking, but especially Hare's performance; so that
Speaker Phillips felt constrained to address an apology to the
Lords for "the most undescreete behauior of an unconsiderat
fyerbrand." [51] Fortunately, James retained his composure. Reply-
ing indirectly through Salisbury, he pointedly rejected the "royal
cistern" image, preferred one of his own: "Account [the king] but
your stewerd of whatsoever you give him," Salisbury reported,
and he will be "fidus depositorius." Let the Commons show their
grievances, knowing "how dangerous a thing it is to sommon
subiects to complaine, but thinking that there was none among

50. C. D. Bowen, *The Lion and the Throne* (1956), p. 311; David H. Willson, *The
Parliamentary Diary of Robert Bowyer, 1606–1607* (1931), pp. 38–41; *Journals of the House
of Commons*, 17 vols. (1803–52), 1 : 269.

51. Bowyer, p. 38, n. 3; *State Papers Domestic, James I (1603–10)*, p. 289, no. 89, 14
February 1606.

you that woulde take on them to be Tribunes of the people"
(Bowyer, pp. 41–42). Even then Hare stood his ground. Assured of
support in the House, he merely requested that his speeches might
not be imputed to himself alone; and in his report the next day,
he did not include the reference to tribunes (ibid., p. 46).
Somehow, incredibly, the temperature of the body politic had
remained in control.

Only one course was possible in the face of Hare's recklessness.
Mildness became the tone of the day. Mr. Recorder and some
others moved that the House "should not send to the Lords in
general but mildly to use some such speach to the Lords'
Committees at the next Conference." Mr. Hyde echoed the mood:

> The Lords ought not to taxe us nor wee them. . . . Let us
> send to the Lords mildly to signifie to them where our greife
> is and to desier them if any thing from us do offend them
> they wil be pleased to signifie it to us and not to censure us
> and that wee with all reverence will respect their Lordships
> as becometh us. [Bowyer, p. 51]

Strange words from one of the "tribunes." And next day, Henry
Yelverton joined the chorus: "The Lords should mildly be
requested to forbeare from hence forwarde to taxe any member
whome this howse should send or use unto them," and further,
that if their Lordships should question why the House should take
their reprehension "in evell parte," we shall answer with silence,
and if they still press for an answer from us, "to every particuler
which their Lordships shall stand on, an aunswere to be given in
mildnesse" (ibid. pp. 52–53).

In such a reversal of mood, the bill against purveyance might
be let sleep, and as Hyde put it, "wee should kill our own child
which weare monstrous" (ibid. p. 63). Instead, it malingered
through a series of exceptions by the Lords, sustained mainly by
the courageous stand of Yelverton, who earned because of it the
jocular title of "the old Tribune of the house." [52] But no jest could
hide the demonstrated strength of the common voice nor the

52. Bowyer, p. 123, n. 1. Dudley Carleton to John Chamberlain, 17 April.

gravity of the issue. These things were clear, even though the
judges who were finally called in for a decision "overruled all on
the Prerogative side." For they had "delivered one Iudgment in
all mens opinions of dangerous consequence, that the prerogative
was not subject to law, but that it was a transcendent above the
reach of parlement," [53] and both sides knew that that was not the
end of the argument.

Day by day, during that relatively short period in 1606 when
purveyance had suddenly become a major point of attack on the
king's prerogative, the ears of Londoners were cocked for reports
of it. By good fortune, we have one such report, given first hand
by Sir Edward Hoby to Sir Thomas Edmondes directly after
Hare's climactic speech of 14 February:

> The House stood much ill-affected towards the lords' car-
> riage, and Hyde yielded many reasons why we should not
> yield more unto the King than we did; with many invectives,
> and so far put the house in distaste, as that an expectation
> grew of the sequel. And if your lordship had heard them, you
> would have said that Hare and Hyde had represented the
> tribunes of the people.[54]

Long after, the king would continue to fulminate against the
"tribunitial Orators" in the House;[55] but it is significant that in
1606, London gossips, like the king, immediately recognized in
Hare and Hyde and the newly discovered power of commons the
rise of the *tribuni plebis* in republican Rome. To Lord Chancellor
Ellesmere, the traditional idea of commonwealth was being
shaken to its foundations. From the dignity of the Exchequer
Chamber he leveled his scorn at those "busy questionists," "new
risen philosophers," who looked at the common law as above the
monarch; "common discoursers" who presumed to cite those
"mislikers of monarchies," Plato and Aristotle, on the framing of

53. Bowyer, p. 134, n. 1. Quoted from Chamberlain's letter to Carleton. *S. P.
Dom. James I*, 20 (1606) : 36.

54. Thomas Birch, *The Court and Times of James the First*, 2 vols. (1848), 1 : 60.

55. John Rushworth, *Historical Collections of Private Passages of State*, 8 vols. (1721),
1 : 47.

states and commonwealths as they walked in Paul's aisle or sat in
ordinaries, "drowned with drinke, or blowne away with a whiffe
of tobacco."[56] Whatever the dire extremities that might come of
such speculations, a new idea of commonwealth, taking shape
from those idle smoke rings, would assert itself again in the *Petition
of Grievances* (1610), the Petition of 1621, and the *Petition of Right*
(1628). The commons had found a voice; and every ordinary in
London when Shakespeare wrote *Coriolanus* was alive with the
news.

The Mutinous Parts

It is in this context of contemporary politics that the audience
appeal of *Coriolanus* can be best understood. On grounds of style,
the play has usually been dated about 1608. But considering the
general public interest in the 1606 debates on purveyance, and
the fact that king and commoner alike recognized in them a
parallel to the rise of popular representation in Rome, there is
good reason to believe that Shakespeare in 1606 or shortly
thereafter made dramatic capital of that interest. Parliament's
business was for the moment Shakespeare's business—"the greatest entertainment that we have."

Characteristically, Shakespeare uses recurrent image patterns
to reinforce the evolution from personal to public tragedy.
Coriolanus despises the commons with a congenital ferocity, and
when his peers, the patricians, and particularly his mother,
impose on him the role of a beggar for the consulship, he has
repudiated his own nature. "Why did you wish me milder?" he
half-petulantly demands of her. "Would you have me / False to
my nature? Rather say I play / The man I am" (3.2.14–17). Yet
this is precisely the role he presently assumes. In yielding to her
specious and disastrous alliance of "honour" and policy, a speech
of Shakespeare's own invention, and mildly donning the robe of
candidatus, he has become traitor to himself. The ironic overtones
of this image of traitorship are echoed throughout the action in

56. *A Complete Collection of State Trials*, eds. William Cobbett, T. B. Howell et al.,
42 vols. (1816–98), 11 : 103.

permutations on his public and private treason. The tribunes
goad him to turn traitor with the hated epithet, and in boyish
rage he becomes beggar to Aufidius to lead the Corioli against
Rome. With Rome at his mercy, he once again yields to his
mother's persuasions, this time to her formula of "honour" and
mercy, which Aufidius reminds us is incompatible with his nature,
and "traitor" is his reward for the compromised peace. Doubly
beggar and doubly traitor, once to the Romans, once to the
Corioli, we find in the end some small measure of sympathy for
this humiliated hero. And these images, dramatically intensifying
the abjectness of his ruin, conspire in the concluding action with a
third image which completes the artistic statement of his degradation. It is announced first in the reluctant admiration of the
tribunes: "Such a nature, / Tickled with good success, disdains
the shadow / Which he treads on at noon" (1.1.263–65). Soon
after, his mother imagines him stamping on the Volscians,
beating Aufidius's head below his knee and treading upon his
neck (1.3.35, 45–50). When he threatens Rome, she sees him as
capable of treading on his country's ruin, even on his mother's
womb. Moreover, she dares him to do it, and his dove-like wife
and vicious little son double and triple the dare (5.3.116, 122–28).
Likewise, in Menenius's eyes, "he walks, he moves like an engine,
and the ground shrinks before his treading" (5.4.19–20). Moments
before the close of the play, the action is sharply reversed, and
symbol combines with image as the beggar-traitor is ground to an
ignoble death under the trampling feet of his arch-rival. Only
then, a nameless lord recalls the image in a final ironic protest:
"Tread not upon him. Masters all, be quiet! Put up your swords."
Aufidius, a soldier like Coriolanus and his peer, recognizes in him
a "sovereignty of nature . . . as is the osprey to the fish"
(4.7.33–35); his personal tragedy rises out of his abdication of his
nature to rule.

Sovereignty, in fact, is the issue which expands the personal
tragedy into the larger tragedy of the commonwealth. So long as
that healthy state of the body politic exists for the mutual benefit
of head and heel, the stomach will not cupboard the viands and
the great toe will not attempt to go foremost. But in the present

bodily distemperature the astute Menenius recognizes fatal symptoms. "Your most grave belly was deliberate," he says, knowing that Coriolanus is neither grave nor deliberate. Yet far more malignant is the commons' bid for political power, for it represents the first time that the sovereignty of the patricians has been seriously challenged. The citizens are fully conscious of their newly won advantage, but without the tribunes, they are incapable of positive action: "We have power in ourselves to do it, but it is a power that we have no power to do" (2.3.4–5). By themselves, they are inclined to excuse Coriolanus's faults, and they do. But the tribunes are exasperated with such "childish friendliness":

> Could you not have told him
> As you were lesson'd? When he had no power
> But was a petty servant to the state,
> He was your enemy; ever spake against
> Your liberties and the charters that you bear
> I' th' body of the weal; and now, arriving
> A place of potency and sway o' th' state,
> If he should still malignantly remain
> Fast foe to th' plebeii, your voices might
> Be curses to yourselves.

> [2.3.183–93]

With your present bargaining power, they argue, you should have demanded promise of concessions, "as you were fore-advis'd"; then, if he had become enraged and refused, you could have "pass'd him unelected." Now, "in free contempt, . . . do you think / That his contempt shall not be bruising to you / When he hath power to crush?" (2.3.198, 207–11). Revoke your "ignorant election," lay the fault on us, and reaffirm him as "your fixed enemy" (2.3.250).

Coriolanus's warning to the senators immediately following makes it clear that he will grant no concessions to the commons:

> I say again,
> In soothing them we nourish 'gainst our Senate
> The cockle of rebellion, insolence, sedition,

> Which we ourselves have plough'd for, sow'd, and scatter'd
> By mingling them with us, the honour'd number,
> Who lack not virtue, no, nor power, but that
> Which they have given to beggars.

> [3.1.66-73]

The citizens are "measles / Which we disdain should tetter us, yet
sought / The very way to catch them." In this mood, Coriolanus
explodes his contempt on Sicinius, "this Triton of the minnows"
with his "absolute 'shall,' " whose ultimate intention is "to turn
[the Senators'] current in a ditch / And make [their] channel
his." But he also lashes out at the senators themselves who remain
supine before Sicinius's attack:

> If he have power
> Then vail your ignorance; if none, awake
> Your dangerous lenity. If you are learn'd,
> Be not as common fools; if you are not,
> Let them have cushions by you. You are plebeians
> If they be senators.

> [3.1.78-80, 97-102]

Such is the plight of the commonwealth "when two authorities are
up, / Neither supreme." As Coriolanus so clearly sees, the struggle
is fundamentally for sovereignty, and popular sovereignty is for
him unthinkable. Like Thomas Elyot and Lord Ellesmere, he
recalls the political eclipse of the Greeks under popular rule:
"Though there the people had more absolute pow'r— / I say they
nourish'd disobedience, fed / The ruin of the state" (3.1.109-10,
116-18). "Pluck out / The multitudinous tongue," he pleads, else
the state will be bereaved

> Of that integrity which should become't,
> Not having the power to do the good it would
> For th' ill which doth control 't. . . .
>   In a better hour,
> Let what is meet be said it must be meet,
> And throw their power i' th' dust.

> [3.1.155-71]

But this new popular power is not to be so put off. The tribunes
have legal status, and they retort shrewdly enough that Coriolanus is "a traitorous innovator" and "foe to the public weal,"
choosing not to remember that they also are innovators, and, for
that matter, subverters of commonwealth. Their audacious question, "What is the city but the people?" reveals their ultimate
aim; and the people, caught by the new doctrine, respond
delightedly, "True! The people are the city" (3.1.175–76, 198–
200). At this critical juncture, sovereignty seems indeed to have
shifted to the commonalty. Commonwealth has for them become
the wealth of the commons. And even as Menenius makes a
desperate gesture to "you worthy Tribunes," Sicinius boldly seizes
the initiative and sentences Coriolanus to be thrown down the
Tarpeian Rock. Since he has resisted law, "law shall scorn him
further trial / Than the severity of the public power, / Which he
so sets at naught." The degree of the citizens' subservience is
confirmed in the voice of the First Citizen: "He shall well
know / The tribunes are the people's mouths, / And we their
hands" (3.1.265–72). Again, Menenius interposes for the traditional order in the commonwealth:

> He's a limb that has but a disease;
> Mortal, to cut it off; to cure it, easy.
> . . . The service of the foot,
> Being once gangren'd, is not then respected
> For what before it was.
>
> [3.1.296–307]

But the tribunes, victorious as voices of the people, have no
interest in the body politic. The popular mouth has become
sovereign, and as the succeeding action demonstrates, it has
brought the commonweal into mortal danger.[57]

57. With his eyes on the Civil War, F. W. Maitland comments in *Selected Essays*,
p. 113; "It is true that 'the people' exists, and 'the liberties of the People' must be
set over against 'the prerogatives of the king'; but just because the King is no part
of the People, the People cannot be the state or Commonwealth." Except for his
equating of State and Commonwealth, his distinction of rival prerogatives is
equally valid for the reign of James I. The people can be the state; they cannot, by
definition, be the commonwealth.

Meanwhile, as an extraordinary parallel, Coriolanus is similarly maneuvered by his mother into a Machiavellian monstrosity
of dialectic. Speak, she says, "with words that are but rooted
in / Your tongue, though but bastards and syllables / Of no
allowance to your bosom's truth" (3.2.55–57). He is to combine
the incompatible: honor and policy. And thus falsely clothed, he
is to beg for the consulship—but mildly, mildly. Like the
Commons, his tongue has been captived. "Never trust to what my
tongue can do / I' th' way of flattery further" (3.2.36–37). The
banishment of Coriolanus is a staged performance in which the
new dictators speak popular slogans behind popular masks: "I' th'
right and strength o' the commons," "insisting on the old
prerogative" (even James would have smiled at that), "i' th' truth
o' the cause"—whatever that might mean (3.3.14–18). He must
now submit "to the people's voices . . . whose great power must
try him." (3.3.4, 79–80). All is to be done "in the name o' th'
people / And in the power of us the tribunes." So managed, there
could be but one result. Speaking as a banished man, Coriolanus
flings back at them a prophetic curse in their newly captured
office:

> Have the power still
> To banish your defenders, till at length
> Your ignorance (which finds not till it feels,
> Making not reservation of yourselves,
> Still your own foes) deliver you, as most
> Abated captives, to some nation
> That won you without blows! Despising
> For you the city, thus I turn my back.
> There is a world elsewhere.

> [3.3.127–35]

The helplessness of the state can be inferred from Coriolanus's
resentful explanation of Roman affairs to his social equal,
Aufidius, in Antium:

> The cruelty and envy of the people,
> Permitted by our dastard nobles, who

> Have forsook me, hath devour'd the rest
> And suffer'd me by th' voice of slaves to be
> Whoop'd out of Rome.

[4.5.79–83]

But the full extent of the tragedy to commonwealth is revealed only after a deceptive calm following the banishment, a calm for which the tribunes flatter themselves that they are responsible (4.6.1–10). The quiet is filled with rumors: that for banishing Coriolanus, the nobles intend to take all power from the people and pluck their tribunes from them; that the Volsces are invading Roman territories; that Coriolanus and Aufidius are leading a power against Rome. When Coriolanus returns with Rome's enemies at his back, the tribunes offer no leadership; their "franchises," indeed, as the patricians remind them, are "confin'd into an auger's bore" (4.6.86–87). They who "stood so much / Upon the voice of occupation and / The breath of garlic-eaters" instead of facing the sudden military crisis, now seek to avoid it. Their obvious ineptness becomes explicit in their surrender of the initiative to the patricians as invasion becomes imminent. A mere Volscian watchman sums up their failure:

> Can you, when you have push'd out your gates the very defender of them, and in a violent popular ignorance given your enemy your shield, think to front his revenges with the easy groans of old women, the virginal palms of your daughters, or with the palsied intercession of such a decay'd dotant as you seem to be? [5.2.41–47]

Indeed, having precipitated the political tragedy, the tribunes retire in utter futility while the nobles, sovereign by default, turn at last to Volumnia to save Rome. But saving Rome does not save her son. By her counsel of duplicity, she has sealed Coriolanus's political as well as personal tragedy quite as effectually as the tergiversation of the tribunes has determined the popular defeat. And the commonwealth, in the meantime, is left to fare for itself.

To the tribune-conscious audience for whom this play was written, its topical impact was inescapable. The tragedy to

commonwealth is repeatedly staged in the image context of the
current parliamentary debates, yet with just enough perspective
to leave the reference inferential. Was James that grave belly,
that "fidus depositorius" he had pictured himself? Was he "the
storehouse and the shop of the whole body," or did he seem more
like "a royal cistern, wherein his Majesty's largesse to the Scots
caused a continued and remediless leak"? And was not the word
"mildly . . . Ay, but mildly. . . . Well, mildly be it then—
mildly" (3.2.139–45) on the tongue of every member of Shakespeare's audience after Hyde's elaborate and apparently sophistical use of it in Commons to soften the intemperate speech of
Hare? When Menenius good-humoredly rallies his popular
audience as "th' discontented members, the mutinous parts"
(1.1.115, 153) and Coriolanus presently castigates them as
"worshipful mutiners" who in "their mutinies and revolts . . .
showed most valour" (1.1.254; 3.1.126–27), Shakespeare was
using a politically saturated byword as familiar in the theatre as it
was to the Earl of Shrewsbury two days before Hare's speech,
when he so misjudged the temper of the House as to report to Sir
Thomas Edmondes:

> The Commons of the Lower House, where yourself was wont
> to be placed amongst the mutineers, are much more
> temperate than they were at the first session, and now spend
> all their spirits and endeavors in devising laws tending to his
> majesty's safety, and suppressing of the dangerous members
> of this State.[58]

One need not make Shakespeare a partisan; we need only
remember that in 1606 his standing as a playwright both at the
Globe and at Whitehall would prevent his making a serious
misjudgment in tact. But it is equally clear that he was making
dramatic capital of a burning current issue.

However allusive this most political of Shakespeare's plays,
broader issues were involved. A politically-minded Jacobean

58. 12 February 1606, "from the Court at Whitehall"; Thomas Birch, *The Court
and Times of James the First*, 1 : 52.

audience would have recognized, above all, the demonstrated failure of representative government. In both *Julius Caesar* and *Coriolanus*, the many-headed multitude is incapable of rule. But the banishment of Coriolanus posed a new question both ponderable and disconcerting: Could a many-headed multitude achieve and maintain a commonwealth with the aid of tribunes to speak for them? The ineffectualness of Sicinius and Brutus, once they have acquired authority, would seem to preclude any such possibility; and their complacence in office (4.6) is as perilous to commonwealth as Brutus's apparent insouciance after the killing of Caesar. It can be maintained that their conduct as popular leaders is not wholly indefensible. They are no less intent on the public good. Unlike Antony, they cannot be said to have acted out of self-interest; nor have they appealed their case, as he did, on purely emotional grounds. Only when they are on their way to control do they use the language of naked power; once they have attained it, they assume a benignity which belies the precariousness of their rule. They are, nevertheless, astute manipulators of public opinion, skilled in quasi-juridical shifts; and their attack on Coriolanus amounts in reality to subversion of the common weal under the unassailable canopy of legality. They begin with the false political premise: "What is the city but the people?" This accepted, they reaffirm their grudgingly won status as representatives of the popular voice: "By the consent of all we were establish'd / The people's magistrates." And finally, armed with "public power," they propose that Coriolanus, not they, "hath resisted law, / And therefore law (that is, the tribunes speaking for the people) shall scorn him" (3.1.202, 267–69). Meanwhile, Coriolanus, who as the arm, our soldier, has by their own admission "served well for Rome," (3.3.83) single-handedly denies their offense to law, his unyielding stand a very audible mockery of their claim to the consent of all the city, a palpable and sharp reminder of their presumption of sovereignty.

Consent, as the tribunes use it, puts an ancient seal on their right to office. It was precise and politically evocative to Shakespeare's audience. Associated with the origin of societies, it was the necessary consequence, as Cicero saw it, of men's first gathering together for their mutual advantage to establish a commonwealth. Consent implied the right of every member of that society to determine the form government should take. Furthermore, it is quite clear in *De Legibus* (3.3.9) that by the establishment of tribunes the rights of the plebeians were not only acknowledged for the first time but protected against invasion in the future. These Ciceronian idealisms, restated in Thomas Smith's *Commonwealth of England* ("The consent of the Parliament is taken to be every man's consent") could be viewed with no less than apprehension in the early years of James. And though in *Coriolanus* the new popular sovereignty will not survive, the demise of the customary idea of commonwealth is already predictable when on both sides duties have been set aside for the rights implicit in initial consent. Aufidius, looking back in a moment of abstracted reflection properly describes the political debacle: "Rights by rights falter, strengths by strengths do fail" (4.7.55).

The defeat of commonwealth brought about by this political impasse gives *Coriolanus* its thematic bond with *Julius Caesar*. In its own way, the intransigence of both Coriolanus and the tribunes is quite as much a public loss as Brutus's uncongenial but well-intentioned sacrifice. At the conclusion of both plays, commonwealth as an ideal is as far away as ever. But while there is no political gap between the two plays, in *Coriolanus* the tragedy is more sharply etched by the unresolved confrontation of the boyish destroyer of butterflies and the popular orators. Shakespeare has perceived and dramatized, as he perhaps could not have done under Elizabeth, the larger issue at stake in the welter of political maneuver at the beginning of James's reign. Beyond the question of the king's prerogative or parliament's—the question that loomed immediately in Shakespeare's mind—was the immense jeopardy to commonwealth when both parties were at fault. "The public power of all societies," said Richard Hooker, "is above every soul contained in the same societies" (*LEP*, I, xvi. 5). It had now become shockingly clear that the validity of this hitherto unshakable concept of government, a body politic whose health depends on the mutual coactivity of each of its members, had been for the first time seriously challenged. *Coriolanus* is the story of that challenge. Had Shakespeare's audience been able to foresee the course of seventeenth-century history as clearly, the upheaval some forty years later might have been averted. The true measure of the stature of Shakespeare's political thought lies in the difference between Menenius's commonwealth and Oliver Cromwell's.

Shakespeare needed no more than *Julius Caesar* and *Coriolanus* to indicate the unattainability of commonwealth. But if commonwealth is merely an ideal, it is a necessary ideal, and from this point of view, Shakespeare was to come back to it once more in the stated opinions of Gonzalo, the old courtier in *The Tempest*, who finds himself safe in a newfound land after what seems to be—and is—a magical reprieve from drowning, and straightway falls into a dream of establishing a perfect commonwealth there. Gonzalo's speculations fall into proper perspective against the background of Brutus's thwarted idealism. His mind leaps at the opportunity to form a government "t'excel the golden age," like Plato's ideal republic or More's Utopia. His immediate inspiration, however, is the report not of Socrates nor of Raphael Hythlodaye but of a simple and rough-hewn servant of Montaigne; and this blueprint he persists in proposing over the mocks and mows of his somewhat less than ideal fellows, Antonio and Sebastian. Like Lord Ellesmere, Shakespeare must have heard their counterparts, idealist and scoffer, envisioning imaginary commonwealths while they walked in Paul's aisle or whiffed tobacco in the ordinaries of London. In *The Tempest* they are unaware that their very speech is under the surveillance of the rightful Duke of Milan whom they formerly served, and who in proper time will release them from the bonds that without their knowledge now hold them. Yet granting freedom, as Prospero's experience illustrates, will not of itself bring commonwealth. Freedom to Caliban too easily suggests knocking a nail into the head of "the tyrant" he serves; freedom to Antonio, usurper of his brother's dukedom suggests a similar course for the brother of the Duke of Milan. Both, by resorting to force for private gain, consciously or unconsciously reject a public conscience: "Ay sir! Where lies that? If 'twere a kibe, / 'Twould put me to my slipper;

but I feel not / This deity in my bosom" (2.1.276–79). So long as men regard the state as a property without societal obligations, so long will commonwealth remain a dream. Which does not make the dream any less necessary to man as a political animal.

Decline of Empire

After the death of Julius Caesar, decline until the peace of Octavius. So the usual historical view in Shakespeare's day, and so Shakespeare's in *Julius Caesar* and *Antony and Cleopatra*. But with an important difference: *Julius Caesar* is a tragedy of state, *Antony and Cleopatra* a tragedy of empire. Elizabethan commentators on Roman history saw in the factional quarrels that followed upon the destruction of the noblest man in the tide of times a classic example of the tragic consequences of repudiation of the monarchical principle essential to commonwealth. In the world of *Julius Caesar*, it was still possible to think of the state of man as a little kingdom, disrupted as much by the political idealism of Brutus as by the pragmatism of Antony and Octavius. In the world of *Antony and Cleopatra*, kingdoms are clay, to be taken in or enfranchised for the mirth of an empress; to piece her opulent throne; to be bargained for by one world contender and kissed away by another. Kingdoms may serve at one moment to grace the deferential courtesy of an emperor's servant:

> Your Caesar's father oft,
> When he hath mus'd of taking kingdoms in,
> Bestow'd his lips on that unworthy place
> As it rain'd kisses.
>
> [3.13.82–85]

Or at another, they may be pawns to keep decorum between equals. In such a world, there is no longer accommodation for Brutus's commonweal. Political idealism has given way to a vaster imperial theme—vaster, but flawed by an amoral grasp for power to which persons and states alike fall victim. *Res publica* has been replaced by *imperium*, the common good by statism.

Empire was no new word when James came to the throne, but

its earlier meanings, as Richard Koebner has observed, tended to deliquesce into ambiguities.[59] When Henry VIII declared unequivocally in the preamble to the Act of Appeals in 1533, "This realme of England is an Impire," his aim was to establish the status of England as a sovereign state. But he never further defined it. Sufficient to say that it had always been so,[60] as manifested in "divers sundry authentic histories and chronicles." Precisely what those old authentic histories were was not made clear, and the vagueness was doubtless intentional,[61] but the declaration authoritively served Henry's purposes in his effort to disentangle himself from papal empery and confirm his own. England as empire could also elevate Henry's status in comparison with that of his kinsman, Charles, titular head of the Holy Roman Empire. Thus, Charles's ambassador was informed that "the King had a right of Empire in his Kingdom." Once stated, the claim of empire became a statutory precedent throughout the Tudor period. Henry's successors were described as "lawful kings and emperors of this realm," [62] and though it was used imprecisely, the title had the effect of reinforcing national sentiment against the threat of rival imperial claims: "How has our most puissant and redoubted king fortressed this his most flourishing monarchy, empire, and kingdom with all things that any man can invent for the prosperous conservation of a commonweal." [63]

> So let thy soueraigne Empire be encreast,
> And with Iberian Neptune part the stake
> Whose Trident he the triple worlde would make.[64]

It is to be noted that the Tudors did not claim empire beyond

59. *Empire* (1961), p. 318, n. 61.

60. G. R. Elton, *England Under the Tudors* (1962), p. 161.

61. Richard Koebner, " 'The Imperial Crown of this Realm': Henry VIII, Constantine the Great, and Polydore Vergil," *BIHR* 26 (1953) : 29–52.

62. I am indebted to Koebner's *Empire*, pp. 40, 47, for the two following citations.

63. Thomas Becon, *The Policy of War* (1542), Parker Society (1843), p. 245.

64. George Chapman, *De Guiana, Carmen Epicum* (1596), ed. P. B. Bartlett (1907), p. 354.

the traditionally presumptive limits of the realm of England, France, and Ireland. At the accession of James, however, the union of England and Scotland gave the idea new historical dimension. In the first of the Statutes of the Realm, Parliament found it expedient to nudge James's memory of that earlier "happie Union and Conjunction" of the two noble houses of York and Lancaster "because there is derived and graven from and out of that Unyon of those two Princelie Families a more famous and greater Union (or rather re-unitinge) of the two mightie famous and ancient Kingdomes (yet ancientlie but one) of England and Scotland under our Imperial Crowne, in your moste Royall Person." [65] Of course, the ceremony doesn't make the marriage. Beneath the grandiose rhetoric proclaiming "the Inestimable and unspeakable Blessinges" of the greater union lurked the delicate question of the *post nati* now that two kingdoms previously sovereign were united under one imperial crown; and before long, it would become apparent that the prerogatives of Crown and Parliament would not be easily resolved. Nevertheless, at the first there were evidences of accommodation, especially on James's part, not to touch tender political nerve ends. In the King's speech to Parliament in 1607, he took pains to reassure some English towns who feared that they might suffer by the union. It may be, he admitted "a Merchant or two of Bristow, or Yarmouth, may haue an hundred pounds lesse in his packe: But if the Empire gaine, and become the greater, it is no matter: You see one Corporation is euer against another, and no priuate Companie can be set vp, but with some losse to another." And he closed on an even more conciliatory note:

> Remember I pray you, the trewth and sincerity of my meaning, which in seeking Vnion, is onely to aduance the greatnesse of your Empire seated here in England; And yet with such caution I wish it, as may stand with the weale of both States. What is now desired, hath oft before bene sought when it could not bee obteined: To refuse it now then, were

65. *Statutes of the Realm*, vol. 4, part 2 (1819), pp. 1017–18.

> double iniquitie. Strengthen your owne felicitie, *London* must
> bee the Seate of your King, and Scotland ioyned to this
> kingdome by a Golden conquest, but cymented with loue.[66]

Thus, a potential crisis of sovereignty was averted by mutual
forbearance, and the union of the two kingdoms had become a
political reality.

Meanwhile, James's golden conquest made it possible to view
the royal estate in broader scope. An "empire of Great Britain"
extending from Brittany to the Virginia plantation invited
comparison with the establishment of the Roman empire under
Octavius Augustus after the struggle of civil war. Francis Bacon,
who was not given to flights of fancy, believed that the battle of
Actium decided the empire of the world,[67] and Shakespeare
apparently felt the same way. He had complimented the new
king's ancestry in *Macbeth*; perhaps the Roman empire in its
greatness would catch the fancy of the king in his new imperial
status. Indeed, Shakespeare may have been scanning the maps of
Ortelius before writing of Antony's delights as dolphin-like,
showing his back above the element they lived in. If any such idea
were in his mind, it had been transfused with other metals by the
time that *Antony and Cleopatra* took form as a play. The grandeur
and magniloquence is there, but the mood and the characters that
induce it are amalgamated with baser stuff. Antony's honor is in
his past, and the cold and callous efficiency of Octavius is no
Vergilian compliment to the emperor of Great Britain. The tone
of the play is retrospective, not prospective. It dramatizes not the
rise of empire but its decay by indulgence. The sense of greatness
is there, but the glory has departed.

Shakespeare was not the first writer to identify idleness as the
cause of that magnificent ruin. In fact, it had long been a
standard literary exercise. Spenser, in translating Bellay's poem
on the subject, stresses the invincibility of the empire before the
civil wars:

66. *The Political Works of James I*, ed. McIlwain, pp. 299–300, 304–05.
67. "Of the true Greatness of Kingdomes and estates," first published in 1612.

> But when the object of her vertue failed,
> Her power it selfe against it selfe did arme;

and the cause of its fall, as in Shakespeare, was in idleness:

> O warie wisedome of the man, that would
> That Carthage towres from spoile should be forborne,
> To th' end that his victorious people should
> With cancring laisure not be ouerworne;
>   He well foresaw, how that the Romane courage
> Impatient of pleasures faint desires,
> Through idlenes would turne to civill rage,
> And be her selfe the matter of her fires.
>   For in a people giuen all to ease,
> Ambition is engendred easily;
> As in a vicious bodie, grose disease
> Soone growes through humours superfluitie.
>   That came to passe, when swolne with plentities pride,
> Nor prince, nor peere, nor kin they would abide.[68]

So for Antony, when a Roman thought hath struck him:

> I must from this enchanting queen break off.
> Ten thousand harms more than the ills I know
> My idleness doth hatch.

> [1.2.132–34]

But when he faces Cleopatra with it, she turns his bitterness off with sentiment: " 'Tis sweating labour / To bear such idleness so near the heart" (1.3.91–94).

The vastness of Roman accomplishment and the trivialities that brought about its destruction were indissociable historic facts, and in this respect *Antony and Cleopatra* covers a larger canvas than the narrower matter of government and politics of *Julius Caesar* and *Coriolanus*. To convey this impression, Shakespeare seems to have exploited every theatrical device. Once before, in the prologue to *Henry V*, he had professed the need and with assumed modesty deprecated the result. Now using techniques which he

68. *Ruines of Rome*, stanzas 21, 24.

would not have occasion for again, he extends the physical properties of the "little O" to match the proportions of empire. By a series of quick, short sequences, which the cinema in a later day has rediscovered, he transports the audience over the entire expanse of the Mediterranean basin. Alexandria, Rome, the corners of the empire, are brought together on the stage by messengers, by formal triumphs, by marching armies—above all, by deft use of montage, a long since mastered technique of focusing into the middle of a conversation. "Nay, but this dotage of our general's . . ." imposes an instant illusion of imperial downfall. Thereafter, in restless movement, the current flows from point to point, then lingers in small pools gathering itself for the next turbulence. And all is done with a beguiling effortlessness which both conceals and reveals the immensity of the fall. At the end, out-policied Caesar, gazing on the body of Cleopatra, is overcome with a feeling of awe, almost disbelief, at the gamester in love and politics that so recently was, and will not longer be:

> But she looks like sleep,
> As she would catch another Antony
> In her strong toil of grace.

[5.2.347-51]

Never again does Shakespeare quite achieve this complexity of trivia and magnitude, of idleness and grandeur.

Yet the style, indeed the whole tempo of the play, rises from a political base, and in this regard much of modern criticism falls silent. Professor Geoffrey Bullough sees Octavius as "political man at his most efficient," though he feels that in the play generally political theory is a minor concern; and while he speaks of the play as "both a tragedy of state and a tragedy of love and honour," he does not expatiate.[69] More recently Professor J. W. Lever has located the compass points of the play in the intense concern of the theatre during the last years of Elizabeth and the first of James with contemporary politics.[70] Lever argues appo-

---

69. *Narrative and Dramatic Sources of Shakespeare* (1964), vol. 5, pp. 249–52.
70. *The Tragedy of State* (1971), pp. 3–4.

sitely that the political plays of the early Jacobean dramatists
reflect a new growth of "state power, . . . a concept of absolutism
which required that all loyalties, all personal obligations and
human bonds be sacrificed to the interests of state." Bussy,
Flamineo, Bosola, Brachiano, and the rest of the statists operate
under their own set of moral values. One may accept the
generalization, yet insist that *Antony and Cleopatra* cannot be drawn
into the same net. Antony's struggle is not with the political
system but with his own inability to conform to it, and this
constitutes his tragedy. Cleopatra and Octavius are the politicians
in the play to whose machinations first Antony and eventually
Octavius himself fall victims. Nor is it possible to accept Lever's
conjecture that Shakespeare postponed writing the sequel of *Julius
Caesar* because of the political risks involved. He had just written
Coriolanus in which the reference to current politics was much
more specific. The simpler explanation is a matter of circumstance: empire had not become a current issue until the accession
of James.

Yet it would be a mistake to assume that the earlier uses of the
word had lost any force. Antony's loss of sovereignty, apparent in
the first words of the play, is reiterated presently in his own report.
"Our Italy shines o'er with civil swords" (1.3.44–55); but "our
Italy" is no longer Antony's, and Antony has long since become
Cleopatra's. He has willingly removed Rome into a corner of his
thought where it rankles as a galling reminder of the Roman he
once was. "Grates me, the sum," is a shorthand dismissal of his
public as well as his private conscience, and his attempts at
self-exculpation succeed only in exposing his failure.

Francis Bacon well understood the dilemma of the private
person in public office:

> To speake now of the true Temper of *Empire*: It is a Thing
> rare, & hard to keep: For both Temper & Distemper consist
> of Contraries. But it is one thing to mingle Contraries,
> another to enterchange them. . . . This is true; that the
> wisdome of all these latter Times in *Princes* Affaires, is rather
> fine Deliveries, and Shiftings of Dangers and Mischiefes,

when they are neare; then solid and grounded Courses to
keepe them aloofe. But this is but to try Masteries with
Fortune. . . . The difficulties in *Princes* Businesse, are many
and great; But the greatest difficulty, is often in their owne
Minde. . . . For it is common with *Princes*, (saith *Tacitus*) to
will Contradictories. *Sunt plerumque Regum voluntates vehementes,
& inter se contrariae.* For it is the Soloecisme of Power, to thinke
to Command the End, and yet not to endure the Meane.[71]

The Antony of *Julius Caesar* admirably mingled contraries in
achieving power; in *Antony and Cleopatra* he has discovered how
rare they are and how hard to keep. Weakness in empire is
systemic, unlike the solid and grounded courses of state; and the
weakness is particularly evident in the Triumvirate in which
Lepidus remains an ass to bear burdens while Antony cannot
muster the power to withstand Octavius's inexorable rise. Sardonic recollection of a more glorious past is an essential element
in the play's structure. The lofty scene which Cassius had
confidently predicted would immortalize the knot of men that
gave their country liberty has long receded, and the memory of
those more heroic times is colored by the new fashion for idol
breaking. Agrippa finds Antony's histrionics at the death of
Caesar a ready subject for lampoon:

> Why Enobarbus,
> When Antony found Julius Caesar dead,
> He cried almost to roaring; and he wept
> When at Philippi he found Brutus slain.

And Enobarbus reduces Antony's sentiment to bathos:

> That year indeed he was troubled with a rheum.
> What willingly he did confound he wail'd,
> Believe 't, till I wept too.
>
> [*Antony and Cleopatra*, 3.3.53–59] [72]

71. *Essays*, ed. W. Aldis Wright (1883), pp. 76–77. The passage is from the 1625
edition. In 1612, Bacon had written: "A true temper of gouernment is a rare
thing."

72. Cf. Aumerle's "hollow parting," *Rich. II*, 1.4.5–9.

The younger Pompey's present fortune is far more personally
bound with the past; but he proves to be something short of a hero
in his self-appointed role of revenger of his father, as he recalls
with a nice blend of reluctant admiration and flippancy Caesar's
revenging ghost at Philippi after "the good Brutus ghosted"
Caesar, the intensity of the legendary revenger, "pale Cassius,"
and the high-mindedness of the "all-honour'd honest Roman,
Brutus, / With the arm'd rest, courtiers of beauteous freedom."
His sarcasm reveals a diminished imitator of those great ones,
living in an age too late for ideals. Even before the scene is over,
he has made ignominious peace with the erstwhile objects of his
revenge. Antony himself, in the midst of present attractions on the
River Nile, also remembers in a ruefully nostalgic mood the high
convictions of "the lean and wrinkled Cassius," and "the mad
Brutus"—"mad" as an old soldier admires heart in an amateur.
Then, the trusting Brutus had offered him "a place in the
commonwealth"; "yet now"—confessing his enslavement to passion—"no matter."

In other ways, Antony's widely publicized loose indulgence, of
which he is only too well aware, has destroyed the popular image
of Roman integrity. The virtues of the Roman soldier were
proverbial, the Roman art of war had been a textbook for modern
warfare. But now the text has been revised. Soldiers, goodly
Roman soldiers, have beheld and trimmed course accordingly.
Ventidius, fresh with victory over the Parthians, refrains from
pursuit for fear of rivaling his captain, Antony, and thus losing
favor. "Who does i' th' wars more than his captain can / Becomes
his captain's captain" (3.1.21–22). Hence, a novel revision of the
rules of war: Ambition is best served by political prudence, not
victory. Machiavelli could do no better. Menas, hireling of
Pompey, practices the same politics for similar personal gain.
"Wilt thou be lord of all the world?" is a question on the answer
to which his future as well as Pompey's rests. In a world without
honor, prudence ironically drives Pompey into rejecting the
opportunity, not because he did not approve the slaughter
involved, but because he was apprised of it before it was done. For

both Ventidius withholding his hand in Parthia and for Menas enjoined not to cut the ship's cable, the empire is involved, yet none of the participants puts it before self-interest.

Nor does Shakespeare's Cleopatra any more than his Richard II ever give a hint that her empire is at stake. Egypt is her estate merely, to do with as she wishes, and she uses it to advantage her personal whim. Wisely, she professes not to understand when after his first defeat Antony solicits his soldiers "to make as much of me / As when mine empire was your fellow too / And suffer'd my command" (4.2.21–23). But personal though her rule is, she is a professional politician, and she plays the game with consummate skill, most apparent after Antony's death, when she knows that she must even with her match in deviousness, Octavius. For let it be stated negatively, her death is no liebestod. If that had been her intention, the match would never have occurred. Like Elizabeth, she had always mixed love and politics, the peculiar prerogative of a woman; but if with Antony, her actions have appeared frivolous, without him she exercises her womanly powers with deadly awareness of her opponent's political capabilities. The death of Leicester was not Elizabeth's death; it did ripen her long demonstrated powers. In the same way, Cleopatra is ready for this final encounter, and this, her last performance, is incomparably her best. Octavius's overture of gentleness does not deceive her, nor his cunning and intricate shift from cause to grievance. He will excuse "the injuries" she did him, "though written in our flesh,"

> but if you seek
> To lay on me a cruelty by taking
> Antony's course, you shall bereave yourself
> Of my good purposes, and put your children
> To that destruction which I'll guard them from
> If thereon you rely.

Against such threats, she is ready to counter duplicity with duplicity, his offer of gentleness with hers of submission. The world is his, she assures him,

and we,
Your scutcheons and your signs of conquest, shall
Hang in what place you please.

[5.2.127–135]

The device works ("You shall advise me in all for Cleopatra"),
and she turns to her treasurer, Seleucus, to yield the spoils of
conquest.

But Seleucus betrays his trust and gives a wholly unexpected
and gratuitous advantage to Octavius. She has every right to fury,
chiefly because her trick has been exposed; but she keeps her
composure with admirable aplomb, appealing to his polished yet
despicable self on their only possible ground for agreement, the
contemptibility of untrustworthy servants. Octavius can afford to
be generous. After all, the empire of Egypt is his, a mere plate in
his pocket, and the trophy that he craves, Egypt's Queen, is at last
within his danger. Moreover, she has confessed freely to "the
frailties of our sex" and accepted his sovereignty. Now he can
return her possessions with a gesture. His only problem is to
prevent her from committing suicide; hence, his elaborate precau-
tion to take her alive—an Egyptian serpent to display in Rome as
the symbol of his conquest. His veiled threats to herself and to her
children are based on this unsatisfied political appetite, as she is
fully aware, and she parries his soporific, treacherous "Feed and
sleep" with equal cunning. Outwardly, she is the perfect figure of
submission to his grace. Her private face is one thing, her public
face as Queen of Egypt quite another; and we know that her
confessions are deceits as soon as Octavius has left the stage.

Whatever her plans after the miscalculation that instigated
Antony's suicide, the Seleucus episode is proof that she still has
them. Suicide has always been the alternative to the parade
through the streets of Rome; and certainly she would have used
the dagger if Proculeius had not prevented it. But just as certainly
she has immortal longings and prepares for immortality—not
death—in her own queenly fashion. Who shall say when she
finally lays the asp to her breast, whether in the labyrinth of her
various mind the saucy lictors, the scald rhymers, and the quick
comedians with their squeaking Cleopatra are not as great a

persuasion as the lover's pinch? She hears Antony call; but we may only conjecture to what degree the satisfactions of the asp lay in calling "great Caesar ass / Unpolicied!" At the last moment would she have taken the asp at all were it not for jealousy that Iras might get to the curled Antony first and spend the kiss which is her heaven to have? Of one thing there is no vestige of doubt: she has outplayed Octavius at his own deadly game.

Cleopatra's vision of heaven is very earthly indeed. She never forgets that she is a queen, and hence can drive a sharp bargain for her merchandise. As long as Antony lives, her art of love is a delicately poised alternation of depreciation and eulogy, so that Antony is made to feel alternately a hero and a fool. On occasions when matters of Rome whip him into the path of virtue, she cheapens him to his face as a Herculean Roman; when he is beyond hearing, she glorifies him as "the demi-Atlas of this earth, the arm and burgonet of men." The fact that his suicide makes no sudden end of the perilous game she plays with Octavius in not the slightest degree lowers her praise of her man of men. In death, he is apotheosized "Emperor Antony," whose "rear'd arm crested the world," in whose livery "walked crowns and crownets." Yet even as he achieves an emperor's status in her mind, by a strange and reverse transmutation which reveals Shakespeare's special mastery of his art, gold becomes homely metal, her deepest urge asserts itself, and Antony becomes what the other lover-emperors had not been—a husband; and then, by the same reverse process, cunning beyond compare, the asp becomes the maternal symbol, the baby at the breast.

The doubled irony of these successive transfigurations of Antony is Cleopatra's willingness to dismiss her part in his personal tragedy (he is never incriminative; she never shows guilt) and her manifest indifference to the larger tragedy of empire behind his dereliction as Triumvir. She can even persuade herself, "O, my oblivion is a very Antony, / And I am all forgotten!" and never remember that his oblivion is of her doing. Philo's invitation to his fellow soldier at the beginning of the play sets the common opinion:

> Take but good note, and you shall see in him
> The triple pillar of the world transform'd

Into a strumpet's fool. Behold and see.

[1.1.11–13]

We behold, and the sight confirms his words while the pillars shake. Octavius, the future emperor, sneers: "He hath given his empire up to a whore," and we cannot reject the accusation. For Cleopatra, love is a game, and politics is a game, and the two are a heavenly mingle. Even in her most romantic reverie, Antony could indeed drop realms and islands from his pocket and still suffer no loss in greatness; but we cannot forget that it was a dream that came to the price of the civilized world. Exasperated by Cleopatra's taunts, he very early falls into the sentimentality that anticipates the irony of the larger tragedy: "Let Rome in Tiber melt and the wide arch / Of the rang'd empire fall! Here is my space" (1.1.33–34). From a political point of view, nothing could be more absurd. Cleopatra at least is not the fool, nor is Rome, where the stories of his profligacy are common gossip. As the world knows, Antony, a hapless victim, succumbs to the serpent of Old Nile long before Cleopatra succumbs to the asp.

Obviously, there is much to blame in Antony, much to extenuate. He is morally lax; but he is also acutely aware of his laxity, and Cleopatra is not the only obstacle to his escape from the fetters of his dotage. His resolves to amend are neutralized quite as much by the sterile atmosphere of the Egyptian court. Chiefly contributory to this effect are the sardonic comments of Enobarbus. His development from a mere name in Plutarch to an instrument of satire serves not merely to demonstrate Antony's predicament but to comment on his decline from the stiff Roman virtues. A frequently cited case in point is Shakespeare's use of Plutarch's imaginative description of the meeting of Antony and Cleopatra on the River Cydnus. Shakespeare is following Plutarch closely, and hence we feel close enough to the creation of art to observe the hand of the artist as it molds the materials. There is no suggestion of satire in Plutarch's account; but in Shakespeare's, luxury becomes luxurious, and innocent wonder becomes sophistical mischievous sensuality (2.2.191–231).[73]

73. The style Shakespeare uses here is strongly reminiscent of Philip Sidney's

Enobarbus, fresh from the sights of Egypt, may well be excused for taking advantage of the credulity of his less privileged friends in Rome, just as Shakespeare may be excused for exercising the ancient literary privilege of borrowing, especially since he returns the property with such rich interest. And the debt is not merely to Plutarch. The lascivious artifice with which Shakespeare clothes Antony's Egyptian revels on the River Cydnus compels recollection of Spenser's Bower of Bliss where Nature and Art are indistinguishable. There idleness is personified in those who have spent "their looser daies in lewd delights," and Phaedria (Jollity) sports on the Idle Lake. It is a place where Acrasia (Lat. *impotentia*) is ruler of misrule, where her womanish tears are a "fine forgery" designed to affect the stubborn heart with "fraile infirmity," and where her lover has removed his warlike arms, "the idle instruments of sleeping praise."

This is the febrile distemper that infects Shakespeare's great ones: "my brave emperor" dancing the Egyptian Bacchanals; a eunuch and Cleopatra's maids managing the war for "Emperor Antony"—a point sharpened by Enobarbus's professional cynicism (3.7), which the casual remark of a soldier later turns back on the reformed poseur: "Your emperor / Continues still a Jove" (4.6.28–29), recalling with a smirk his master's present unmanliness. Such barbs merely penetrate the surface. The stakes, passed comically off, are nonetheless enormous when Antony and Octavius, peers in empire, meet to patch their differences in a diplomatic marriage, only to find themselves engaged to their mutual chagrin in a ridiculous game of chairs which the younger of the two abruptly terminates with a "Nay, then" as he seats himself first, victor in protocol as he will be later at Actium. But for sheer arrogance Octavius's first stab on meeting with Cleopatra tents to the quick: "Which," he asks in the presence of the imperial court, "is the Queen of Egypt?" In diplomatic parlance, this is the ultimate insolence in the man who has already won all the world. The wide arch of the ranged empire has fallen in

extravagant sensuality in the bathing of the princesses in the River Ladon. *Arcadia* (ed. Feuillerat), vol. 1, pp. 215–18.

punctilio. In a rare moment of reflection this sole sir of the world
wonders that the death of Antony should not have made a greater
crack. Like the death of Julius Caesar,

> The round world
> Should have shook lions into civil streets
> And citizens to their dens.
>
> [5.1.15–17]

But the news that Cleopatra has been captured, and alive,
quickly cuts off any further lament for "my competitor / In top of
all design, my mate in empire," and he takes up the practical
politics of cajolery and threat which is his natural habitat. To his
underlings, he has long been "universal landlord." Yet he has
failed to take Antony alive as he had ordered (4.6.2). To fail now
to capture his other quarry would be a tactical defeat; yet despite
his extraordinary pains, he fails in that too. In the end, his "glory"
will not be diminished. He will see to that (5.2.365). But in total
effect, his behavior is picayune, and debases the traditional
benign image of Octavius as a restorer of peace after civil war.
Only once does he refer to that glowing future:

> The time of universal peace is near.
> Prove this a prosp'rous day, the three-nook'd world
> Shall bear the olive freely.
>
> [4.6.5–7]

But imminent battle quickly sweeps him away. What must be
said is that *Antony and Cleopatra* represents an empire damaged not
merely by Antony's idleness but by Octavius's unscrupulous climb
to power—a power suggested in *Julius Caesar* but omnipresent in
its sequel.

If *Antony and Cleopatra* be viewed from this political base, the
issues that concern much of recent criticism of the play will fall
into their proper perspective. The play neither subscribes to nor
inveighs against immorality except as it affects the decline of
empire. It is not Antony's love but the political cost of his love
that frames and articulates the action. Octavius does not hunger
for Cleopatra but for sovereignty, and as everyone in Shake-

speare's audience knew, he gets his way. "The transcendental humanism" which G. Wilson Knight sees in Shakespeare's play completely ignores its political realities. To John Danby, the reality Shakespeare is writing about is "the vast containing opposites of Rome and Egypt, the World and the Flesh." But though Rome by contrast with Egypt is "the sphere of the political," and though in his mind Octavius represents it, Danby still denies him the lust for power. Traversi barely allows the political orientation of the play though he recognizes Octavius's "controlled, ungenerous dedication to the pursuit of power." [74] What must be remembered about its expansiveness, a quality which many critics comment on, is that while Shakespeare has moved successively in the earlier Roman plays from the destruction of commonwealth in *Julius Caesar* to the failure of representative government in *Coriolanus*, both plays clearly operate within the idea of a city state (πόλις) conceived as a morphological entity operating much as the human body does, bound by duties to the whole and subject to demands by its members. The political expansion represented by the idea of empire in *Antony and Cleopatra* refuses such limitations, together with the moral limitations they imply. In such a spacious atmosphere, kings and kingdoms lose their identity as organisms, and this is what Parliament viewed with concern in the union of England and Scotland. *Antony and Cleopatra* operates from the political base of Rome, but it is a base no longer strong enough to support the accretion of its own weight.

In common usage, both "commonwealth" and "empire" were extensible beyond the boundaries of the realm, though "commonwealth" within or without the nation involved ideal and ethical social relationships incapable of attainment. "The commonwealth of the realm" was a customary phrase, though Shakespeare made no use of it in either *Julius Caesar* or *Coriolanus*. "Empire," on the other hand, fell solely within the political sphere, unrestrained by

74. G. Wilson Knight, *The Imperial Theme* (1931), p. 199; John Danby, *Poets on Fortune's Hill* (1952), pp. 140–44; Derek A. Traversi, *An Approach to Shakespeare* (1938, reprint ed. 1956), pp. 240–41.

ethical content; and it easily associated with ideas of grandeur. The imperial crown was therefore a phrase to conjure with throughout Shakespeare's writing career. It is hard to be a king of infinite space, whereas the rise from "king and commander of our commonweal" to "the wide world's Emperor" is perceptible as early as *Titus Andronicus* (1.1.247–48). Furthermore, as Gonzalo in *The Tempest* had to be reminded, while the politics of common-wealth implied no sovereignty, the politics of empire by definition rested on it. Before *Antony and Cleopatra*, the railing of Apemantus and Timon against Athens bridges the verbal gap:

> *Apemantus.* The commonwealth of Athens is become a forest of beasts.
> *Timon.* Set them into confounding odds, that beasts
> May have the world in empire!
> [*Timon of Athens*, 4.3.351, 392–93]

If Athens had indeed become a forest of beasts, it was no longer a commonwealth. Scratch the veneer of *Antony and Cleopatra*, and the struggle for sovereignty is just as beastly. The union with Scotland posed a new departure in empire, testing Timon's sour rejection.

Again, the first statute in James's reign celebrating the reuniting of the two kingdoms of England and Scotland may have been in Shakespeare's mind in directing a retrospective glance to early British history when Britain was united with the Roman Empire in peace and concord. "We submit to Caesar, / And to the Roman Empire" (*Cymbeline*, 5.5.460–61). In the new dynasty, one might believe that England would again be an empire in a way that Henry VIII could not have anticipated. Koebner has alleged that "the territorial confines" of Britannia during Tudor and Stuart times were "not imposing enough to qualify as an 'empire.'" [75] But if the erstwhile James VI of Scotland soon after his accession to the throne of England could contemplate "our imperial monarchy of two great kingdoms," Shakespeare may well be allowed the even larger prospect in Antony's reference to the "empire of the sea."

75. *Empire* (1961), p. 61.

3

EQUITY

Mercy Seasons Justice

Any brushes that Shakespeare may have had with the law before William Wayte craved sureties of the peace against him for fear of death in November 1596, are purely apocryphal; and it is hardly likely that this case would have put him in mind of *The Merchant of Venice*. But then, it is hardly likely that we have recovered all the records, or for that matter, assuming that we had recovered them, that we could establish any more than we already know—that Shakespeare was familiar with legal procedure. Nor would such knowledge enable us to say with any greater certainty that Shakespeare had any more than the ordinary London citizen's awareness of the nature and degree of his own legal protection. There is no record, in fact, that Shakespeare ever threw himself on the mercy of the court, though the writ of attachment filed by Wayte is certain and adequate evidence that he understood the limits of mercy.

The sterilities of those who have sought in Shakespeare's knowledge of the law a reason for wresting his plays out of his hands are a monument to misplaced energy, remarkable chiefly because it is so frequently lawyers otherwise of impeccable judgment who are so ready in this case to suspend it.[1] What makes Shakespeare's familiarity with the law significant is that in *The Merchant of Venice* and later in *Measure for Measure* he dramatizes what was unquestionably the most important legal

1. One notable exception is Mark E. Andrews, *Law vs. Equity in The Merchant of Venice: A Legalization of Act IV, Scene I*, with Foreword, Judicial Precedents, and Notes, ed. J. K. Emery (1965). The publication date is misleading since Andrews' work was done 30 years earlier.

development of the sixteenth century, and probably to his audience the most familiar: the adjustment of the common law to the practice of equity in the Court of Chancery.[2] Shakespeare uses the term only four times in the plays, and only once in association with the king's conscience (2 *Hen. VI*, 3.1.141). The idea of equity, however, is at the heart of both *The Merchant of Venice* and *Measure for Measure*, and a review of the state of Tudor thinking on the subject is a necessary approach to Shakespeare's use of it.

It is not surprising that acceptance of the competence of equity in a native legal system should have been achieved slowly. Encroachments of Chancery on the common law had been occurring throughout the fifteenth century, and a principle of equity to temper the rigor of the common law had actually been in practice long before Cardinal Wolsey set up a court of conscience for the trying of "poor men's causes." Still, the common law continued as common practice, and what Vinogradoff calls "the sixteenth-century crisis"[3] was only formally resolved when with James's support Sir Thomas Egerton as Lord Chancellor (1603–1617) established a code of equity free of the common law and consequently juristically capable of challenging its decisions.[4]

The strength of equity as a legal concept derives from the fact

2. S. E. Prall gives a brief history of the subject in "The Development of Equity in Tudor England," *AJLH* 8 (1964) : 1–19; D. E. C. Yale's edition of Edward Hake's *Epieikeia, A Dialogue on Equity in Three Parts* (1953, late Elizabethan but not previously published) includes a valuable preface by S. E. Thorne; G. R. Elton, *The Tudor Constitution* (1960), pp. 150–51, who quotes the pertinent passage from Sir Thomas Smith, *De Republica Anglorum*, pp. 154–55.

3. Paul Vinogradoff, "Reason and Conscience in Sixteenth-century Jurisprudence," *Law Quarterly Review* 24 (1908) : 377, later reprinted in *Collected Papers*, 2 vols. (1928), 2 : 190.

4. Halsbury's *Laws of England*, second edition (1907–17), 13 : 5, cites Egerton's judgment in the Earl of Oxford's case, 1615. According to Holdsworth, Francis Bacon consolidated the victory. James claimed absolute power and the privilege of "judge of all judges." W. S. Holdsworth, *A History of English Law*, 13 vols. (1922–52), 1 : 463–69, 5 : 238; Theodore F. T. Plucknett, *A Concise History of the Common Law* (1956), pp. 194–95; H. D. Hazeltine, "Early History of English Equity," *Essays in Legal History*, ed. Paul Vinogradoff (1914), p. 285.

that it is equally congenial in the Aristotelian context of
ἐπιείκεια, that sweet reasonableness which observes the spirit
rather than the letter of the law, and in the Christian context of
doing unto others what you would have them do unto you. Legal
writers contemporary with Shakespeare cited the *summum ius* of
Aristotle as "exact or precise law" with "no allay in it to qualifie
the harshenes and seuerity of it, . . . unpleasant and sower in tast,
and repugnant to equitie." It was *ius subtile*, "when men stande
more upon the letter of the Law, then upon the meaning of the
wrighter, or maker of the Law." [5] But in John Gerson's populari-
zation of Aristotle, due weight had already been given to *aequitas:*
"Aequitas quam nominat philosophus epiekeiam praeponderat
iuris rigori." [6] And it was mainly through Gerson that ἐπιείκεια
implemented and amplified by conscience, became the law within
one's heart, applicable wherever in human conduct man-made
laws do not extend or are inadequate.[7]

Evidence for relief from the harshness of the common law can
be found inter alia in the Year Books of the fifteenth century, but
it is chiefly through Christopher St. Germain's *A Dialogue betwixt a
doctor of divinity and a student in the laws of England*, commonly called
Doctor and Student, that the concept of equity became known to
Englishmen. Its extraordinary popularity is attested by the
number of times it was reissued in the sixteenth century: twice in
Latin and no less than twenty times in English. It was without
doubt the most important legal commentary during the Tudor
period. Vinogradoff wrote of the two dialogues that compose the
work: "One can hardly do better in order to realize the conflict of
legal ideas in the reigns of the early Tudors than to study these
tracts with some attention." It is not too much to say that the
principle of equity in the common law won acceptance largely
through the fact that St. Germain's unpretentious little book was

5. William West, *Symboleography Pars Secunda* (1594), sig. A–Aiᵛ.

6. *Regulae morales*, as cited by Vinogradoff, "Reason and Conscience," p. 374.

7. W. J. Jones (*The Elizabethan Court of Chancery*, 1967) finds the word *conscience*
more appropriate than *equity* in legal thinking during the sixteenth century when
equity was still "a system of remedies," not a formalized theory. See especially pp.
418–20.

in every man's hand. The immediate source of *Doctor and Student* was John Gerson's *Regulae morales*. Thus, St. Germain's definition of equity partakes of both Christian and classical traditions: "a right wiseness of the deed, the which also is tempered with the sweetness of mercy . . . ordained to temper and mitigate the law." [8]

This refrain echoes and reechoes through the rest of the century. John Rastell cites Aristotle in calling equity "the correction of a law generally made, in that part wherein it faileth." [9] William Fulbecke advised students at the Inns of Court: "Justice is rightly administered . . . when hatred is away and conscience is present, when rigor is tempered with mercy." *Aequum & bonum* in his classification of laws is "that which doth mildly interprete, amend, and mollifie the hard and rigorous speaches and ansures of the other Laws." [10] Equity was mainly on Spenser's mind in book 5 of *The Faerie Queene* (1596), which while it defends the rigorous justice of Lord Grey in Ireland, reanimates the classical legend of Astraea, "most sacred vertue she of all the rest," as instructor of Artegall, the thinly disguised portrait of Elizabeth's Lord Deputy:

> There she him taught to weigh both right and wrong
> In Equall ballance with due recompence,
> And equitie to measure out along,
> According to the line of conscience,
> When so it needs with rigour to dispence.
>
> [*The Faerie Queene*, 5.1.7]

Astraea holds the balance (Libra) in her hand, but Spenser makes sure that it will not be understood as popular equality (5.2.30). True equity is represented by Isis, under whose feet the crocodile

---

8. Christopher St. Germain, *A Dialogue betwixt a doctor of divinity and a student in the laws of England* (1531), ch. 1, sec. 16; hereinafter cited as *Doctor and Student*.

9. *An exposition of certaine difficult and obscure words and termes of the laws of this Realme* (1579), sig. K7.

10. *A direction or preparative to the study of the law*, sig. B1ᵛ, K2. Not printed until 1620, but the introductory epistle to law students is dated from Gray's Inn, September 9, 1599.

Osyris sleeps "To shew that clemence oft in things amis, / Re-
straines those sterne behests, and cruell doomes of his" (5.7.22). As
Artegall later discovers, Prince Arthur himself serves a maiden
queen, Mercilla, "For her great bounty knowen ouer all, / And
soueraine grace, with which her royall crowne / She doth support" (5.8.17). Whether sixteenth-century commentators base
their position on classic or Christian ethics, whether on the
written law or the law within one's heart, they uniformly agree on
the necessity for tempering the rigor of the common law.

Within this muddy vesture of decay, however, conscience can
play strange tricks. Thomas More was aware of them when, as
William Roper reports it, certain judges accused him of granting
too many injunctions. More retorted tartly that such orders would
cease to be issued, "if the Justices of every Court, unto whome the
reformation of rigour of the Law, by reason of there office, most
specially appertained, would, upon reasonable considerations, by
there owne discretions (as they were, as he thought, in conscience
bound) mittigate and reforme the rigor of the Law themselves.[11]
When Edward Hake follows Philip Melanchthon's description of
equity as a mitigating element residing in every interpretation of
laws, so that "wher need is, they may be bowed and turned to the
gentler sentence," he is defining equity in the language of the
day.[12] As Melanchthon put it, the law is a mind without
covetousness.[13] But then Hake like More lays out the dangers of
conscience as arbiter: "If the lawe . . . be a good lawe and well
grounded, then the Equity that must be used to the correction of
the generalitye thereof cannot be said to be the Equitye of the
judge, but of the lawe, for otherwise the lawe muste be a lawe
without Equitye." There speaks the voice of the common law
against the law of Chancery. To the common lawyers attempting

11. *The Life of Sir Thomas More*, printed in J. Rawson Lumby's edition of More's
Utopia (1922), pp. xxvi–xxvii.

12. *Epieikeia* (ed. Yale), p. 11.

13. *A ciuile nosgay, wherein is contayned not onelye the office and dewty of all magestrates
and Judges but also of all subiectes* with a preface concernynge the lyberty of Justice in
this our tyme newly collected and gathered out of latyn and so translated in to the
Inglyshe tonge, by J. G. [n.d.], sig. Ci–Ci^v, Cvii.

to reduce St. Germain's philosophic strictures to the more pragmatic considerations of case law, conscience as a basis for litigation was a queasy thing: "Some men think that if they tread upon two straws that lie across they offend in conscience, and some man thinketh that if he lack money, and another hath too much, that he may take part of his with conscience; and so divers men, divers conscience." [14]

In 1597, possibly the same year in which Shakespeare wrote *The Merchant of Venice*, Richard Hooker had wrestled with the same problem of the two straws in ecclesiastical law and arrived at the same conclusion: Private judgment is no safe guide. (*LEP*, v.ix.4–x.1). "It is natural unto all men to wish their own extraordinary benefit, when they think they have reasonable inducements so to do; and no man can be presumed a competent judge what equity doth require in his own case." Hence, it is necessary "that he which useth the benefit of any special benignity above the common course of others must needs administer that which in every such particular shall appear agreeable with equity," and further, that "for common utility's sake, certain profitable ordinances sometime be released, rather than all men always strictly bound to the general rigour thereof." If therefore, "against the discretion of the Church in mitigating sometimes with favourable equity that rigour which otherwise the literal generality of ecclesiastical laws hath judged to be convenient and meet," men would be free to reject its laws, "what other effect could hereupon ensue, but the utter confusion of his Church under pretense of being taught, led, and guided by his Spirit?"

Whether in ecclesiastical or secular context, private judgment was no practical substitute for existing law. The familiar words of John Selden in the next century aptly fix the shortcomings inherent in the administration of a law of conscience: "Equity is a roguish thing. For law we have a measure . . . equity is according to the conscience of him that is Chancellor, and as that is larger and narrower, so is equity. 'Tis all one as if they should make the

14. *A Replication of a Serjaunte at the Lawes of England*, in Hargrave's *Collection of Tracts relative to the law of England* (1787), p. 326.

standard for the measure a Chancellor's foot." [15] Nevertheless
Selden nor anyone else doubted its indispensability.

William Lambard well represents the amiable rivalry of the
two traditions when Shakespeare wrote *The Merchant of Venice*. He
finds that as far back as pre-Conquest law, the king judged "not
only according to mere right and law, but also after equity and
good conscience." He does not question the sovereign power by
which the king may both supply the want and correct the rigor of
positive law. But it should be used only rarely, "lest, as Aristotle
saith, a beast should bear the rule," and in any case he should not
overthrow the courts of common law: "He will rather suffer the
Common Law to have her just honour, and not to be interrupted
in her right course; and will yet withall provide that the gate of
Mercy may be opened to all Calamity of Suite: to the end, (where
neede shall be) the rigour of Right may be amended by the
Iudgement of Equity." In this respect, he praises Elizabeth for
allowing access to the courts of "mere law," and at the same time
placing "in that Pretoricall Roome, or Chancery, men no less
learned in the Common Lawes of this Realme, then accomplished
with the skill of this Moderation of Equity." [16]

Lambard's words are more than a graceful compliment to a
queen who was very much aware of the limits of the royal
prerogative. They bear out at the close of her reign the report of
the Spanish ambassador to his far from disinterested employer on
the occasion of her coronation, that in her entire demeanor she
expressed "mildness with majesty." She herself had become the
image of the conscience that now resided in the common law and
which would persist after her death as her most precious bequest,
a substantial bulwark against the stresses that would follow.
Equity had become, in the words of William Perkins the year
after James's accession, "the marrow and strength of a common

15. Holdsworth, *English Law*, 1 : 467–68; S. E. Thorne's preface to Hake's
Epieikeia (ed. Yale), p. 8.

16. *Archion, or, A Commentary upon the High Courts of Justice in England* (1635), sig.
C2–C2ᵛ; F6ᵛ–G2. Completed, but not published, in 1591, according to Conyers
Read, *Bibliography of British History* (1959), p. 133.

weale." [17] "Without the practise of it, no house, familie, society, citie, commonwelth, kingdome, or Church can stand or continue." Against the indiscriminate exercise of it, Perkins like Lambard recommends moderation. Some justices, "as by a certain foolish kind of pittie, are so carried away, that would have nothing but *mercy, mercy.*" Though "there are few that offend in this kind," he allows, "this is the way to abolish lawes." On the other hand, there are others "as have nothing in their mouthes, but *the lawe, the lawe:* and *Iustice, Iustice:* in the meane time forgetting, that Iustice alwaies shakes hands with her sister mercie, and that all lawes allowe a mittigation" (sig. Aviii–Aviii").

Once, when Perkins cites cases, one can almost imagine that he is recalling *The Merchant of Venice* rather than court records: A man bound to pay fifty pounds in a day, breaks his day, not by negligence, but by some necessity; "now to take the forfeiture," in his opinion, "is in this case, extremitie: though the law doth yield it." But the court records confirm it as a case falling specifically within the jurisdiction of Chancery.[18] Is it familiarity with Portia's bland concession of the forfeiture—"The court awards it, and the law doth give it . . . The law allows it, and the court awards it" just before her cautionary "Tarry a little"—that makes Perkins's comment so like Shylock vs. Antonio? Whether or no Shakespeare in creating *The Merchant of Venice* was drawing from contemporary case histories of debt forfeiture is less important than that the play is steeped in the very language of equity. Mercy does finally season justice, though in the course of it, appeals to "The Law! The Law!" become as much Portia's merry sport as that of the relentless Jew.

17. 'Επιείκεια, *or a treatise of Christian Equitie and moderation* (1604), sig. A1ᵛ.

18. Cecil Monroe, *Acta cancellaria* (1847), pp. 487–88: *Franclyn* vs. *Watkins* (1579). Holdsworth, *English Law*, 5 : 330, quotes Cary's *Reports*, pp. 1–2: "If a man be bound in a penalty to pay money at a day and place, by obligation, and intending to pay the same, is robbed by the way; or hath intreated by word some other respite at the hands of the obligee, or cometh short of the place by any misfortune; and so failing of the payment, doth nevertheless provide and tender the money in short time after; in these, and many such like cases, the Chancery will compel the obligee to take his principal, with some reasonable consideration of his damages."

The Tricker Tricked

Portia's speech is the ethical center of the play. But as Shakespeare's title indicates, it is Antonio, not Portia, who stands at its structural center. Shylock scoffs at his "low simplicity," his "humility," and if Shakespeare is stressing Antonio's unaccountable melancholy in the opening lines of the play, it is an anticipation of his Christian Stoicism markedly apparent throughout the action. Contrasted with Shylock's stage flamboyance, Antonio's sober deportment and quiet resignation become more and more the major dramatic statement as the action proceeds. If he has spit upon Shylock and called him dog, such conduct is wholly conformable to the general distaste for the tribe of usurers, not for the man; and the greater fault is in Shylock's vindictiveness, not his usury. But credibility is strained when in the face of Shylock's obvious use of the letter of the law for a cruelty, Antonio makes not the slightest effort to plead his own case. On the contrary, he enters the court room prepared to suffer the Jew's "rigorous course," opposing fury with patience, and "armed / To suffer with a quietness of spirit." He views his predicament with calm dispassion; he is a willing sacrifice, a tainted wether of the flock, meetest for death; his only requirement an epitaph which he hopes the strangely inert Bassanio will compose. His valedictory is a model of selfless martyrdom, and he urges the court to proceed with judgment. With Shylock's knife at his breast, he is ready to accept death stoically as no more than a release from poverty and old age, eager to pay the debt instantly with all his heart. When Portia springs the trap which reverses the situation, and Shylock is at Antonio's mercy, he merely eases the conditions of the Duke's pardon. And in the comic antistrophe at the end of the action, when Portia has laid hard conditions on Bassanio, and Antonio in the same spirit once more undertakes surety for his friend's good conduct, the behavior of both aggressor and victim strain the bounds of belief.

It would be a mistake to take sympathetically this confrontation of arrogance and humility. Melodrama depends primarily on suspense; it has very little need for motivation. Sharp contrasts, bold strokes from a rich palette accomplish equally important purposes. Antonio's extraordinary forbearance played against the splendor of Shylock's heartlessness is wholly consistent with, and in fact essential to, the artistic intent. In the playhouse, we do not ask why a merchant who has been so obviously astute in trade should be so lacking in shrewdness as to expose his fortune to the hazards of the casket choice; or why, knowing Shylock's reputation for sharp practice, he would not only lay himself open to it but call it kindness. Sufferance may be the badge of Shylock's tribe, but Antonio has plainly caught more than a touch of it. He doesn't understand his sadness at the opening of the action, and at the end of the play we have no need to recall it.

What Shakespeare's audience would understand in Antonio's conduct is the love principium: "Charity suffereth long, and is kind; charity envieth not; charity vaunteth not itself, is not puffed up, / Doth not behave itself unseemly, seeketh not her own, is not easily provoked, thinketh no evil; / Rejoiceth not in iniquity, but rejoiceth in the truth; / Beareth all things, believeth all things, hopeth all things, endureth all things" (1 Cor. 13 : 4–7). It is this quality in Antonio that excites Shylock's irascible jibe: "If a Jew wrong a Christian, what is his humility?" His question is pointedly satiric to Londoners long accustomed to the literalism of Puritan adherence to the Mosaic code. For the Jew represents in an exaggerated form the revenge which characterized the Old Law, which the New Law of Christ, the law of mercy, should long have superseded (Matt. 5 : 38–42). Shylock is far from making a humanitarian plea at this point; rather, he is justifying his own insentient conduct "by Christian example," and it is his intent to "better the instruction." Shylock is not, like Jonson's Ananias, primarily a caricature of Puritan strictness. He is no more a Puritan than Malvolio, though a great effort has been made to make him one. He is closer to a morality figure, one of Spenser's deadly sins brought to life on the stage, a symbol of revenge. He exists mainly to set in the sharpest possible perspective Antonio's comely role of Christian humility, the charity that suffers long and is yet kind, the law within one's heart, the source and substance of Christian equity.

Now it is perfectly apparent that in the world of Shylock, a world of sharp business practice protected by law, the discrepancy between Christian ethics and practice is laid bare. He recalls with evident relish the Biblical account of Jacob's smart deal to get the better share of his father-in-law's flocks; but again the crux of his defense is that he is merely following Christian example. Shakespeare's audience, searching their conscience, would have turned from the dubious business ethics of Jacob to Christ's injunction in the Sermon on the Mount where Christian conduct is judged in terms of the Rialto: "And if ye lend to them of whom ye hope to receive, what thank have ye? for sinners also lend to sinners, to receive as much again. / But love ye your enemies, and do good, and lend, hoping for nothing again; and your reward shall be great" (Luke 6 : 34–35).

This amalgam of Christian self-effacement and worldly success is fundamental in determining the impact of Antonio's conduct; it becomes understandable when his confrontation with Shylock is placed in its legal context. Shakespeare quite pointedly stresses the invulnerability of Shylock's legal stance. In spite of the fact that the money lender is an alien, he presses his case wholly within the laws of Venice, as he insists again and again in the trial; and the court, in the person of Portia, sustains his legal rights. In fact, in common law, his foreign status is substantively to his advantage, as Antonio is very well aware. Long familiar with the Jew's hate, Antonio has hitherto delivered other of his victims from forfeiture; yet he is equally aware that Shylock is now making a stand on law which the Duke understandably would not contravene:

> For the commodity that strangers have
> With us in Venice, if it be denied,
> Will much impeach the justice of the state,
> Since that the trade and profit of the city
> Consisteth of all nations.

[3.3.27–31]

Shakespeare here guides the action in close conformity to contemporary legal opinion. Defenders of the common law stated

as one of its advantages that it did not interfere with the
commodities or liberties of other trading nations.[19] What more
illustrious example of cosmopolitanism than Venice? Shylock
knows as well as the Duke that he is legally secure, and he
obviously intends to take full advantage of his protection as a
stranger.

But his greatest advantage lies in the absence of a court of
equity. It is apparent from the beginning of the trial, that for all
Portia's eloquence, her plea for mercy is not sustained in the legal
code of Venice, and that if he persists in demanding the law, the
state is helpless to intervene. In the eyes of the audience, since she
has no case, she can only enter a personal plea for mercy. She
admits—and Antonio does not protest—that despite the strange
nature of the suit, "Venetian law cannot impugn you," and "this
strict court of Venice / Must needs give sentence 'gainst the
merchant here." Bassanio beseeches the judge to "wrest once the
law to your authority. / To do a great right, do a little wrong."
But Portia, like Shylock, stands on law:

> There is no power in Venice
> Can alter a decree established.
> 'T will be recorded for a precedent;
> And many an error by the same example
> Will rush into the state. It cannot be.
>
> [4.1.218–22]

Any hopes of the audience must therefore rest solely on Portia's
veiled hint that she has found a remedy of some sort before she
enters the court room, though her "whole device" she intends to
keep secret from Nerissa and—provocatively, of course—from an
audience of small learning in Venetian law, of less in Roman civil
law on which the oft told tale of the pound of flesh is based. That
she isn't revealing her knowingness is the strongest kind of
suggestion that the action will come short of tragedy; there is
more if insubstantial evidence in the behind-the-hand jocularities

19. William Fulbecke, *A parallele or conference of the Civil Law, the Canon Law, and
the Common Law of this Realme of England* (1601), sig. xxi.

which she trades with Nerissa, who is obviously by now party to the plan from which the audience continues to be excluded. We will hardly be deluded into taking too seriously Bassanio's profession of esteem for Antonio beyond his life, his wife, and all the world, when she retorts, "Your wife would give you little thanks for that / If she were by to hear you make the offer." In brief, Antonio will somehow be relieved from the rigor of the law, and the audience relieved of anxiety for Antonio's fate. There will be no such shocking hoax as the comic byplay in Kyd's *Spanish Tragedy* when the boy holds up a box supposedly containing Pedringano's pardon to encourage him in insolencies to the judge that make his hanging sheer macabre. In Kyd's device, grim farce is close to the surface, since the audience knows that the box is empty. In Shakespeare's melodrama, the tricker will be tricked even if we don't know how. Long before Antonio's trial opens, we have had adequate assurance that he will not be a sacrifice to the law's severity.

So secured against misapprehension, the audience is free to enjoy Portia's straight-faced control of the action. She exudes self-confidence as she announces with gravity that "the intent and purpose of the law / Hath full relation to the penalty," and with every appearance of innocence inquires if Shylock has remembered a balance "to weigh the flesh" and a surgeon to prevent Antonio's bleeding to death. Since the victim is standing by, such preoccupation with last moment details would seem to be the height of inconsideration; even worse, she remains silent while Antonio, in an affecting valediction forbidding mourning, requests Bassanio to "bid her be judge / Whether Bassanio had not once a love."

Had Shakespeare any intention at all to depict normal human motivation, Antonio would be expected to show chagrin or outrage at such needless offer of his life, and Portia some temptation to reveal her identity. But of course in Shakespeare's comic design, neither Portia nor Antonio are under any such compulsions. Shakespeare's interest is centered not at all on feelings but very much on arranging the principals in the action in postures that will best display the legal dilemma created by strict adherence to the law. And of course it is important to observe that in terms of contemporary legal practice, Portia's conduct throughout the trial is meticulously correct toward both Shylock and Antonio. As a judge, she exercises the rigor that the law demands—"the liberty of justice," as Melanchthon puts it in *A ciuile nosgay.* "Equite is to be added to publike iustice" only after positive law fails (sig. Civ^v), and Portia follows the same strategy. After three hundred lines of suspense laced with light badinage during which the rigor of the law is pursued to its extremity of harshness, her "Tarry a little" signals the major legal reversal of the play. Only then it appears that a law nullifies a law,[20] rigor in the prosecution has been defeated by its own weapon, and Portia's "whole device," so long postponed, has effectively turned the tables on Shylock's vindictive abuse of his legal rights. Once having gained the advantage, Portia's insistence on the letter of the law is as relentless as Shylock's. "Is that the law?" Shylock asks incredulously, and Portia's response is inflexible, "without mitigation of any circumstances":

> For, as thou urgest justice, be assur'd
> Thou shalt have justice more than thou desir'st.[21]
>
> [4.1.315–16]

When Shylock in full retreat attempts to settle for Bassanio's previous offer of thrice the sum, Portia forbids it. The Jew shall have all justice, nothing less than the penalty. Refusing the forfeiture, Shylock is still held by the laws of Venice against aliens who directly or indirectly seek the life of any citizen. He is thus reduced, by the sole agency of positive laws operating against each other, to throw himself on the mercy of the court.

The battle of the statute books has thus resulted in a victory of justice; but the fact remains that the laws by themselves have proved inadequate. The lack of a law of equity would have

20. Andrews, *Law vs. Equity*, p. xii, distinguishes *judgment* in common law and *decree* in Chancery. But Portia resorts wholly to common law to defeat Shylock.

21. Ibid., pp. xiv, 346, identifies Portia's move in common law practice as a "cross action."

proved a tragedy were it not for Portia's device, but it is no more than a device, serving at best as a temporary stay to vengeance. Conscience must now effect a resolution. Since Shylock has come within danger of the law, and the rigor of the law itself thus prevented from doing an injury, it is for the Duke to substitute for the law's inadequacy "the gentler sentence." Vengeance must give way to mercy, the tangible law to an intangible spirit above the law conformable to Christian conduct—as the Duke reminds Shylock, "that / Thou shalt see the differences of our spirit." Simply spoken, he enacts that spirit by substituting the New Law of mercy and forgiveness for the Old Law of revenge; or, to put it in legal terms, the Duke's conscience, as equity, intervenes to temper and mitigate the rigor of the law. Even to Shylock, "uncapable of pity, void and empty / From any dram of mercy," he renders the deeds of mercy; and one experiences a feeling of quiet justice in recollecting Antonio's "Content, in faith. I'll seal to such a bond, / And say there is much kindness in the Jew" (1.3.153–54). Significantly during the mitigation of Shylock's sentence, both parties use the same phrase, "I am content," in submitting to the judgment of the Duke. The case rests on common law even as common law is made mild by equity. Shakespeare makes use of the conventional phrases of business contracts, but they convey also a sense of that larger accommodation for man's frailty which in Christian ethics constitutes the divine comedy.

Season Season'd

The socially-minded eighteenth- and nineteenth-century theatre made of Shylock a tragic figure, and the image has persisted. Denied the prop that sustains his house and the means by which he lives, he is content with the judgment perforce; and on this note of tragic despair, he leaves the stage, a broken victim of Christian vindictiveness and anti-Semitism. To maintain such a view is to ignore not only the equitable base on which judgment of Shylock rests, but the comic structure which supports it.

An early hint of Shakespeare's method is perceivable in Launcelot Gobbo's struggle with his conscience on the occasion of his running away from the Jew, his master. No conscience ever worked harder or suffered more ignominious defeat. Bassanio's rare new liveries may have had something to do with his decision, and if so, the order to give his new servant a livery "more guarded than his fellows" inadvertently worked in the devil's interest. Launcelot's conscience, admittedly "hard," is made of more penetrable stuff than the Duke's. The part is extrinsic to the play's structure, perhaps invented for William Kempe to do with as he liked. But it is not irrelevant. The fact that conscience may speak and fail, as it does with Launcelot, lends perspective to that crucial moment when in the person of the Duke, the statutes being silent, it speaks with the authority of law.

In the ring plot, on the other hand, conscience does not fail. As it exists in Shakespeare's adaptation from Fiorentino's *Il Pecorone*, it becomes a highly sophisticated sprightly parallel to the main action, closely connected with the trial scene to which it supplies witty confirmation. The atmosphere of comedy has been formally asserted by the banishment of Shylock from the action after his conviction. His hatred of the wry-necked fife would indeed make him bad company at Belmont where song is the food for love and even the music of the spheres is audible. In such a night, while the escapers, Lorenzo and Jessica, are celebrating the most famous escapades of history—Cressida and Thisbe and Dido and Medea —the unheeding heavens proclaim the glory of God, and the firmament showeth his handiwork. They are witness to that law whose seat is the bosom of God, whose voice is the harmony of the world.

> All things in heaven and earth do her homage, the very least as feeling her care, and the greatest as not exempted from her power: both Angels and men and creatures of what condition soever, though each in different sort and manner, yet all with uniform consent, admiring her as the mother of their peace and joy. [*LEP*, i. xvi. 8]

The voice is the voice of Hooker and Lorenzo's echoes it:

> There's not the smallest orb which thou behold'st
> But in his motion like an angel sings,

> Still quiring to the young-ey'd cherubins;
> Such harmony is in immortal souls;
> But whilst this muddy vesture of decay
> Doth grossly close it in, we cannot hear it.
>
> [5.1.60–65] [22]

This harmony is presently interrupted, however, by the return of Portia who has purportedly been straying about by holy crosses, kneeling and praying for happy wedlock hours; and now with a gleam in her eye and a careful injunction to the household to keep silent about the Venetian affair, she is ready for tricks. As for Bassanio, like many another young and innocent husband, he helps, from the moment of his first appearance, to build his own trap.

Shakespeare's comic strategy in the confrontation to follow is to replay the trial scene with Portia in the role of Shylock, aided by the language of bond forfeiture and forgiveness. In the process, the atmosphere of melodrama gives way to the kind of merry sport which in Shylock is a disguise for vengeance, in Portia for mercy. But first, she must exult over her unhappy victim with the same satisfaction that Shylock does over Antonio. As with another no less triumphant lady, disdain and scorn ride sparkling in her eyes, misprizing what they look on. In the newly wed heiress of Belmont, Shakespeare uncovers—and not for the first time—the rich vein of comedy derivative from feminine domination over the helpless male. Katherine the shrew finds her match; but shall not the same be said for Beatrice and the terrifyingly ebullient Rosalind? And by comparison what falsetto abjects do Bassanio—and Benedick—and Orlando prove themselves to be!

In *The Merchant of Venice*, it is only after the melodramatic tricking of the moneylender and the release of the merchant from the jeopardy of the law that the play dissolves into comedy. Shakespeare here reaches a high level of design, executed with extraordinary ingenuity and with exquisite comic reassertion of the theme already established in the main plot. Actually, not one

22. Cf. *LEP*, I. ii. 4–5.

but three bonds are forfeited and in due course forgiven, the minor action characteristically echoing on a comic level the action of the main plot. Just as Shylock "in a merry sport" held Antonio to the letter of his bond, so Portia will hold Bassanio to his, and Nerissa will hold Gratiano to his. Revenge will be exacted with gusto; nor will there be any hope for mercy on the part of the defendants. Shylock was willing to bring Antonio to the point of the knife; now Portia will indulge a like penchant for civilized torture to the point of comic desperation. With the vengeance of a Shylock, she will dangle the hapless Bassanio until she has exhausted the comedy of his inability to give a credible explanation for giving away the token of his love. Likewise, and on a slightly lower level, Nerissa will face Gratiano with the same charge of disregard for the marriage bond and echo her mistress's artifice.

The verbal pattern of legalisms follows the structural parallel. Bassanio introduces Antonio to Portia as the man "to whom I am so infinitely bound." Whereat Portia, in apparent innocence responds, "You should in all sense be much bound to him, / For, as I hear, he was much bound for you." Perfect decorum indeed! But this harmony of souls is interrupted immediately by Nerissa's forthright accusation that her husband has broken oath, apparently over a paltry ring "whose posy was / For all the world like cutler's poetry / Upon a knife, 'Love me, and leave me not.' " He had sworn to wear it till death, but confesses now to have given it away to "a little scrubbed boy, / No higher than thyself, the judge's clerk." With her own ring—never to be plucked from his finger for the wealth that the world masters—safely stowed on her person, Portia now summons her most imperious manner to make an example for Gratiano and Nerissa in her own husband with the calamitous results which she has anticipated. Bassanio has given his ring away too—"not that, I hope, which you receiv'd of me." Alas, Bassanio is forced to show the ringless proof of his perfidy. The broken bonds now plainly confessed, Portia pursues her advantage with the ruthlessness of a Shylock, despite Bassanio's humiliating efforts at escaping the rigor of the sentence. As Portia countered law with law in the main action, so she now counters broken bond with broken bond. Henceforth, she will become as "liberal" as Bassanio, deny "the worthy doctor" from Padua nothing; and Nerissa promises the same liberality for the doctor's clerk. The case is at stand unless mercy can season justice. Once again, Antonio intercedes in his friend's behalf, and amidst prostrate pleas for mitigation of Portia's cruelty, he offers himself as a sacrifice in words that explicitly bind his first loan to his second:

> I once did lend my body for his wealth,
> Which, but for him that had your husband's ring
> Had quite miscarried. I dare be bound again,
> My soul upon the forfeit, that your lord
> Will never more break faith advisedly.

[5.1.249–53]

Only then is mercy seasoned with justice, mildness with majesty, as Portia withdraws the knife from Bassanio's throat and produces the ring which obviates the forfeiture for Antonio and extricates Bassanio from further discomfiture. The spectator to this restoration of harmony may well ask as the play ends whether Shylock or Portia exercises the greater persistence in revenge, or whether baiting fish or baiting husbands is the merrier sport.

Whatever incidental effect Shakespeare may have gained by the comic parallel in obliterating the potentially serious overtones of the main action—and I think that is considerable—its main result is to display to advantage the theme of the play. In Fiorentino, Shakespeare found the bond plot and the ring plot already associated in the same tale; but the theme of equity is Shakespeare's own. His adroitness in deploying both plots to dramatize the paramount legal question of the day exhibits a new found skill which he continues to use to advantage, but never more effectively than when some years later he returned to the same theme and the same cumulative effect in *Measure for Measure*.

Equity Reviewed

In *Measure for Measure* mercy reseasons justice with profoundly different result. The years between represent the period of

Shakespeare's greatest dramatic activity, and his maturity appears in every aspect of the play's construction and style. In both plays, the rigor of the law is employed to exact extreme cruelty; in both, the means of alleviation are at hand but withheld; in both, the remedy of mercy is eventually applied to mitigate rigor in the law; and in both, forgiveness heals the wound of injustice. Even the figure of lending is in Shakespeare's mind as he writes the Duke's extravagant praise of his newly appointed deputy in the opening lines of the play:

> Nature never lends
> The smallest scruple of her excellence
> But, like a thrifty goddess, she determines
> Herself the glory of a creditor,
> Both thanks and use.

[1.1.36–40]

But while the pattern is the same, a graver tone precludes the easy, lighthearted assurance of the earlier play. In the first half of *Measure for Measure*, justice appears to be irreparably overthrown by gross misuse of authority, and though in the second half the escape from tragedy is foreseen, it is achieved at greater cost. From the beginning of the action, situations and characters impress us as tragic; they cannot be passed off easily as merely melodrama, in spite of the fact that there is much that is melodramatic in the action. Indeed, the human predicament is so overpowering that caricature, a major device in *The Merchant of Venice*, is no longer tolerable. Most of all, one is increasingly persuaded that the atmosphere of the play is redolent of allegory, as if, having deliberately exploited the tragic situation beyond the point of human resolution, Shakespeare had said, "There is yet something."

This last quality troubled criticism long before W. W. Lawrence called the play a problem comedy. But the problem has always been with the critics. Baffled by its representation of earthly justice, they resort—in my opinion rightly—to more heavenly solutions, though even among those who take the play as a religious allegory—and may I say that I am not one of them—there is inevitably a wide difference of opinion not only as to what that allegory is but as to how the characters fit into it. The Biblical title, drawn from the Sermon on the Mount and recalled specifically in the crucial moment of the action,[23] encourages a figurative approach; so does the godlikeness of the Duke, who has been interpreted by one critic as the Lord Incarnate, by another as the good ruler standing for God.[24] But whether the play be viewed as religious or political, the Duke's allegorical significance in the action is inferred. Amidst a welter of interpretations, one might be disposed to adopt the wiser stance that the play has meanings rather than a meaning, and that in any case one should beware of "imposing a pattern on Shakespeare's thought." Certainly this attitude is safer than that of the unfortunate critic who came to the conclusion that Shakespeare himself was confused.

As a matter of fact, it is not necessary to assume that Shakespeare spoke in tongues. He had always exploited the emotive power of Christian analogues, and they are an important part of his theatrical resources here. In the climactic moment of the play, Angelo, substitute for the absent Duke, is publicly revealed as abusing his trust. Not the fallen angel, but certainly a fallen angel, he perceives the Duke's omniscience and submits to it. Like the psalmist, he asks only to be judged according to his righteousness. "God judgeth the righteous, and God is angry with the wicked every day." He corresponds to the psalmist's wicked man who "travaileth with iniquity, and hath conceived mischief, and brought forth falsehood. / He made a pit, and digged it, and is fallen into the ditch which he made. / His mischief shall return upon his own head, and his violent dealing shall come down upon his own pate" (Ps. 7 : 8, 14–16). When his evil dealing is exposed, he seems to invoke the psalmist's acknowledgement that there is

23. Matt. 7 : 1–2: "Judge not, that ye be not judged. / For with what judgment ye judge, ye shall be judged: and with what measure ye mete, it shall be measured unto you again."

24. R. W. Battenhouse, "*Measure for Measure* and Christian Doctrine of the Atonement," *PMLA* 61 (1946) : 1029–59; Elizabeth M. Pope, "The Renaissance Background of *Measure for Measure*," *Shakespeare Survey* 2 (1949) : 66–82.

no escape from the omnipresence of God: "Whither shall I go
from thy Spirit? or whither shall I flee from thy presence? / If I
ascend up into heaven, thou art there: if I make my bed in hell,
behold, thou art there" (Ps. 139 : 7–8). And as the psalmist lays
himself open to the judgment of God, so does Angelo to the
judgment of the Duke:

> O my dread lord,
> I should be guiltier than my guiltiness
> To think I can be undiscernible
> When I perceive your Grace, like pow'r divine,
> Hath look'd upon my passes!
>
> [5.1.371–75]

Without doubt Shakespeare expected his audience in such a
passage to equate the all-knowingness of God and of the Duke, as
well as the uselessness of any attempt of as wicked a man as
Angelo to hide from the Duke's justice.

But granting that the Christian analogy recurs throughout,
there is greater advantage in viewing the Christian elements as an
ideological extension of the theme of equity in *The Merchant of
Venice*. Here again we may turn with profit to St. Germain's *Doctor
and Student*. Conscience, says St. Germain, is not always a sure
guide, but one must distinguish conscience, "an applying of any
science or knowledge to some particular act of man," from
synteresis (συντήρησις) "a naturall power of the soule sette in the
hyghest parte thereof mouynge and sterring it to good and
abhorring euil." Conscience may sometimes sin, either through
ignorance, negligence, pride, singularity, following one's own wit,
insubordinate affection to oneself, pusillanimity, or perplexity.
Synteresis never sins, and "maye not wholy be extincted neither
in man ne yet in dampned soules." It is sometimes called the law
of reason "for it ministreth the pryncyples of the lawe of reason,"
and indeed by reason, the noblest among God's gifts, man
"precelleth al beastes, and is made like to the dignitie of Angelles,
discernying trouth from falshed, and evyl from good." But only
Angels are of a nature "to understand without serching of
reason," and when synteresis is observable in man, it constitutes

that modicum of perfection which even if "it may be lette for a tyme eyther thorughe the darkenesse of ygnoraunce or for undiscrete delectacion, or for the hardnes of obstynacye," it can on occasion elevate him to a station of understanding with angels. The presence of this angelic quality makes the exercise of equity something more than an application of the law of conscience. For where conscience may misjudge, "sinteresis ministreth a universal principle that never erreth."

In this perspective, the Duke, important though he is in the structure of *Measure for Measure*, plays an assisting role to Isabella. Through much of the action he exercises almost godlike power over his fellow creatures. Legally, he stands in relatively the same position in *Measure for Measure* as Portia does in *The Merchant of Venice*, but with one notable difference. While in both plays justice remains within the area of earthly jurisdiction, Portia never relinquishes the power to dispense it; the Duke at one critical juncture does, and in so doing raises the concept of equity above the competence of man-made law to the point where synteresis in the person of Isabella may come into play. Portia's plea for mercy is no more than a Christian reminder of human inadequacy:

> Though justice be thy plea, consider this—
> That, in the course of justice, none of us
> Should see salvation.
>
> [4.1.198–200]

But conscience takes on a larger dimension in Isabella's first verbal encounter with Angelo, still new in his robes of office. When he brusquely turns off her appeal for her brother's life on the bare legalism that Claudio is "a forfeit" to the law, Isabella finds her proper response in Christian doctrine:

> Why, all the souls that were were forfeit once,
> And he that might the vantage best have took
> Found out the remedy.
>
> [2.2.73–75][25]

25. Cf. Shylock's insistence on foreclosing Antonio's forfeit of the bond

Suddenly, Isabella's theologically oriented eloquence has made earthly law craven.

We shall therefore be at a central point of vantage if we consider *Measure for Measure*, not primarily as a Christian allegory, but as an equitable resolution of the human predicament when the laws of man are used to violate the laws of God. In such a circumstance, the Duke's "remedy," unlike Portia's, can be no more than dispensatory. Shakespeare's audience would have compared his conduct as judge with that of his deputy-judges, Escalus and Angelo, who violate their charges with the respective worldly errors of unconscious stupidity and deliberate malfeasance. But though he preserves a certain aura of divinity until he reveals himself to pronounce judgment, he no more than prepares the way for Isabella. Justice in *The Merchant of Venice* is achieved solely within the area of common law; in *Measure for Measure* it exceeds the bounds of human justice by Isabella's act of voluntarism whereby man "precelleth all beasts, and is made like to the dignity of angels."

It is on this distinction of human and divine law that the whole play's structure sharply divides. Tillyard first perceived the entrance of the Duke in act three, scene one, line 151 as a new point of departure in the play. After noting that the Duke "does not begin to interpose" in the action until this point, he remarks:

> The simple and ineluctable fact is that the tone in the first half of the play is frankly, acutely human and quite hostile to the tone of the allegory or symbol. And however much the tone changes in the second half, nothing in the world can make an allegorical interpretation poetically valid throughout.

Tillyard concludes that the play is not of a piece but changes its nature halfway through. He sees a reflection of this division in the literary style: the first half of the play is "predominantly poetical," whereas after the Duke's entrance there is "little poetry

---

(4.1.206–07): "I crave the law, / The penalty and forfeit of my bond." Angelo observes the amenities.

of any kind." He admits grudgingly that the episode of Mariana and Isabella pleading to the Duke for Angelo's life "does rise somewhat as poetry"; but it is exceptional, and counts for little "in the prevailing tone of lowered poetical tension." [26]

With this point of division in the play, I heartily concur. But to call it an inconsistency overlooks the legal issues which hold the two parts together. For the first part poses a problem in legal chicanery which the second part resolves. What happens at midpoint in the play is the interposition of "divine" justice where human justice has failed. The first half of the play places Isabella in the intolerable position of having to decide whether she should save the life of her brother by yielding herself to the desires of Angelo, the judge who condemned him, or reject his advances at the expense of her brother's life. She chooses to remain chaste, thus calling down generations of critics on her cruelty.

But there is no room for sentimentality here. On purely moral grounds, her stand is arguably reprehensible, and Shakespeare forces her inflexibility on the audience with great power. But it is equally apparent that from the point of view of divine law, Isabella has no choice: yielding to her brother's judge would mean the loss not merely of her chastity but of her soul, to say nothing of her brother's. By comparison with Angelo, who has been commissioned "to enforce or qualify the laws. / As your soul seems good," yet finds himself quite differently disposed, Isabella in her innocence offers to "bribe" him to save Claudio with "prayers from preserved souls, / From fasting maids whose minds are dedicate / To nothing temporal" (2.2.153–55). Angelo would dismiss her talk of soul, yet her mind continually returns to it; and when he proposes as "the voice of the recorded law" that there might be "charity in sin" to save her brother's life, she naïvely and ironically agrees to consider "it," i.e., forgiving Claudio, "as a peril to my soul . . . no sin at all, but charity." Aware at long last that he is "bidding the law make curtsy" to either "condemnation or approof" as he chooses, that he is in fact "hooking both right and wrong to th' appetite," Isabella remains firm: the state of her

26. E. M. W. Tillyard, *Shakespeare's Problem Comedies* (1949), pp. 129–31.

own soul as well as her brother's is her single and sufficient
criterion:

> Then, Isabel, live chaste; and, brother, die!
> More than our brother is our chastity.
> I'll tell him yet of Angelo's request,
> And fit his mind to death for his soul's rest.
>
> [2.4.184–87]

If the laws of man and the laws of God are set at variance, if the
laws of man, as here, are hooked to appetite, earthly justice has
indeed come to a stand. As Shakespeare was writing elsewhere,
perhaps at the same time, once justice has given way to power,
power is translated to will and will to appetite, "an universal
wolf " (*Troilus and Cressida*, 1.3.117–21). Portia could match a law
with a law and cancel out the law's injustice in *The Merchant of
Venice*; in *Measure for Measure*, there is no such choice. Human
equity unavailing, for their souls' rest Isabella must live chaste
and Claudio die.

Isabella vs. the Critics

It should not be necessary to defend Isabella's decision. Yet
more than one critic feels that she was a bit straitlaced about the
matter. Though some reservation should be made—I should
suppose—for the fact that she was preparing to enter the
sisterhood of the votarists of Saint Clare, she has been accused of
"narrow-mindedness and self-righteousness" because she refuses
the proposal to sacrifice her virtue to save her brother's life. She is
made out to "storm . . . like a virago" when she sees the obvious
signs of Claudio's weakening of resolution to die rather than to see
her "virginal righteousness" stained. She is willing—so the
indictment continues—to submit Mariana to the same offense
that Claudio has committed, and shows no regret at her
"harshness" to her brother. We are told that she is a good match
to Angelo who is also "virginal and self-righteous." She comes
through the experience of the play "a wiser and finer woman,"
and we are expected to put reservations on Lucio's enthusiastic

description of her at the beginning of the play as a "thing enskied and sainted." [27]

This studied denigration of Isabella's character is, if nothing more, distressingly ungallant; it also ignores or underrates her primary motivation, her overriding concern for the world of the spirit. Her critics have been too ready to accept the sufficiency of Claudio's very human appeal and too ready to condemn her indignant rejection:

> *Claudio.* Sweet sister, let me live!
> What sin you do to save a brother's life,
> Nature dispenses with the deed so far
> That it becomes a virtue.
> *Isabella.*   O you beast!
> O faithless coward! O dishonest wretch!
> Wilt thou be made a man out of my vice?
> Is't not a kind of incest to take life
> From thine own sister's shame? What should I think?
> Heaven shield my mother play'd my father fair!
> For such a warped slip of wilderness
> Ne'er issued from his blood. Take my defiance!
> Die, perish! Might but my bending down
> Reprieve thee from thy fate, it should proceed.
> I'll pray a thousand prayers for thy death,
> No word to save thee. . . . O, fie, fie, fie!
> Thy sin's not accidental, but a trade.
> Mercy to thee would prove itself a bawd.
> 'Tis best that thou diest quickly.

[3.1.133–51]

But what seems like inhumanity in this speech is in fact from a Christian point of view irreproachable, and Shakespeare has calculated its dramatic impact with all the adroitness of Shylock's denunciation of Christian conduct in *The Merchant of Venice.* Its provenance is Christ's words: "What is a man profited if he shall

27. Harold S. Wilson, "Action and Symbol in *Measure for Measure* and *The Tempest,*" in *Shakespeare Quarterly* 4 (1953) : 375–84.

gain the whole world and lose his own soul?" But the immediate point of reference in judging Isabella's conduct is St. Germain's *Doctor and Student*. For her soul is in jeopardy. The principle of synteresis moves and stirs conscience to love good and abhor evil. Claudio has in effect asked her to sin at the cost of her soul and his own. At the beginning of the play she has already separated herself from the world and no longer measures life by worldly standards. She has returned to it for one reason only, to save her brother's life. As for her own, she would willingly sacrifice it for his salvation:

> O, were it but my life,
> I'd throw it down for your deliverance
> As frankly as a pin.
>
> [3.1.104–06]

This spirit of *contemptum mundi* would be expected of one who has dedicated herself to the imitation of Christ; but her devotion to it so far exceeds normal human expectation as to suggest the Christian paradox: "Whosoever will save his life, shall lose it: and whosoever will lose his life for my sake, shall find it."

For this latter role, Claudio is unprepared, as Isabella well knows and fears (2.2.84–87; 3.1.74–81). Unknown to her, the Duke, in the guise of friar, likewise anticipates man's proneness to fall, and thoroughly schools him in an elaborate monologue preparing him for death. At the end of it, Claudio seems resigned to lose his life for his sister's sake:

> I humbly thank you.
> To sue to live, I find I seek to die
> And seeking death, find life. Let it come on.
>
> [3.141–43]

Yet no sooner is he absolute for death than he is confronted with the news that he must die tomorrow. His instant response (in a characteristic image recall) is to "encounter darkness as a bride / And hug it in mine arms." His fears quickly overcome his resolution, and his plea for life at his sister's expense exposes his moral insufficiency to Isabella's icy vituperation.

The dilemma to which Claudio responds with weakness, Isabella with strength, is only partially reducible to personal choice. It involves forces beyond the control of either, forces for which there is no human remedy. In *The Merchant of Venice*, we are constantly made aware that the remedy is safely tucked away in the mind of Portia, ready for use when the proper dramatic moment arrives. In *Measure for Measure*, we have as yet no such assurance, and consequently we cannot so easily slough off the predicament in which both Claudio and Isabella find themselves. "Is there no remedy?" Claudio cries despairingly to his sister, and again, "Has he affections in him / That thus can make him bite the law by th' nose / When he would force it?" But Isabella knows too well the "devilish mercy in the judge." As we know, she has already posed the same question to Angelo, "Must he needs die?" and reminded him of "the remedy" for human frailty that Christ himself used (2.2.73–75), only to receive Angelo's cold rebuff, "It is the law, not I, condemn your brother." Knowing Angelo's devilish mercy, and defeated by Claudio's weakness, she faces the dilemma for which there is no remedy short of divine intervention.

Within this broader area of divine law, human law either because of man's weakness (Claudio) or contumacy (Angelo) can hardly be more than a dim reflection. Isabella's rejection of Claudio's plea, so abhorrent to the critics, condemns both positions with cold precision and no little heroism. She is now as inexorable for the soul's rest as she has hitherto been indefatigable in seeking human equity. Starkly, without the mitigating factor of mercy, she proclaims him for what he is, and her reasoning, however bleak is impeccable. Between the angel and the beast, man continually wavers, and it cannot be denied that Claudio has momentarily yielded to the beast. He has earned her castigation of his cowardice. He could even be called dishonest, since in effect he has played the role of bawd to his sister. Such is her zeal that she will doubt his mother's honesty, withhold mercy where before she had begged it, postulate that his single act of honest love is habitual. We are not asked to believe that Isabella believes these accusations. Her conduct to this point has been and is still a true index of her character, as her later conduct will prove. Nor should we misinterpret her present bitter vehemence. Her refusal of Claudio's plea not so much condemns the beast in Claudio as it condemns the beast in mankind; its immediate effect, crucial in the action, is to assert the limitation of human mercy. The quality of Isabella's mercy is not strained, but its quantity must be.

As we have learned to expect, the minor plot is patterned to confirm this assertion on a comic level. William Perkins, it will be recalled, condemned those who "have nothing in their mouths but 'The Law! the Law!' " but also those who "by a certain foolish kind of pity are so carried away that would have nothing but 'Mercy! Mercy!' " This, he observes, "is the highway to abolish laws." In the world of bawdry that is Vienna, the laws have long been let slip. Escalus, like Angelo commissioned to enforce them, has on a lower level enjoyed the confidence of the Duke ("The terms / For common justice, y'are as pregnant in / As art and practice hath enriched any / That we remember"); and one could hardly suppose a more deserving pair for his prosecution than those inveterate bawds, Mistress Overdone (nine husbands, "overdone by the last") and Pompey ("in the beastliest sense, Pompey the Great"), by lawful trade Overdone's tapster. Escalus makes a half-indulgent effort to wheedle an admission from Pompey of his real profession, but Pompey is an old hand at evasion: "Truly, sir, I am a poor fellow that would live." Escalus's exasperation is understandable: "How would you live, Pompey? By being a bawd? What do you think of the trade, Pompey? Is it a lawful trade?" But the force of reason cannot disturb Pompey's impudent composure: "If the law would allow it, sir." "But the law will not allow it, Pompey," retorts Escalus, now completely out of patience, "nor it shall not be allowed in Vienna." He might better have saved his heat for Pompey's innocent and wholly disarming question: "Does your worship mean to geld and splay all the youth of the city?" (2.1.234–43).

We cannot wholly condemn such verbal dexterity. In a hearing before the disguised Duke and Elbow, the ridiculous constable, Pompey exhibits the same imperviousness to instruction. Elbow faces him with the simple truth: "You will needs buy and sell men and women like beasts"; the Duke is equally explicit:

> Say to thyself,
> 'From their abominable and beastly touches
> I drink, I eat, array myself, and live.'
> Canst thou believe thy living is a life,
> So stinkingly depending?
>
> [3.2.24–28]

When Pompey takes exception: "Indeed, it does stink in some sort, sir / But yet, sir, I would prove—" the Duke breaks off his proof by sending him to prison with the ruffled comment: "Correction and instruction must both work / Ere this rude beast will profit." Yet even for this "beast" Shakespeare allows more than a degree of pity. Lucio, who has in times past made generous use of Pompey's services, refuses to bail him out with the flippant comment: "Bawd is he doubtless, and of antiquity too; bawd-born" (3.2.71–72) and leaves him to suffer the penalty, and us in a degree to sympathize.

The comic parallel of Pompey, professional bawd, and Claudio, bawd by circumstance, is both curious in its seventeenth-century use of verbal echo and functional in generating sympathy for Claudio. Shakespeare would expect his audience, attentive to intricate image patterns, to remember Pompey's "Truly, sir, I am a poor fellow that would live" when Claudio pleads with his sister, "Sweet sister, let me live!" They would extenuate Isabella's epithet "Beast!" having heard the same term applied to Pompey. The humor of Lucio's scoff at Pompey's birth lends poignancy to Isabella's aspersion on Claudio's parentage. And Pompey's dispute on the lawfulness of his trade of bawdry softens her description of Claudio's sin as

> not accidental, but a trade.
> Mercy to thee would prove itself a bawd.
> 'Tis best that thou diest quickly.
>
> [3.1.149–51]

In aggregate, the comparison sharpens the essential problem of the play: Is the application of equity to the rigor of the law unlimited? When Pompey's appeal is rejected by Lucio and Claudio's is rejected by Isabella, they both have arrived at extremities properly subject to equitable review. Unknowingly, both use the same language in asking for mercy, and both are accused of making bawdry a trade. In either case, mercy would open "the highway to abolish laws."

Yet even if one is inclined to conclude at this midpoint in the play that for quite different reasons there are mitigating factors for both Pompey and Claudio, what exercise of judgment will be acceptable for Angelo who has not merely transgressed the law, not even lived by it, but consciously abused it to further his own vice? Not only is justice here plainly overturned, but any effort that Isabella might make to expose Angelo's guilt would be admittedly circumvented. In the action of *The Merchant of Venice*, Portia's "Tarry, Jew" assures the audience that Shylock will not win his claim though the law allows it and the court awards it. There is a significant structural difference in *Measure for Measure*: Isabella faces her court of appeal with no answers. She is in fact convinced before the entrance of the friar-Duke that her cause is lost. But the Duke applies strange remedies cloaked in the language of the friar:

> The hand that hath made you fair hath made you good. The goodness that is cheap in beauty makes beauty brief in goodness; but grace, being the soul of your complexion, shall keep the body of it ever fair. [3.1.184–88]

Her beauty rather than her grace has "softened" Angelo (1.4.70), but both the earthly and the heavenly quality still remain to her. Her hope must rest in the friar's plan, and the plan as far as she knows has not succeeded in saving her brother's life by the time the Duke "returns." Isabella could say with good reason: There comes a time in human affairs when all that man can do is not enough. As for the audience, who know that Claudio is alive, they are left to wonder why the Duke does not say so publicly. Why is it necessary for him to work such a cruelty on the innocent Isabella?

The Fantastical Duke

Except for the Duke's bizarre gamesmanship, there is nothing mysterious about his moral stance. It is true that he busies himself in dark corners—that is, he is not exposing his tactics any more than Portia did. Judging by the conduct of that astute lady, we should surmise that whatever the Duke is up to, it is he who will resolve the dilemma Isabella is faced with in his own good time. Meanwhile, his presence assures us that the outcome will not be tragic. His return corresponds closely to Portia's entry to the courtroom. The Duke, like Portia, has complete control of the action and need merely reveal his identity to resolve the dilemma. Quite obviously he is postponing such a resolution in order to arrange a climax involving clerical disguise and elaborate stage managing, not without occasional misrepresentation, and not without what appears to be wholly unnecessary obfuscation of his original motive for retirement from public view. His declared intention at the beginning of the action is to enforce laws long disregarded in Vienna; but at the end, there is still no evidence of an effort at general civic reform, let alone any substantial progress toward Pompey's suggestion of gelding and splaying the youth of the city. Indeed, at the close of the play, no one, not excepting the reforming Duke, seems to give Vienna a moment's thought. What does occupy the Duke's attention from beginning to end is Angelo's capacities as a judge, an interest which makes his temporary retirement plausible as a means of observing Angelo's uninhibited use of authority. Dressed as a friar, he would have access to all, his sincerity would not be questioned, and more particularly, he would be able to see "if power change purpose, what our seemers be" (1.3.53–54). Angelo's death sentence to Claudio is an early indication that law will be administered with rigor. Isabella has not yet entered into his calculation, and it is only after Angelo has made vicious use of the powers granted him for reforming vice that the Duke undertakes the stage preparations, the purpose of which will not be clear until the final tableau. Meanwhile, the action and the actors are wholly at his disposal, either willingly, as in the case of Isabella, or unknowingly, as in the case of Angelo.

To an audience alert to the Christian analogy, this intervention when human affairs have reached an impasse, this apparently sudden shift from his role of counsellor to active director of affairs, should cause no surprise. The fact is that at no time has the Duke relinquished his sovereignty: Angelo is merely appointed deputy for the time, and the predicament for Isabella and Claudio, real for them, is nevertheless for the time merely in their own minds, to be terminated at the Duke's discretion. Until he chooses to identify himself, the whole design of the friar-counsellor is to set up a situation which requires a choice of Claudio's death or Isabella's violation of conscience. In this context, all the Duke's acts are explicable. His outwardly mysterious original retirement was a necessary expedient to allow the exercise of free choice, and his subsequent busyness was directed to the same end, his visitations in the garb of priest amounting to confessionals of conscience. His approach to Juliet early in the action was the first of such trials, and it is significantly couched in legal language:

> I'll teach you how you shall arraign your conscience,
> And try your penitence, if it be sound
> Or hollowly put on.
>
> [2.3.21–23]

She acquiescing, he tells her that Claudio must die tomorrow, and her anguished reply proves her soundness of soul:

> O injurious law,
> That respites me a life whose very comfort
> Is still a dying horror!
>
> [2.3.39–41]

The audience knows that the law that seems so "injurious" to her, could at any moment be made inoperative by the Duke. But she has no way of knowing that in her steadfastness in the face of the law's rigor she has been the first success in the Duke's elaborate stratagem.

Thus, for Juliet, as presently for Claudio, the Duke intervenes at the moment of despair, but he leaves no comfort beyond the relief of conscience through the confession of guilt as outwardly he prepares them for death. But Isabella is being prepared for a different and more difficult role. The net result of her long and frustrating debate with Angelo for the life of her brother has been the misprision of justice. Confronted with the evidence that she has been stalemated by the injurious law, her choice is clear; her brother must die, and she must make public Angelo's attempt at subornation. The Duke, like Portia, chooses to present a remedy, and with it the tragic tone of the play changes abruptly to suspense.

The essence of his plan is a substitution, what has come to be known since W. W. Lawrence as a bed-trick. As Lawrence showed, such tricks were traditional; medieval literature offers parallels not intended to do more than titillate the fancy, certainly not to invade propriety; and for the chaste Isabella, the scheme is credible since it is proposed by a friar and has his sanction. What is worth attention is that it is not the only substitution nor even the first. Up to this point in the play, Angelo has been acting as substitute for the Duke who "lent him our terror, dress'd him with our love" (1.1.20–21), and now so describes him in his leading question to Isabella: "How will you do to content this substitute and to save your brother?" (3.1.192–93). Her refusal to "content" Angelo prepares the way for further tactical substitutions designed to permit freedom of decision for both Angelo and Isabella. The success of this strategy depends wholly on concealment of the fact that Claudio is alive, and it demands ingenious shifts. Since Angelo has ordered his immediate execution in spite of a promise made at his assignation with the supposed Isabella, Barnardine's head must be substituted for Claudio's; and when Barnardine (like Claudio) declares he is not prepared for death, Ragozine's head must be substituted for Barnardine's. Both substitutions, by preserving the life of Claudio, make it possible for the Duke to fulfill his promise to Isabella that acquiescence in the bed-trick would "redeem" her brother from "the angry law."

It is a complicated business, much more complicated than Portia's ruse, though the dramatic effect is the same, amazing to the participants but immensely interesting to the audience who are silent but knowing observers, as unperceived the Duke finds out the remedy for the anger of the law and prepares Angelo and Isabella for their role in the final action. No sooner has Isabella agreed to the bed-trick than he aids and abets Lucio in hanging a noose of slander about his own unsuspecting neck. He lets Claudio continue to believe that he will die, and at the same time postpones Angelo's order for execution, using his own signet to stay the provost's hand. Having dispatched the head of Ragozine to Angelo in order to deceive him into thinking that Claudio is dead, he deceives Isabella to the same purpose. Only then does he give out to them both that the Duke is returning shortly, and that there will be a court of appeal. Except for the unexpected recalcitrance of Barnardine in not consenting to the removal of his head, the Duke has managed to control every moment of the action, not neglecting occasional hints which while they tantalize more than satisfy, yet reassure the audience of an expected dispensation of justice. Once again his conduct conforms to Portia's and fulfills the same function. There is even time as the final tableau is being readied for some rather broad humor at the expense of the inexcusable bawds.

When what turns out to be the arraignment of Angelo begins, all the participants have been properly disposed to suit the Duke's purposes, yet none know what those purposes are. Claudio, after shrinking from death, "professes to have received no sinister measure from his judge, but most willingly humbles himself to the determination of justice . . . and is now resolv'd to die" (3.2.256–62). Angelo, though he is outwardly "so severe" that "he is indeed justice" (3.2.266–68), now inwardly much regrets ordering Claudio's death. He rationalizes the deed as preventing some future revenge; yet—and here he himself analyzes the weakness of his case precisely—"once our grace we have forgot, / Nothing goes right! we would, and we would not" (4.4.35–36). Isabella, deliberately misinformed that her brother has been executed, is tutored to vengeance by the ubiquitous Duke. Assured of his grace, she is ready now to carry out her earlier threat to declare publicly the perfidy of Angelo. Each of them in his own way, all else failing, has at the last come to grace, as indeed, from the Christian point of view, every man must. But though Claudio and Isabella are both resolved, Angelo still stands outside it in a state of dreadful moral uncertainty. In this state of suspended judgment, wholly of the Duke's contrivance, Lucio will act as the spring to release the final action. From the first, we have known him as a scurrilous slanderer, least deserving of grace. With a pun on grace at table, he has asserted with unwarranted assurance that "grace is grace, despite of all controversy." To which the audience might well respond: Despite his self-allowance, his time of judgment too is close at hand.

Inward and Spiritual Grace

It was a fantastic trick of the Duke of dark corners that the calumniator Lucio in jerking off the hood of a friar should have exposed the judge who would sentence Angelo as well as himself to judgment—a trick worthy of the angels' laughter. At that moment, they might well have laughed themselves mortal at man's greater madness, in his pride and ignorance. For the trespass which, so far as Angelo and Lucio know, has cost Claudio his life, they must now pay the same penalty, and the Duke's sentence for each reaches to the extremity of the law. Both expect it, and indeed anticipate no less (5.1.371–79; 510–19).

"This may prove worse than hanging," exclaims the still far from discountenanced Lucio, contemplating only such mercy as could be expected from the person he has just unsuspectingly described as a "bald-pated lying rascal" with a "knave's visage" and "sheep-biting face." And indeed there is no seeming mercy in the judge. Yet Lucio's sentence to be married to the whore he has gotten with child, and afterward to be whipped and hanged, is immediately remitted by the whipping and hanging, on the grounds, one might venture to hope, of his neck-verse wit: "Your

Highness said even now I made you a duke. Good my lord, do not recompense me in making me a cuckold" (5.1.521–23).

By comparison, Angelo's conduct is patently unforgivable. Shall we expect remission for him who has not only committed Claudio's offense but ordered his execution to conceal his own guilt? A hint as to the Duke's purposes is his own care to conceal from all but the audience the fact that Claudio is alive, for it is clear that the Duke's intention is not to be satisfied by the mere public exposure of Angelo's abuse of office. Obviously, his stratagem also permits the unrestricted operation of Angelo's conscience and what must follow, a test of his present worthiness of grace—whether, that is, he is in a state of repentance, a prerequisite to attainment of that "inward and spiritual grace" by which alone man becomes new made.

The Book of Common Prayer at this point in the action is a very specific guide to the central idea of the play. In the Sacrament of Baptism, inward and spiritual grace is "a death unto sin, and a new birth unto righteousness: for being by nature born in sin, and the children of wrath, we are hereby made the children of grace." [28] We remember Christ's words, "Verily, verily, I say unto thee, Except a man be born again, he cannot see the kingdom of God (John 3 : 3). Though at this moment Shakespeare's strategy has contrived Angelo's contrition as something of a surprise, the imagery in fact has long prepared us for it. "How would you be," Isabella had pleaded with him on their first meeting,

> If he which is the top of judgment should
> But judge you as you are? O, think on that!
> And mercy then will breathe within your lips
> Like man new made.
>
> [2.2.75–79]

Angelo himself had condemned Claudio in similar terms:

> 'Tis all as easy
> Falsely to take away a life true made

28. Cf. Eph. 2 : 3–5.

> As to put metal in restrained means
> To make a false one.
>
> [2.4.46–49]

The despicable Lucio offers the appropriate counterpoint. Lucio has committed slander, Angelo allowed it. Now by the unfrocking of the Duke, both are in the same plight. But whereas Lucio shows no change of heart, and seeks only to elude judgment, Angelo asks for it and thereby demonstrates his capability for reformation:

> No longer session hold upon my shame,
> But let my trial be mine own confession.
> Immediate sentence then, and sequent death,
> Is all the grace I beg.
>
> [5.1.376–79] [29]

But the secret of Angelo's responsibility for Claudio's death remains unexposed, and he is therefore ineligible for grace though the Duke now sets the stage for it. Acting with strict justice on Angelo's confession, the Duke hurries him off to marry Mariana. When the newly-wedded man returns, he is instantly condemned to "the very block / Where Claudio stoop'd to death," to be executed solely by the *lex talionis*:

> The very mercy of the law cries out
> Most audible, even from his proper tongue,
> "An Angelo for Claudio! death for death!"
> Haste still pays haste, and leisure answers leisure:
> Like doth quit like, and Measure still for Measure.
>
> [5.1.412–16]

Commentators have had no difficulty in agreeing that Shakespeare is here putting his audience in mind of the Sermon on the Mount, and that the point has now been reached where the New Law must be substituted for the Old. That greatest of substitutions, mercy for vengeance, must surely be at hand. To a certain point, the structural and ethical pattern of *The Merchant of Venice* is

29. Cf. St. Jerome's "spark of conscience" (*scintilla conscientia*) not lost by original sin.

here reenacted. The Duke's technique has hitherto closely resembled that of Portia in carrying the law to its permissive extremity. When she seems most to encourage the Jew's cruelty ("You must prepare your bosom for his knife . . . Are there balance here to weigh / The flesh? . . . Have by some sur- geon . . . / To stop his wounds, lest he do bleed to death"), she is really postponing in the interest of dramatic suspense the legal remedy which as audience we have little doubt she possesses—else her nonchalance and her thinly veiled references to the ring and to the husband and wife situation presently to be faced would strain audience toleration. Likewise, at the corresponding mo- ment in *Measure for Measure*, an Aristotelian pattern of recognition is followed by reversal, and the revelation of Angelo's concealed evil removes the prop that alone sustains his boldness.

But here the later play diverges notably from its prototype. Shylock makes no confession; offered mercy by the Duke, he is "content" only in a legal sense to accept the mitigated sentence. Plainly, he remains unregenerate, and even though in a Christian spirit his death sentence is commuted before he asks for it, the Duke in granting pardon then regarded it as an illustration of "the difference of our spirit" (*The Merchant of Venice*, 5.1.368–69). By contrast, Angelo in confessing his guilt and by his own free choice both refusing grace and asking sentence of death before the Duke imposes it, has shown himself to be indeed a man new made. At the same time, the Duke, by pronouncing sentence, has removed himself from further action at a moment when justice for the other characters is still at sixes and sevens. For all that they know, the repentant Angelo has been placed beyond mercy ("The very mercy of the law cries out . . .") by a rigorous execution of justice wholly within the propriety of the law; but in so satisfying the formal claims of both Mariana and Isabella, the Duke has seemingly left Mariana without a husband, Isabella without a brother. Thus the Duke's administering of the law has brought about an overt injustice. It is the moment toward which his strategy has been directed. The insufficiency of strict administra- tion of man's law is manifest, and he dispenses his power to the two who have suffered grievance at the hands of Angelo. In this new dispensation, they will plead mercy for him even though mercy has been denied.

For Mariana, forgiveness under present circumstances is understandable as the tide of human feelings welling up to Angelo's callous rejection brings her to her knees. But for Isabella, mercy to Angelo requires a moral decision of extreme difficulty. For this climactic decision, the Duke as friar has maneuvered all the previous action. Her part was to proclaim Angelo publicly for his perfidy, and to the very moment when Mariana pleads for her mercy, the Duke has seen to it that she is provided every legal and human encouragement to the opposite course. This part she has played, trusting wholly in the friar-Duke's promises:

> you shall have your bosom on this wretch,
> Grace of the Duke, revenges to your heart,
> And general honour.
>
> [4.3.139–41]

At the same time, to protect Mariana, she has blackened her own character by omitting the bed-trick from her account and accepting thereby the doubtful, and to her mind reprehensible, role of yielding to "the concupiscible lust" of Angelo for the sake of her brother (5.1.92–101).[30] To make her decision even more dramatic, Angelo is not only the deceiver, the hypocrite, the virgin-violator she denounces from her own experience, but the murderer of her brother, as she has been led to believe. What then must be her state of mind when her accusations in the presence of the "returned" Duke are rebuffed, and she herself accused of blackmail, declared mad, and by the Duke's apparent whimsy stifled and imprisoned for her pains? Despite his enigmatic assurances and his advice that she "give [her] cause to heaven,"

30. An admirable summary of the common law behind Isabella's "repair i' the dark" has been composed by J. W. Lever in the Arden Edition of *Measure for Measure* (1965), pp. li–lv. He there indicates that Shakespeare's audience would have seen in her willingness to comply with the duke's plan to reclaim Mariana's espousal rights "no breach of the traditional moral code." It should be added in her defense that she was following the advice of a seeming friar, whose device she had no reason to doubt.

she must rightfully assume that since earthly justice has been
subverted—and worse, by the very ones who should have upheld
it—she can hope only for the intercession of a higher justice, "you
blessed ministers above," who will "with ripened time / Unfold
the evil which is here wrapt up / In countenance" (5.1.115–18).
Earlier in the action, she had refused to save her brother's life at
the price of her soul; but now with Mariana asking for Isabella's
interposition to save the life of her brother's murderer, she makes
the hard choice of grace, resisting the Duke's powerful persuasions
to both revenge and conscience, even as the Duke rebukes
Mariana for requesting it.

> Against all sense you do importune her,
> Should she kneel down in mercy of this fact,
> Her brother's ghost his paved bed would break
> And take her hence in horror.
>
> [5.1.438–41]

Yet in spite of his words, she brushes personal feelings aside and
kneels with Mariana in a symbolic act of forgiveness. For her,
conscience has proved to be an insufficient guide. The rationale
for her judgment on Angelo must rest on her willingness to believe
that his will had been overcome by appetite. As Hooker had put
it:

> The object of Appetite is whatsoever sensible good may be
> wished for; the object of Will is that good which Reason doth
> lead us to seek. . . . Wherefore it is not altogether in our
> power, whether we will be stirred with affections or no:
> whereas actions which issue from the disposition of the Will
> are in the power thereof to be performed or stayed. [LEP,
> I.vii.3]

Such is the agonizing choice Isabella now makes as "against all
sense" in a sheer act of will she pleads for Angelo's life:

> Look, if it please you, on this man condemn'd
> As if my brother liv'd. I partly think
> A due sincerity governed his deeds

> Till he did look on me. Since it is so,
> Let him not die. My brother had but justice
> In that he did the thing for which he died.
> For Angelo
> His act did not o'ertake his bad intent,
> And must be buried but as an intent
> That perish'd by the way. Thoughts are no subjects,
> Intents but merely thoughts.
>
> [5.1.449–59]

Once in *The Merchant of Venice* Shakespeare was close to this selfless emanation of inward and spiritual grace. "On what compulsion must I be merciful?" asks the vengeful Shylock, unable to conceive of a justice which is not strained, and failing to understand not only that the very nature and substance of mercy is dispensatory, but that conversely, it would be entirely possible to dispense justice within the legal code yet remain unbound by considerations that might involve salvation (*The Merchant of Venice*, 4.1.197–202). Such considerations are explicit in the crucial stage tableau. Isabella's decision has called forth a higher power than conscience and synteresis must now govern, "as in a parke / With hys tables in hys hand her dedys to marke." [31] Earlier, she had leveled scorn on proud man. Conscience had then served her, and she had let Claudio die. But news of the execution of Angelo's threat has dissipated her contempt, and now, his authority shorn from him, man, proud man, has rather become the object of pity, for whom there is no laughter, only the immense and angelic grace.

And grace we now perceive, has been her quality from the beginning. She has indeed proved herself "enskied, ensainted," even before Lucio first appealed for her grace to soften Angelo (1.4.69–70). The provost had prayed that Heaven give her "moving graces" (2.2.36). The Duke also was careful that his machinations would "do no stain to [her] own gracious person" (3.1.208–09). And Angelo could not have become new made

---

31. John Lydgate, *The Assembly of the Gods*, Early English Text Society, extra series, no. 69 (1896), stanza 134.

without her help. Of his unredeemed situation, Angelo was very well aware, even before his guilt was made public (4.4.35–36); now that the natural power of the soul has stirred it to good, grace has by natural consequence interposed for his salvation. The focus is not on Angelo but on Isabella. "He dies for Claudio's death," the Duke insists until the very moment that her kneeling figure, symbol of synteresis, establishes the sovereignty of grace over her deliberate mercy.

It remains for the provost to reveal that he has saved Claudio from death, and hence, by happy inadvertence, saved Angelo from the burden of his newfound conscience. Earthly justice does in truth show likest God's when it has been seasoned by mercy; but beyond the framework of earthly justice as administered by the Duke, equity has found its sufficient extension in grace both inward and spiritual.

4

CIVILITY

A Gold Spear on a Bend Sables

Shakespeare's title went back to Adam, though on 20 October 1596, he had been a gentleman "any time these four hours." There is no evidence that his elevation in status had any further effect on him, in either repute or bearing. No person was more deserving. Gentleness was a temper in Shakespeare, not a title, equally applicable to the man and his work. To the admirers of his sonnets—the plays were hardly to be spoken of as literary pieces—*honey-flowing, honey-tongued* seemed right for his style. But for the style of the man as his fellows knew him, *gentle* came oftenest to their tongues. And so he seemed when shortly after his death they collected his work. In the rough-and-tumble world of the theatre, the quality of gentleness distinguished him from his fellows. Heminges and Condell remembered him as "a most gentle expressor of Nature." Jonson, prone to regard his fellow-creatures as either knaves or fools, broke custom to speak unaffectedly and affectionately of "my gentle Shakespeare." As his friends and contemporaries, they were certainly in the best position to describe the temper of the man. But we too at this distance note it everywhere in the plays: an acute sensitivity to the anomaly of man's gentleness and his beastliness, in public as well as familial relations. "Tigers, not daughters," King Lear concludes after denouncing what seems to him filial ingratitude; had he been other than kith, "unkindness" would still have hit near the mark. Goneril and Regan at the last are unkindly in the beastly sense. Quite beyond their unkindness to their father, they devour each other in their jealousy, like monsters of the deep, and the kingdom as a result is "gor'd."

Gentle is an ambivalent word. Indeed, *kindness* and *gentleness* lend themselves naturally to dual meanings, and Shakespeare constantly plays on them: kindness as kinship and as gentleness; the quality of gentleness and the quality of gentility; and inversely, ungentleness where gentility should be expected. "A little more than kin and less than kind" are the first words of that character who above all of Shakespeare's creations confronts the paradox of the vicious mole of nature in men otherwise "as pure as grace, / As infinite as man may undergo." For Hamlet, the natural association of kinship and kindness no longer obtains. The age gives it proof: Nature is turned against itself, outward seeming becomes inward reality, and the tragic consequence of this self-torture is that he must be cruel only to be kind. If neither Gertrude nor Ophelia is what she seems to be, if both are victims of seeming, so also is Hamlet, whose assumption of their moral insensitivity is real, his cruelty a moral inversion of his love.

Equally ambivalent and closely interwoven in the texture of Shakespeare's thought was the concept of civility. Ideally, civility (*civilitas*) might and should exist with gentleness (*gentilitas*), but the relationship often breaks down in the plays. Gentleness obviously exists without civility, and unkindness in those whose birth would seem to preclude it. To be civil is not to be kind. What possesses Shakespeare's mind throughout his writing career is the outbreak of barbarity in those who are superficially at least civil—in Rome (*Titus Andronicus*), in Florence (*All's Well that Ends Well*), in Venice (*Othello*), in Athens (*Timon*), in Milan (*The Tempest*), the centers of culture in Europe. And the paradox was complicated almost from day to day by the news of other cultures in peoples unacquainted with culture in the European style and perhaps antedating any of those previously known.

How then could civility be defined? The question had been debated since the discoveries began. Thomas More, who knew the cities of Europe as well by his own observation as by his friends, notably Erasmus, deplored among the princes of Europe and their counsellors that "other philosophye more cyuyle" than that taught in the schools, "whyche knoweth as ye wolde saye her

owne stage," and acts accordingly.[1] Frequently, the debate
focused on the origins of society. Thomas Starkey, leading
political theorist of Henry VIII's reign, incorporated More's
argument and extended it in his *Dialogue between Pole and Lupset*,
the authenticity of which there is no reason to doubt. When
Lupset defines civility as "the best kynd of lyfe and most
conuenyent to the nature of man, wych ys borne to commyn
cyuylyte, one euer to be redy to helpe another, by al gud and
ryght pollycy," Pole takes him up on his premise and postulates
superior living conditions before the establishment of civility:
"For as much as man at the begynnyng lyuyd many yerys
wythout any such pollycy; at the wych tyme he lyuyd more
vertusely and more accordyng to the dygnyte of hys nature then
he doth now in thys wych you cal polytyke ordur and cyuylyte."
Moreover, we see now in our own day that "thos men wych lyue
out of cytes and townys and haue fewyst lawys to be gouernyd by,
lyue bettur then other dow in theyr gudly cytes neuer so wel
byldyd and inhabytyd." Their study is of "vertue and veray true
symplycyte" rather than of vice, subtlety, and craft, of adultery
and murder, of gluttony and all pleasure of the body as practiced
in the "socyety and cumpany of men togydur." It would be better,
Pole concludes, "Rather to lyfe in the wyld forest, ther more
folowyng the study of vertue, as hyt ys sayd men dyd in the golden
age, where in man lyuyd accordyng to hys natural dygnyte."
Lupset, who here carries the burden of Starkey's argument,
vigorously dissents to such a nostalgic view. He insists that civility
is not "a multytude conspyryng togeddur in vyce" but in all virtue
and honesty. If men give themselves to vice in cities, the virtuous
man should not therefore be driven "to the woodys agayne and
wyld forestys wherein he lyuyd at the fyrst begynnyng rudely."
The fault—and here he is closest to More's real life dilemma—is
with "such as be grete, wyse, and polytyke men"[2] as fly from

1. *Utopia* in Ralph Robinson's translation, ed. J. Churton Collins (1927), p. 39.
Edward Surtz's translation, *Utopia* (1965), p. 49; "another philosophy more
practical" blots the important word.
2. Starkey had first written "as you be."

office "by whose wysdome the multytude myght be conteynyd
and kept in gud ordur and cyuylyte." So as "in the begynnyng,
men were brought from theyr rudenes and bestyal lyfe, to thys
cyuylyte so natural to man," they must now be kept therein by
the like wisdom. Pole takes issue with Lupset's definition of
civility as a "conspyracy in honesty and vertue" on the grounds
that it is equally acceptable to Turks, Saracens, and Jews as well
as Christians, and he insists that by Lupset's definition "the veray
true polytyke and cyuyle lyfe" must remain a matter of opinion.
To this cavil, Lupset responds that the virtues that incline man to
the civil life are common to all men: "Thes vertues stond not in
the opynyon of man, but by the bunfyte and powar of nature in
hys hart are rotyd and plantyd, . . . wych though al men folow
not, yet al men approue." [3]

That there were other opinions about the origins of civil life is
apparent from the works of Machiavelli which were becoming
known to Pole's circle at the time that the *Dialogue* was written.[4]
Machiavelli describes no Golden Age, when men were said to
study virtue.

> At the beginning of the world the inhabitants were few in
> number, and lived for a time dispersed, like beasts. As the
> human race increased, the necessity for uniting themselves
> for defence made itself felt; the better to attain this object,
> they chose the strongest and most courageous from amongst
> themselves and placed him at their head, promising to obey
> him.[5]

3. Thomas Starkey, *Dialogue between Pole and Lupset*, PRO, SP 1/90, x.i.2816 fols.
34–41. A similar passage, assigned somewhat inconsistently to Pole in the *Dialogue*
(fols. 89–91), was developed from a treatise, *What ys pollycy aftur the sentence of
Arystotyl* (PRO, SP 1/89, fols. 220–30), presented to Thomas Cromwell but
intended for the king's eye. For the circumstances, see my *Foundations of Tudor Policy*
(1948), pp. 142–44, and G. R. Elton ("Reform by Statute: Thomas Starkey's
Dialogue and Thomas Cromwell's Policy," *Proc. of the British Academy* 4
[1968] : 165–88), whose views, particularly as to dating, differ from my own.

4. See my *Foundations of Tudor Policy*, pp. 14–16, 46, 76–77 (particularly n. 155),
184–89, 232.

5. *The Discourses*, ed. Max Lerner (1940), p. 112.

Between these extremes, sixteenth-century thought tended to
gravitate. La Perrière flatly equates civility and policy: "Policie is
derived from πολιτεῖα which in our tongue we may tearme
Ciuilitie, and that which the Grecians did name Politicke
gouernement, the Latines called, the Gouernment of a Commonweale, or Ciuile societie." [6] Adam Islip who was apparently the
translator as well as the printer, reflects current usage. In the
popular mind, civility, unlike gentility, could not predate the
origin of societies; but neither were all present societies civil. Loys
Le Roy, following the argument of Lupset in Starkey's *Dialogue*,
assumes:

> An universall and everlasting Law printed in mens hearts,
> and sowen in their brests long time afore there was any
> ordinaunces written, or any citie founded; upon the which
> Lawe all other particular, locall, and temporall Lawes ought
> to be grounded, and by the same also ruled, moderated &
> expounded. It hath derived equitie from nature . . . and
> hath made us truly to understand, that Law & Justice consist
> not in opinion, but are naturally graffed in humane crea-
> tures.

However, in spite of this unschooled capability, Le Roy sees no
evidence to support the theory of a Golden Age. If we look into
antiquity, we shall find that

> the people which inhabited in old time the Countrie where
> wee dwell now, were as rude and uncivill three thousand
> years agoe, as are Sauages that have lately beene discovered
> by the Spaniards and Portingales towards the West and
> South parts of the world. They dwelt scattered here and
> there in caves of mountaines, and in Forrests under Cabines,
> without law, without Iustice, without Counsell, without
> magistrate, without Religion, and without any forme of
> marriage.

6. Translated in 1598 as *The Mirrour of Policie: A Worke nolesse profitable than
necessarie, for all Magistrates, and Gouernours of Estates and Commonweales*, sig. A.

Only gradually they began to draw into companies, into hamlets and villages induced for friendship's sake and enforced by necessity and adversity. Eventually, they also made laws, for though by intent men are civil, yet they are subject to passions.[7] And though Le Roy does not specifically say so, passions, the vestiges of barbarity, remain to jeopardize man's long gain of civility.

Peter Martyr of Angleria was even less sanguine of the civil capability of the inhabitants of the New World. While he was willing to venture that the aborigines might "cheflyer bee allured to the Christian fayth, for that it is more agreable to the lawe of nature then eyther the cerimonious lawe of Moises, or portentous fables of Mahometes Alcharon," the experience of the Spaniards in their conquest of the Indies seemed to deny any such expectations. He has only praise for "the manhodde and pollicie" of the conquistadores who have "consumed these naked people . . . this deuelysshe generation . . . partely by the slaughter of suche as coulde by no meanes be brought to ciuilitie, and partly by reseruynge such as were ouercome in the warres, and conuertynge them to a better mynde." [8] Plainly, to Peter Martyr, a dead Indian is better than an uncivil one.

Yet it was intoxicating to imagine that the classical Golden Age of Hesiod and Ovid was no mere myth, that the supposedly long lost innocence of the Garden of Eden might somehow have persisted in some hitherto unknown region.[9] In this primitivistic spirit, there were those who found or professed to find gentleness, not barbarity, in alien peoples. No one, least of all the worldly-wise Thomas More, knew where Utopia was. "I am ashamed to be ignorant in what sea that island standeth." "Who euer heard

7. *Aristotles Politiques or Discourses of Government*, translated . . . into French by Loys Le Roy . . . into English [by John Dickenson], 1598, sig. B, Bii^v–Biii.

8. *Decades of the New World*, trans. Richard Eden (1555), sig. Cvii^v, Aii^v.

9. The exhaustive account of classical primitivism by A. O. Lovejoy and George Boas, *A Documentary History of Primitivism and Related Ideas in Antiquity* (1935), has been recently supplemented by Harry Levin, *The Myth of the Golden Age in the Renaissance* (1969). Our paths, I note with pleasure, have crossed on more than one occasion.

of th' Indian Peru?" Edmund Spenser asks, guilefully concealing
the whereabouts of his golden land of Faery. As for the voyagers,
they saw what they wanted to see. To Columbus, they were "the
best people in the world, and the gentlest"; Europeans could not
be compared with them. Philip Amadas and Arthur Barlow,
whose expedition to Virginia had been fitted out by Spenser's
patron at court, Raleigh, marveled at the discovery of "a
handsome and goodly people, . . . in their behavior as mannerly
and civill as any in Europe." The classic ideal was now a reality:
"We found the people most gentle, loving and faithful, void of all
guile and treason, and such as live after the manner of the golden
age." [10] In such archetypal perfection, it was pleasant to find
proof that even before the European patterns of civility had
emerged, the world was governed by a law of nature established
by God and written in the heart of man.

No Golden Court

Spenser suffered under no such delusions, though there are in
The Faerie Queene persons of no court breeding who providentially
come to the rescue of distressed ladies: Satyrane, the unschooled
but innately civil schoolmaster to beasts; Tristram, the "tender
slip . . . in woodsman's jacket of Lincoln green"; and the wild
man, who until the moment when he heard a lady's "loud and
piteous shright . . . did taste of pittie, neither gentlesse knew."
All, despite their lack of courtly training, exhibit the courtly
virtues. In all three, virtue is inherent, and either expressly or by
implication, all are of noble blood; yet all are in need of the civil
training of life at court.

Satyrane conforms to the pattern, but peripherally. He is the
child of "a lady mild" and a Satyr,[11] "noursled up in life and
manners wilde, / Emongst wild beasts and woods, from lawes of
men exilde." He has an instinctive impulse to rule, and he makes

10. *First Voyage Made to the Coast of Virginia*, Hakluyt Society Publications, extra
series, no. 8 (1904), pp. 297–310.

11. She has fallen into his hands while searching for her husband, Therion
[wild beast], "a loose unruly swayne," who preferred chasing savage beasts to
serving his lady's love (1.6.21). Cf. Shakespeare's Thurio.

it his duty to tame the wild beasts. Knowing only the laws of the
forest, he has compelled the wildest of them to bow to his will "as
a tyrans law." As he widens his conquests, his repute for never
being overthrown spreads throughout the land of Faery. His
gentler qualities do not appear until he happens upon Una
teaching "trew sacred lore" to the Satyrs. Instinct rather than
intellection moves him at first to listen, and later, without the
benefit of courtly training, to defend her against the "knightlesse
guile and trecherous train" of a Saracen knight, Sans Loy. He is
quite obviously a virtuous primitive who in spite of his lack of
education, exhibits the manner of a knight and the qualities of
courtesy. Both Sans Loy and Satyrane have made their will their
law. But Satyrane, who takes no delight in "vain sheows . . . and
courtly services," preferring "to be, then seemen sich" (3.7.29),
has by nature established law whereas Sans Loy has by the art of
courtly love tried to destroy it (1.6.3–5).

Tristram is also a type of innate nobility pitted against
discourtesy in knightly armor. Calidore, the titular knight of
courtesy, first comes upon this youth fighting on foot and without
armor against an armed knight on horseback. His whole bearing
is such that he seems of noble race in spite of his woodsman's
jacket of Lincoln green, his hunting horn, his boar spear, and
other evidences of forest life. What most catches Calidore's eye is
the boy's skill in dispatching a knight who for his graceless
conduct to his lady well deserved his fate. When Calidore accuses
him of breaking the law of arms in killing a knight, the boy's
well-spoken defense of his action confirms Calidore's conviction of
his nobility. Tristram presently reveals that he is, in fact, the son
of Meliogras, King of Cornwall, dispossessed by his uncle at his
father's death. But his royal birth has already been proved by
combat, and Calidore makes him his squire forthwith (6.2.3–39).

The clearest example in Faery land of innate nobility, however,
is the savage man of no name. Spenser's editorial comment on his
unexpectedly noble action in rescuing Serena from the discour-
teous, craven knight Turpin points up the courtesy that exists far
from court as well as "in Princes hall," that virtue "which of all

goodly manners is the ground, / And roote of ciuill conuersation"
(6.1.1).[12]

> O what an easie thing is to descry
>   The gentle blood, how euer it be wrapt
>   In sad misfortunes foule deformity,
>   And wretched sorrowes, which haue often hapt?
>   For howsoeuer it may grow mis-shapt,
>   Like this wyld man, being vndisciplynd,
>   That to all vertue it may seeme vnapt,
>   Yet will it shew some sparkes of gentle mynd,
> And at the last breake forth in his owne proper kynd.
>
> That plainely may in this wyld man be red,
>   Who though he were still in this desert wood,
>   Mongst saluage beasts, both rudely borne and bred,
>   Ne euer saw faire guize, ne learned good,
>   Yet shewd some token of his gentle blood,
>   By gentle vsage of that wretched Dame.
>   For certes he was borne of noble blood,
>   How euer by hard hap he hether came;
> As ye may know, when time shall be to tell the same.
>
>   [6.5.1-2]

In the same vein, Serena describes him to Prince Arthur and
Timias, who appear on the scene after the rescue:

> In such saluage wight, of brutish kynd,
>   Amongst wilde beastes in desert forrests bred,

12. There is no hint of egalitarianism here or elsewhere in Spenser's ideal of
society, as Donald Cheney believes (*Spenser's Image of Nature* [1966], p. 210, n. 15).
The giant and the scales (5.2.30–50) had already settled that. The *Viewe* would
confirm it. To see in the presence of the savage man an argument that "a
flourishing society" should "unite [man's] brutish and gentle natures to achieve a
cultured mildness of manner which is constantly being invigorated, strengthened,
and defended by contact with the rigors of nature" is equally alien to
sixteenth-century thought. When Arthur presently constrains the savage man's
impulse to tear Turpin in pieces (6.6.39–40), he gives not the slightest evidence of
endorsing brutishness as defensible social policy.

> It is most straunge and wonderfull to fynd
> So milde humanity, and perfect gentle mynd.
>
> [6.5.29]

His inborn gentleness exhibits itself also in his courage. Lacking the "needfull vestments" of a knight, "the saluage nation" makes a naked frontal assault, and the mounted knight flees. Serena, though she is now rid of Turpin, is at first just as apprehensive of the savage's rude efforts at courtesy.

> But the wyld man, contrarie to her feare,
>   Came to her creeping like a fawning hound,
>   And by rude tokens made to her appeare
>   His deepe compassion of her dolefull stound,
>   Kissing his hands, and crouching to the ground;
>   For other language had he none nor speach,
>   But a soft murmure, and confused sound
>   Of senselesse words, which nature did him teach,
> T'expresse his passions, which his reason did empeach.
>
> [6.4.11]

True to his instinctive kindness, he performs all the knightly offices, skillfully staunching Calepine's wounds with native herbs, making the while "great mone after / His saluage mood," and offering them the crude hospitality of his mossy bed and vegetarian diet. And when Calepine in recovered health presently strays away into the forest, wrests a baby from the jaws of a bear, and exits temporarily from the narrative, the wild man dons Calepine's armor after his untutored fashion and sets forth as her squire, "a saluage man matcht with a Ladie fayre." In the subsequent invasion of the uncivil Turpin's castle, the wild man and Prince Arthur fight side by side, the wild man flying at Turpin's retainers with tooth and nail, tearing them into pieces and roaring as he tears. Undisciplined as Tristram and the savage man are in the art of courtiership, the sparks of gentle mind break forth under stimulus of human distress, and then they act "in their own proper kind." Shakespeare's Arviragus and Guiderius react in the same fashion.

But as the idealisms of the second book of *Utopia* must be measured against the realities of the first, so the innate gentilities of *The Faerie Queene* are sharpened by Spenser's years in Ireland, a country seemingly so resistant to civility that nurture could never stick. And this in spite of its natural beauty. *The Faerie Queene*, it must be stressed again, was written far from the English court, amidst such physical loveliness that it was hard to imagine its people to be anything but gentle. Yet Spenser found in Ireland a present example of inveterate barbarity. Here were no sparks of gentle mind, even though the wild Irish had been long exposed to culture. Looking for ethnological reasons—and perhaps with Tamburlaine in mind—he prefers to think of them as Scythians. They are, he is forced to concede, "a salvage nacion . . . accounted the most barbarous nation in Christendom" in spite of their literacy.[13] And their barbarism is infectious. Hard as it is to believe, many of the English who had come to Ireland in the reign of Henry II are just as rude: "Is it possible that an Englishman broughte up naturallye in suche swete Civilytie as Englande affordes can finde such likynge in that barbarous rudeness that he shoulde forgett his owne nature and forgoe his owne nacion?" (*Viewe*, p. 96). The answer must lie in that other side of man's nature to which by birth he is bound. As Grill will be Grill, so Galloglasse and Kerne, as Spenser regards them, have

> the most loathelye and barbarous tradicions of anye people I thinke under heaven; for from the time that they enter into that Course they doe use all the beastlye behaviour that maye be. The[y] oppress all men; they spoile aswell the subiecte as the enemye; they steale; they are Cruell and bloddye, full of revenge and delightinge in deadlye execucion, licentious swearers and blasphemous Comon ravishers of weomen and murderers of Children. [*Viewe*, p. 123, punctuation supplied]

Such lawlessness, Spenser believes, has persisted since "the firste evill ordinaunce and institucion of that Comon wealthe" (*Viewe*, p. 96).

13. *Viewe of the presente state of Irelande*, Variorum Edition (1932–49), vol. 9, ed. Rudolph Gottfried, pp. 43, 90.

Where civility has been so sharply resisted, sharp remedies are
necessary. Ireland has remained so backward that English policy,
harsh though it has been, can be justified. But mere suppression is
no cure, and indeed has operated to the disadvantage of those
who have attempted it. The solution, in Spenser's view, lies in the
establishment of a viable legal system. England, he recalls,
acquired civility by the imposition of Norman law; and just as
present Irish law can only be compared to the law of the Saxon
kings when England was still in an uncivil state, "annoyed
greately with Robbers and outlawes which troubled the whoole
state of the Realme euerie Corner haueinge a Robin hoode in it
that kepte the woodes and spoilled all passengers and inhabit-
antes as Ireland now hathe" (*Viewe*, pp. 202–03),[14] reformation of
Irish law might well be the means of bringing "swete Civilitie" to
that benighted country.

Spenser's perplexity over the obdurate barbarity of the Irish
was in part semantic. The imposition of culture on alien peoples
was as old as the Roman roads that insected barbarous England.
But the word for it was not on English tongues, nor would be until
the eighteenth century.[15] Not until civility could be conceived as
an exportable commodity, could "civilizing" as a concept be
possible. The occasion for it is obviously in his mind. As the
Normans once civil-ized the English, the English should now
civil-ize the Irish. Precedent for it went back to the Roman
civilization from which the Normans inherited theirs. But Spenser
does not use the word, nor does Shakespeare, though the
techniques of the Spaniards in conferring the benefits of civilization on the Incas in Peru were already advertised in Peter
Martyr's *Decades of the New World* where gentling a nation was
synonymous with Christianizing it—or, by the inscrutable methods of civilized man, with destroying it. That the word did occur

14. See the Variorum Spenser, 9 : 412, which cites Cal. Carew MSS 3. 227 and
Moryson's *Shakespeare's Europe* (1903), p. 194.

15. Boswell reports Johnson's comment on the word in 1772 (Boswell's *Life of
Johnson*, eds. G. B. Hill and L. F. Powell, 6 vols. (1934), 2 : 155) : "He would not
admit *civilization* but only *civility*. With great deference to him, I thought *civilization*,
from to *civilize*, better in the sense opposed to *barbarity* than *civility*.

in a work that Shakespeare knew well will presently appear. But to Spenser the gentling of the wild Irish had to be accommodated with the reports of Raleigh's expeditions to America. The moment had arrived when a standard of culture, hitherto stemming mainly from Roman civil life, was challenged by firsthand scrutiny of newfound lands not so oriented whose manners were un-Roman yet gentle.

It is clear therefore why Spenser was especially sensitive to the disparity between predisposition and observed fact, his experience having been at such sharp odds with theory. Fortune had thrown him for an extended period with the Irish people. Revolted by their rudeness, he not unnaturally retreated in relief to his English and for the most part London upbringing. But not wholly. The Mutability Cantos and the Pastorella episode in book VI of *The Faerie Queene* throw an idyllic coloration over the Irish landscape; they are indulgences, like all pastoral poetry, consciously ignoring the realities. In this, Spenser was two persons. Calidore's happy land of Faery is the invention of the poet; *Viewe of the presente state of Irelande* is the factual report of the secretary of Lord Grey. It represents the utmost that an English expatriate could hold in prospect for the establishment of civility in a barbarous land that he had learned to love. Yet seduced by its primitive natural beauty, he envisioned it as the haunt of Diana. Inappropriate as it might be "to sing of hilles and woods mongst warres and Knights," he could nevertheless abate the epic style to exalt venerable Arlo, "best and fairest Hill . . . in all this holy-Islands hights," and setting patriotism aside, commemorate a time

> when Ireland flourished in fame
> Of wealths and goodnesse, far aboue the rest
> Of all that beare the British Islands name.
>
> [7.6.38]

One senses here the central paradox that permeated both Spenser's and Shakespeare's thought—that a nation at one time so civil should at another time be so barbarous. But whereas Spenser conceived of the phenomenon as primarily cyclical, Shakespeare saw civility and barbarity as synchronous.

There were others, however, whose definition of civility was similarly oriented but who were less bemused by the mirage of a Golden Age and who also affected Shakespeare's thinking. Even if one grants that the law in men's hearts is innate and not a matter of opinion, has not recent experience in previously unknown lands confirmed the traditional thesis that civility which is derived from it is variable from country to country? In 1601, Gerard de Malynes observed:

> Men account that civil which is according to the manner of euery countrey, as the Prouerbe is: (Countries fashion, countries honor,) yet reason must rule herein, with a due consideration of Gods good creatures and gifts. . . . The same civility must be reduced to the good of the common-weale, and for the upholding thereof, living together in Christian society, giving so farre place unto reason that every man may endeuor himselfe to the preservation of the weale publicke, and conceive generally that other nations not indued with so much reason, are alwayes inferiour unto us in that regard, even considering all men alike in an estate of politicke government.[16]

Malynes's comfortable assurance of the inferiority of other nations is based mainly on their economic naiveté ("the simplicity of the West Indians, Brazilians and other nations, in giving the good commodities of their countries, yea, gold, silver, and precious things, for beades, bels, knives, looking-glasses, and such toyes and trifles"). Viewing the natives of the New World as little more than a commodity, Malynes could easily impersonalize civil differences altogether.

Montaigne, in his essay *Of the Cannibals*, begins with a similar relativistic premise: What is civil for one country may not be civil for another. But civility in Montaigne's view breaks through Malynes's pragmatic delimitations to the fundamental considera-tion: If it be assumed that national laws are grounded on the law printed in men's hearts, who is to judge the laws of one nation to

16. *A Treatise of the Canker of Englands Commonwealth*, sig. F2–F2ᵛ.

be superior to those of another? The country we live in always seems to have perfect religion, perfect government, perfect use of all things; others seem savage

> as we call those fruits wilde which nature of her selfe and of her ordinarie progresse hath produced; whereas indeed, they are those which ourselves have altered by our artificiall devices, and diverted from their common order, we should rather terme savage. In those are the true and most profitable vertues, and naturall properties most lively and vigorous, which in these we have bastardized, applying them to the pleasure of our corrupted taste. And if notwithstanding, in divers fruits of those countries that were never tilled, we shall finde that in respect of ours they are most excellent, and as delicate unto our taste; there is no reason art should gaine the point of honour of our great and puissant mother Nature.[17]

Having thus blandly asserted the principle of "equity derived from nature," he proceeds through a principle of cultural primitivism to a further impish assertion that the races discovered in the New World may well be superior in civility to those of the Old:

> Those nations seeme therefore so barbarous unto me, because they have received very little fashion from humane wit, and are yet neere their originall naturalitie. The lawes of nature doe yet command them which are but little bastardized by ours, and that with such puritie, as I am sometimes grieved the knowledge of it came no sooner to light, at what time there were men that better than we could have judged of it.
> [1 : 219–20]

Furthermore, Montaigne makes deft use of the proverb, *Country's fashion, country's honor*, against those who rest the case for civility on the law of nature printed in men's hearts:

17. Florio's translation (1603), repunctuated from Everyman Edition, 3 vols. (1910, reprinted, 1946), 1 : 219.

> But there was never any opinion found so unnaturall and immodest, that would excuse treason, treacherie, disloyaltie, tyrannie, crueltie, and such like, which are our ordinarie faults. We may then well call them barbarous, in regard of reason's rules, but not in respect of us that exceed them in all kinde of barbarisme. [1 : 224]

Montaigne's influence on Shakespeare has long been known; its nature and range need further attention. Whether Shakespeare had Montaigne's *Essayes* open before him when he wrote Gonzalo's description of an ideal plantation is of secondary importance compared to the reverse English that both Montaigne and Shakespeare imposed on current speculation about the inhabitants of the New World. Were they gentle or savage, rude or cultivated? Reports of voyagers were contradictory, depending on the motivation of the reporter, who often, like Malynes, considered gentleness as incidental to exploitation. But if the gentleness of the savage was "simplicity" to the profit-conscious adventurer in prospect of a new voyage, it was quite otherwise to Montaigne, whose view was humane like Spenser's, yet critical of the inhumanity and incivility of presumptively civil nations. This view, evident at the beginning of Shakespeare's career, becomes the characteristic and pervasive theme of his late plays, particularly those written after 1603. It is significant of the ideological affinity of Montaigne and Shakespeare that the paradox of civility and barbarity in mankind should be reflected most clearly in *Othello*, written in the same year as the publication of Florio's translation of the *Essayes*, that it should burgeon in the dramatic romances, and that it should culminate in the play that stemmed most directly from the voyages, *The Tempest*.

Montaigne's benign speculation on the inhabitants of the New World was only one—a late though a most congenial one—of the mediacies by which Shakespeare was to arrive at his own perspective of civility. Unschooled gentleness was much closer at hand: another less obtrusive symbol, English to the core, added its weight to the amount. That self-appointed dispenser of social justice, traditional flouter of all constituted civil order while serving scrupulously the law within himself, was Robin Hood, perennial popular image of innate nobility.

Lincoln Green

Spenser's reference to every corner of Ireland as having a Robin Hood in it needed no gloss. Robin Hood, Scarlet, and John had long since sung and played their way into every Warwickshire man's heart. A case has been made out for the popularity of the Robin Hood legend as an indirect response of the fifteenth-century deprived classes to the social injustices of their day,[18] just as some future social historian might find in the societal victimization of Mack Sennett's Keystone Cops a subliminal urge to outlawry in our own. Grant that, and a sound historical case may still be made to account for its healthy survival and broad acceptance in the late sixteenth century. John Manwood, in 1598 addressing *A Treatise and Discourse of the Lawes of the Forrest* to "the Right Honorable, Charles, Lord Howard, Earle of Nottingham, Constable of the Castle and Forrest of Windsore, and Iustice in Eire of all her Maiestries Forrestes, Chases, Parkes, and Warrens, by south Trent," sees fit to caution him that although by royal permission or sufferance inhabitants had long been tolerated in the royal forests, of late hunters and trespassers had become a nuisance, "so many do daily, so contemptously commit such heynous spoiles and trespasses therin, that the greatest part of them are spoiled and decayed." Recent research has shown that local justice in Warwickshire as in many other counties in Shakespeare's lifetime was much disturbed by banditry among forest dwellers who had settled in squatters' communities "far from any church or chapel." According to one London observer of the day, outlaws were "as ignorant of God or of any civil course of life as the very savages amongst the infidels." People bred amongst woods, he averred, "are naturally more stubborn and uncivil than in the champion countries." [19] All the more reason

18. Maurice Keen, *The Outlaws of Mediaeval Legend*, 1961.
19. Joan Thirsk, *The Agrarian History of England and Wales*, vol. 4 (1967), pp. 111, 411–12.

for close administrative control, certainly in the north and west marches. At the same time, indulgence must be allowed for a legend which in the popular mind possessed a vitality of its own and persisted as a rustic pastime entirely aside from any sting of private revenge or public danger. In May Day games on a hundred rural greens, the outlaw of the Greenwood regaled the populace by his discomfiture of the Sheriff of Nottingham. Old custom had not precisely legitimized Robin's conduct; it had merely given allowance to an area of human conduct to which the norms of legal judgment did not apply. In that green world, civility reverted to its primitive dimensions, and native justice seemed more equitable, certainly more enforceable, than the Laws of the King's Forest, which for the occasion might be suspended with impunity. What the Prince of Purpool was to the Inns of Court, the merry jests of Robin Hood were to May Day in the country.

Since Henry VIII's reign, even "the golden court" by long social custom had memorialized and indulged without sanctioning Robin's unorthodox behavior. Shortly after the coronation while the king was at Westminster with the queen,

> therles of Essex, Wilshire, and other noble menne, to the nombre of twelve, came sodainly in a mornying, into the Quenes Chambre, all appareled in shorte cotes of Kentishe Kendal, with hodes on their heddes, and hosen of the same, euery one of them, his bowe and arrowes, and a sworde and a bucklar, like outlawes, or Robyn Hodes men, whereof the Quene, the Ladies, and al other there, were abashed, aswell for the straunge sight, as also for their sodain commyng, and after certain daunces, and pastime made, thei departed.[20]

On a later occasion, the king and queen gave gracious permission to an exhibition of shooting skill by "a company of tall yomen, clothed all in grene," in real life archers of the king's guard, but for the occasion impenetrably disguised as the outlaw and his meinie:

20. Edward Hall, *The Union*, sig. AAavi[v].

Robyn hood desyred the kynge and quene to come into the grene wood, & to se how the outlawes lyue. The kyng demaunded of ye quene & her ladyes, if they durst aduenture to go into the wood with so many outlawes. Then the quene sayde, that if it pleased him, she was content, then the hornes blewe tyl they came to the wood vnder shoters hil, and there was an Arber made of boowes with a hal, and a great chamber and an inner chamber very well made & couered with floures & swete herbes, which the kyng much praysed. Then sayde Robyn hood, Sir Outlawes brekefastes is veny-son, and therefore you must be contente with suche fare as we vse. Then the kyng and quene sate doune, & were serued with venyson and wyne by Robyn hood and hys men, too theyr great contentacion. Then the kyng departed and hys company, & Robyn hood and hys men them conduicted. [Sig. KKkii^v]

Thus early, the Robin Hood tradition had been reduced to an innocuous pastime, suitable to entertain a queen of an afternoon.

Nevertheless, local administrators of justice were inclined to take a more sober view. Though Henry's gesture that the queen place herself under royal protection in the forest would hardly have shaken the even course of justice in county assizes the next morning, it was a tacit reminder of the threat implicit in this temporary suspension of customary law. One could wink at the fact that throughout the countryside on such occasions, Robin's ale flowed freely, whetted no doubt by rustic Maid Marians; but what such indulgences could lead to, every country sheriff knew. Robbing the rich to give to the poor, however appealing to popular discontent, could in no way excuse Robin's taking the law into his own hands and dispensing justice according to his own code. Understandably, Henry's officers were more inclined than their royal master to take exception to the invitation to lawlessness in the legend. The evidence is in a draft of *A Discours touching the Reformation of the Lawes of England*, written in a clerk's hand with corrections in the handwriting of Richard Morison, propagandist for Henry VIII during the Pilgrimage of Grace.[21] It was addressed to the king, probably not later than 1537, when Morison's mind was still much taken up with the residual effects of the Northern rebellion. In the course of a general critical appraisal of the present state of the common law, Morison expresses explicit concern over the widespread subversive effect of the Robin Hood plays: "In somer comenly on the holy daies in most places of your realm, ther be played of Robyn hoode, mayde Marian, frere Tuck, wherein besides the lewdenes and rebawdey that ther is opened to the people, disobedience also to your officers, is taught, whilest these good bloodes go about to take from the sheref of Notyngham one that for offendyng the Lawes shulde haue suffered execution." The solution, Morison concludes, is a substitution of more suitable outlets to popular exuberance: "How moche better is it that those plaies shulde be forebodden and deleted and others dyuysed to set forth and declare lyuely before the peoples eies, the abhomynation and wickedness of the bisshop of Rome.[22] Exasperation over the problem of law enforcement may have been responsible for an order in 1537 prohibiting May games,[23] though there was very little likelihood that the traditional indulgences on May Day could be eliminated, far less, that they could be translated into antipapal exhibitions. As might be expected, they continued unabated as an essential part of the summer folk festivals long after punitive measures had proved ineffectual.[24]

Clearly, there was no eradicating Robin as a popular symbol of excusable lawlessness, and so he remained throughout the sixteenth century. For the most part, the history of the legend is a

21. For his career, see my "Richard Morison, Public Apologist for Henry VIII," *PMLA* 55 (1940) : 406–25, and *Foundations of Tudor Policy*, pp. 227–33. For the commoners' resistance to enclosure during the Pilgrimage, see Thirsk, *Agrarian History*, p. 408.

22. Brit. Mus., Faustina C II, fol. 18.

23. *L&P*, XII, pt. 1, no. 557. See E. K. Chambers, *The Mediaeval Stage*, 2 vols. (1903), 2 : 220.

24. For references well into the seventeenth century, see John Brand, *Observations on Popular Antiquities* (1877), pp. 137–42.

history of the gentling—or one might say regentling, of a social
exile. It is no surprise that by the end of the century, the yeoman
of the popular ballads had acquired the title of Earl of Hunting-
don. John Major follows tradition in describing him as "the
prince of robbers and the most humane." An aura of civility had
by that time surrounded him, and in this glow he is reincarnated
as Valentine in Shakespeare's *Two Gentlemen of Verona*, and again
as Orlando in *As You Like It*.

Lo the Poor Indian

For Shakespeare, as for all Englishmen, the historic image of
civility was Rome. Padua could be the nursery of arts, Urbino of
courtesy, Venice of commonwealth, but *civis Romanus* memorialized all of these and the Roman *ius civile* still seemed the closest
approach to a law of nations. When Shakespeare first turns to it
in *Titus Andronicus*, the image is flawed. Titus, the admirable
Roman soldier, worthy of rule, concocts a Thyestean feast that
matches the rape and dismemberment of Lavinia in barbarity.
Thus by juxtaposition of the euphoric standard of Roman culture
turned barbarous and Moorish barbarity belying its own name,
Shakespeare creates a rough but potent irony. Implicit in
Shakespeare's thought, even at this early time, is the inexplicable
paradox in man's nature that civility and incivility should be so
inextricably intermingled. Thus early, Goths and Moors, by
expectation barbarous, may show civility; and Romans, by
expectation civil, may exhibit the utmost barbarity. And though
in *Titus Andronicus* the primitivistic pattern seems more casual than
calculated, the pattern of civility vs. barbarity is already discern-
ible.

There is danger in making too much of it. The vogue for
primitives is a familiar characteristic of every civilized culture.
Ovid among the Goths. Shakespeare, with Africa and the New
World to choose from, was more fortunate than the Roman poet,
though his mental picture of a primitive is far from clear. Live
"Indians" he could have seen without crossing the seas, but
Titania's Indian boy could hardly be offered as proof that he ever
saw one. As for Moors, Pory's translation of *Leo Africanus*, the

standard reference book to Africa in Shakespeare's time, describes
them in all shades and characteristics, and one quails before the
task of drawing a composite of Aaron, the Prince of Morocco, and
Othello. Scythians, Goths, Turks, and other barbarous folk seem
even more peripheral. Nevertheless, their stage value is estimable
from a woodcut in a late edition of the ballad of *Titus Andronicus* at
the Folger Shakespeare Library and in Henry Peacham's illustration from the play itself. Shakespeare was too much the showman
not to make use of such popular interest in other races, a contrast
apparent in both literary and environmental contexts from *Titus
Andronicus* onwards. And he takes obvious delight in the stage
spectacle of *exotisme* matched with *savoir-vivre*.

Against the backdrop of civility vs. barbarity, the revolting
cruelty of Shakespeare's earliest Roman tragedy becomes something more than a tale of revenge like Kyd's *Spanish Tragedy*. Two
decades after, Jonson sniffed off both plays as antiquated,[25] but
what Jonson's classical stomach could no longer tolerate had long
been food for the general, and our latter-day barbarities have
prepared our own generation to view it with new understanding.
"Cruel and true," says Jan Kott, too easily identifying the play
and the playwright. Plainly, if we concur with Kott's judgment,
we need not reject that of Shakespeare's friends and contemporaries. And we shall also have to review the opinion of the
stationer, John Danter, who entered *Titus Andronicus* in the
Stationers' Register in 1594 as "a Noble Roman Historye" and
printed it in the same year as a "most Lamentable Romaine
Tragedie." Jonson's observation that the play had indeed gone
out of fashion in the twenty-five or thirty years since it was written
had been attested in the meantime by Shakespeare's own
practice. Cruel it is. But to see the cruelty and not the nobility
and pity engendered by it is to miss its essential irony.

Shakespeare could expect that his audience would immediately
recognize in the Romans and Goths the conventional symbols
respectively of civility and barbarism. On this understanding, the
cruelties in the play take on meaning. Whereas cruelty could be

25. Jonson's Induction to *Bartholomew Fair*.

expected of the Goths, it is the barbarity of the Romans, exemplars of the civil life, that is scandalous though hardly novel. Precedents in both Greek and Roman drama come to mind. Viewed simply in the name of revenge, the cruelties recall the Orestean cycle and the Senecan horrors leading up to the feast of Thyestes, and indeed outdo them to the point of stage tolerability. There is more than a casual suggestion of the Antigone motif in Titus's refusal to allow an honorable burial to the son he has killed for interfering with a hastily contrived political marriage of Titus's daughter Lavinia to the new Emperor whose roving eye has already rested on Tamora, alien Queen of the Goths and Shakespeare's Medea. But classical dramatists, not excepting Seneca, are concerned only peripherally with the concept of civil barbarity within which the action of *Titus Andronicus* moves. Among Shakespeare's contemporaries, we will come perceptibly closer to its central interest if we keep in mind Jonson's association of *Titus Andronicus* with *The Spanish Tragedy* in which the irony is developed around Hieronymo's forced dual roles of revenger and judge. For the irony of Titus's professed position as preserver and servant of the commonwealth is that he too finds himself in the irreconcilable role of private revenger, and that in the course of his revenges he commits a series of acts which all but obliterate order in the state he sought to preserve, and which, were it not for the extremities of cruelty practiced on him, would leave little to choose at the end of the action between the barbarity of the Goths and the barbarity of the Romans.

In this context, Tamora, Queen of the Goths, fulfilled Elizabethan expectations as the barbarous revenger. There is excuse for the revenges she plans for the sacrifice of her son as a propitiation to the Roman gods; but as instigator and witness to the stabbing of the Roman emperor's son, she richly deserves Lavinia's epithet: "Barbarous Tamora! / For no name fits thy nature but thy own!" (2.3.118–19). She exhibits the cruelty and lust of the tiger, qualities that her cubs have learned well. "The milk thou suck'dst from her did turn to marble; / Even at thy teat thou hadst thy tyranny" (2.3.144–45). For her lust, she will die still the "ravenous tiger," and Lucius speaks her proper epitaph:

No funeral rite, nor man in mourning weeds,
No mournful bell shall ring her burial;
But throw her forth to beasts and birds of prey.
Her life was beastly and devoid of pity,
And being dead, let birds on her take pity!

[5.3.195–200]

The barbarity of her Moorish lover, Aaron, is also not unexpected, and it is compounded with other villainies. That black figure of the Moor in what is in fact the only stage picture we have of Shakespeare's plays in production is a sharp reminder of the preconceptions of the Elizabethan audience. His blackness proclaims his devilishness, which his aspirations confirm ("If there be devils, would I were a devil"). But he is also Shakespeare's first Machiavellian. Contriver of a dozen devilish tricks, he regrets not performing ten thousand more. He boasts that he has no religion, no conscience. He is a ravenous tiger (5.3.5), which binds him to his mistress, Tamora, in lust as well as barbarity. Thus he adds another dimension to the structure of civil revenge set up by the Roman–Gothic contrast. After his free admission that he has laid the plot for Tamora's sons to ravish, cut, and trim the hapless Lavinia, Lucius's shocked protest, "O barbarous beastly villains like thyself!" (5.1.97), once more reminds us of the bond of barbarity shared by Goths and Moors. Yet, as with Tamora, Aaron is not without human instincts. Though he would bring up his child on primitive fare "to be a warrior and command a camp" (4.2.175), he displays an almost animal instinct for the protection of his black springald. So roused, by his own admission, "the chafed boar, the mountain lioness, / The ocean swells not so as Aaron storms" (4.2.138–40). And for an alien, he exhibits remarkable literary discrimination. Not every Moor hearing Horace's "Integer vitae" would recognize the wound dealt by it.

One may confess the misgiving that the character as an artistic creation does not quite come off, and still not doubt Shakespeare's main intent. For though Aaron is repeatedly described as barbarous (2.3.78; 5.1.97)—and the epithet seems quite insufficient for the enormities that he recites in the jocose mood of the

Barabas and Ithamore crime recital in *The Jew of Malta*—nevertheless, in the context of the whole play his conduct must act as a
countermeasure to that of the Roman Lucius, who can call him
"barbarous Moor," "ravenous tiger," "accursed devil," and yet,
were it not for Aaron's confession, would have hanged his black
child as the "fruit of bastardy" so that Aaron might "see it
sprawl." Nor is Lucius's sensibility so shocked by Aaron's recital
of villainies that he cannot order him down from the ladder "for
he must not die / So sweet a death as hanging presently"
(5.1.145–46). It is impossible to distinguish the barbarities of
Moor and Roman.

The same moral ambivalence invests the character of Titus. At
the beginning of the play, the Roman general is loaded with
honors. He has returned victorious after ten years of "weary wars
against the barbarous Goths" to find the commonwealth headless
and torn by the rivalries of the late emperor's two sons. Offered
the emperorship, he chooses in the interests of res publica to
disregard the popular voice and instate the elder son. But this
picture of Roman statesmanship is immediately reversed by his
decision to revenge the loss of his sons in battle by permitting the
murder of the noblest of the Goths, the eldest son of the Gothic
queen, and this in spite of her eloquent and reasonable plea:

> O, if to fight for king and commonweal
> Were piety in thine, it is in these!
> Andronicus, stain not thy tomb with blood.
> Wilt thou draw near the nature of the gods?
> Draw near them then in being merciful.
>
> [1.1.114–19]

When Titus insists that sacrifice must be made, *ad manes fratrum*,
the queen understandably cries out against the act as a "cruel
irreligious piety," and her surviving sons agree: "Was never
Scythia half so barbarous." Yet the sacrifice goes on, and the stage
is set for the excesses that follow in the name of revenge.

Blinded to his own inhumanity by the news that his remaining
sons have been condemned to death for murder they did not

commit, the honored Roman conqueror of the barbarous Goths
turns the image of incivility on Rome itself:

> Dost thou not perceive
> That Rome is but a wilderness of tigers?
> Tigers must prey, and Rome affords no prey
> But me and mine.

$$[3.1.53-56]$$

And ironically, before the play is played out, Titus, the erstwhile
revered Roman soldier, will chop the sons of the Gothic queen
into messes, the image of the tiger as a symbol of barbarism
uniting all alike (5.3.4–5, 195). That civil wilderness will continue
to haunt Shakespeare's mind to echo again in Lear's cry: "Tigers,
not daughters!" and in Timon's crazed and misanthropic diatribe
against the Athenian wall "that girdles in these wolves." But the
paradox of civil barbarity is already clear. As Titus tells his son
Lucius, if Rome, the apex of ancient civility has become a
wilderness of tigers, "How happy art thou then / From these
devourers to be banished!" (3.1.56–57).

The play begins with a military flourish: "Royal Rome" is
about to crown a new emperor. It closes with Lucius's order to
throw Tamora to the beasts for her beastly life. In the later
quartos, Lucius further orders that justice be done on Aaron,
"that damn'd Moor, / By whom our heavy haps had their
beginning" (they didn't), "then, afterwards, to order well the
state," thus softening to the play's disadvantage the sheer
brutality of an action in which the rapid succession of enormities
gives the lie to Rome's fabled nobility. Dramatic necessity forces
the conclusion that at the close of the action, gentleness has been
blotted out by a Roman revenge comparable in its ferocity to that
of the most barbarous of races.

A Man Cross'd with Adversity

Rome is not far from Verona; and though Titus and the two
gentlemen of Verona bear no other resemblance, they embody the
same pattern of incivility removed to a courtly context. Put to the
test in the rude conditions of the forest, one of the two, Proteus,

the changeable, violates the laws of friendship, dishonoring the name of gentleman and thereby living up to his own. Valentine, by contrast, banished when his elopement with the Veronese duke's daughter is betrayed by his friend, remains constant in spite of Proteus's perfidy. The reinstatement of their friendship at the end of the play puts the case for courtly conduct in its most extravagant form.[26] In the interim he seeks safety in the woods, a sojourn which gives the play a character quite different from its courtly source. There he joins a band of outlaws as "king" of their "wild faction" after exacting from them the promise that they "do no outrages / On silly women or poor passengers" (4.1.37, 71–72). They accept him the more readily since, as they profess, some of their band are also gentlemen born, but "thrust from the company of awful [lawful?] men" because of acts of such youthful lawlessness as conniving to steal away a lady (Valentine's gambit though the lady is his own), stabbing a gentleman, and other "such-like petty crimes as these" (4.1.46–52). Whatever gentlemanly reservations may be made for such social peccadillos, they would have identified Valentine as a figure of Robin Hood, even without the broad hint in the oath of one of the outlaws: "by the bare scalp of Robin Hood's fat friar" (4.1.36). Mainly by this innovation, deliberately introduced in the story as Shakespeare found it, a romantic tale becomes domesticated without destroying its foreign charm.

If, as has been suggested, there is any underlying social protest in the Robin Hood legend, it is not detectable in the almost casual confessions of Shakespeare's outlaws. They are after all, by definition, merry men, "thrust" into a strange adventure. Always their conduct must be judged on the important consideration that they are gentlemen, brought up in one of the centers of Italian culture. Their present condition, living au naturel, is a novelty; not a permanent state of affairs but an enforced estrangement

26. The tone of the play is sufficient warrant that Silvia's victimization in the process is to be disregarded in favor of her dramatic function as a sacrifice to Valentine's impulsive generosity to his friend. In *The Merchant of Venice*, a similarly extravagant proof of friendship is saved by wit.

from civil custom. And though they are outlaws, they have not
become beastly like some of Spenser's unneighborly Robin Hoods
in Ireland. On the contrary, their response to banishment from
civil life is to organize a commonwealth of their own with an
informal code of laws. Thus, by setting up a primitive society,
they have given proof that man is by nature a political
animal—in Thomas Starkey's words, "borne and of nature
brought forth to a cyuylyte, and to lyue in polytyke ordur.[27] But
human nature being what it is, Valentine has difficulties in law
enforcement. Though they have chosen a king, they have
continued to "make their wills their law," especially when they
"have some unhappy passenger in chase," and Valentine has
"much to do / To keep them from uncivil outrages" (5.4.14–17).
In spite of their gentle birth, living in a state of nature in the
Veronese woods is obviously far from conducive to civility.

Nor have the two gentlemen from Verona arrived in the forest
with any such expectation. Quite simply, the civil life is lived in
cities, not in the country, and Shakespeare was too much a
country man to entertain false notions of an ideal life to be found
there. There were those who did. It will be recalled that in
Starkey's *Dialogue*, Pole holds to the primitivistic view that life is
more virtuous in the wild forest, as in the Golden Age, whereas
Lupset maintains that vice is not the fault of cities so much as the
"malice" of their inhabitants (*Dialogue*, fol. 35). Pole concedes the
force of Lupset's argument without challenging the essential
paradox in man's nature: Allowing, as both parties to the debate
do, that civility in man is innate, the question remained whether
primitive man was inspired to civil life primarily by his prelapsar-
ian dignity or defensively against his lapsarian malice. If Lupset
was indeed right, speculation about either a past or a still
surviving *aurea aetas* would be frivolous; but it would not follow
that the odds for civility would rest with the Machiavellians.
What would follow is that Valentine's role as king of the outlaws
is indispensable, not merely in keeping them from "uncivil
outrages," but in recognizing that as "men endued with worthy

27. *Dialogue between Pole and Lupset*, fol. 34.

qualities" they are capable of reformation and a return to civil life.

The pattern is thus set in Valentine which will be repeated with variations from Orlando in *As You Like It* to Prospero in *The Tempest*. Valentine is a banished man, but far from adopting the ways of outlaws, he carries his civil customs with him and in time can be expected to return to Verona as a model of the civil life. Further, his continuing love both for Silvia and for his friend Proteus, even after Proteus has acknowledged his perfidy, confirms his identity with the society from which he has been temporarily excluded—this in spite of the fact that he devotes as much linage to his love for Silvia as to his concern for his sylvan companions. He is, as he confesses, a man crossed with adversity; but his crosses are those of a distressed lover rather than those of a Robin Hood at odds with the society which bred him. The greenwood becomes little more than a convenient but momentary backdrop for his euphoria, in which he follows the fashion of the ideal courtier, as constant as he is content with a vision of the girl back in Verona, who in his absence has been serenaded with the most delicate lyric grace by the renegade Proteus. "Beauty lives with kindness." But if Silvia excels in kindness each mortal thing upon the dull earth dwelling, so Valentine by "giving" her to the friend who has betrayed him is excellent in that kindness which is the mark of civility. By this quality, Valentine dispels the less savory aspects of the Robin Hood legend. In a rough society, he is an advocate of the law rather than a truant from it. For Falstaff, spending a bibulous evening at the Boar's Head tavern with a Maid Marian on his knee, acquaintance with the Robin Hood ballads is appropriately broad and convivial. For Valentine, they serve a gentler purpose.

In this regard, the two gentlemen of Verona become something more than the pasteboard figures of a romance. Not very clearly, certainly not artistically perfected, the contrast between them penetrates below the mere and preposterous love rivalries of Shakespeare's sources[28] to the capability of man in an unculti-

28. *PMLA* 65 (1950): 1166.

vated environment to live up to his natural dignity and civil estate. However tentatively, but quite as much as in *Titus Andronicus*, the paradoxical nature of man's supposed civility is here being tested. It was not surprising that with the discovery of strange customs of living in hitherto unknown lands, *The Two Gentlemen of Verona* should reflect the new parochialism in social outlook. As Montaigne put it: "We have no other ayme of truth and reason than the example and Idea of the opinions and customes of the countrie we live in" (*Of the Cannibals*, 1 : 219). Bacon, surveying the same phenomenon from Plato's cave, observed: "Although our persons live in the view of heaven, yet our spirits are included in the caves of our own complexions and customs, which minister unto us infinite errors and vain opinions, if they be not recalled to examination." [29] So Shakespeare's Valentine, setting out to broaden his education by travel, advises his friend Proteus: "Home-keeping youth have ever homely wits." But later, after he has experienced the unconventional life in the forest, he wonders at his present condition:

> How use doth breed habit in a man
> This shadowy desert, unfrequented woods,
> I better brook than flourishing peopled towns.
>
> [5.4.1–3]

In this, his first encounter with the anticipated rigors of banishment from civil life, he has discovered that peopled towns and civility are not necessarily synonymous. As yet, Shakespeare does not challenge Montaigne's seductive corollary that primitive peoples whom we regard as savage may in actuality live more virtuously than ourselves. Valentine's acceptance of "unfrequented woods" for "peopled towns" is romantically inspired, his distresses tuned to the nightingale's complaining notes. The greenwood is no political paradise. The uncivil outrages of the band of civil outlaws who make their wills their law merely accent the paradox of civil barbarity without modifying it.

English tradition was indulgent in this respect. How else would

---

29. *Advancement of Learning*, bk. 2, sec. 14, ¶10.

it have been possible, despite the Sheriff of Nottingham, for a Robin Hood to provide entertainment in the forest for Henry VIII, that inveterate searcher for legalities? Yet it was a limited indulgence. No one could believe that the action in *The Two Gentlemen of Verona* would end in the forest. The forest could be no more than a sojourn in a green world of unreality, pleasant to wish for, hardly to be hoped for. At his return, Valentine will find Silvia in the mansion of his own heart, "so long tenantless" as to have grown ruinous and in danger of falling, to "leave no memory of what it was" (5.4.7–10).[30] Now restored to his proper home, he will resume his place in Veronese society, forgive Proteus's "rude, uncivil touch" (5.4.60), and plead the return of his erstwhile banished companions. As he assures the Duke of Verona in begging for their forgiveness:

> They are reformed, civil, full of good,
> And fit for great employment, worthy lord.
>
> [5.4.156–57]

We have no reason to doubt it. Outlawry has yielded to civility, and Verona and "one mutual happiness" wait just over the next hill.

Yet Am I Inland Bred

In *As You Like It*, the action moves again from court to forest and back. The set and characters are thematic variations on *The Two Gentlemen of Verona*: Arden for the Veronese woods; Orlando for Valentine. Again the theme is civil barbarity—Oliver for Proteus—and the statement is made with even more clarity and markedly greater finesse. Structurally, Shakespeare gains in depth by handling the story on two parallel levels which join at the close in an identical resolution. There are in fact two banishments of two brothers, the Duke Senior by Duke Frederick, Orlando by Oliver. Both are victimized by persons and in settings superficially civil; both are relegated to the inhospitality of the forest; both are

---

30. The same image was to carry over presently into *Romeo and Juliet*, 3.2.26–27, 85; 3.3.107–08; 5.3.106–08.

constrained by conscience to forgive the inhospitality of their
brothers; both ultimately regain their proper positions in society.
As in *The Two Gentlemen of Verona*, the removal to the forest is
merely a sojourn, but it is catalytic to the action; and in the key
sequence, where Orlando intrudes into the presence of the
banished duke, incivility is denied and civility affirmed in both
word and symbol.

To both Orlando and the Duke Senior, the Forest of Arden
suggests a primitive state of society, but the image of it as created
in their minds is utterly different. Orlando, long depressed by his
arrogant brother, sees it as only another rough test of his
self-reliance. He has been deprived of the benefits of his deceased
father's will and kept "rustically at home," his gentility "mined"
for lack of education. Yet he has exhibited an innate gentility
which even the overbearing Oliver grudgingly acknowledges:

> He's gentle; never school'd and yet learned; full of noble
> device; of all sorts enchantingly beloved, and indeed so much
> in the heart of the world, and especially of my own people,
> who best know him, that I am altogether misprised. [1.1.
> 172–77]

Rosalind unwittingly states the obverse of his case: "Fortune
reigns in gifts of the world, not in the lineaments of Nature"
(1.2.44–45). Orlando's natural lineaments in fact elicit such
loyalty in the ancient household servant Adam that he willingly
gives up his long retainership to endure with his banished master
whatever rigors forest life might impose.

They expect no Garden of Eden. Armed against adversity, they
find life away from the court wholly conformable to their
expectations—"uncouth" and "savage." It is a shelterless desert
from which, in view of Adam's starving condition, Orlando must
wrest food or become it. His drawn sword symbolizes this hard
primitivistic view, presently to be confirmed by the menace of
gilded snake and hungry lioness. Little wonder that Adam,
disappointed with court and country alike, should in imitation of
his primal namesake yearn backward in time to an ideal "antique
world, / When service sweat for duty, not for meed" (2.1.57–58);

and that Orlando should assume the role of a Robin Hood in a desperate attempt to enforce courtesy at sword point.

Banishment to the other brother, the Duke Senior, expects no such hardship; however rigorous the inclemencies of nature, they will be preferable to the unkindness of man. If in this respect, his image of the forest is antithetic to Orlando's, his behavior is just as much a recoil from court incivility. In his own sophisticated way, he too plays Robin Hood in the Forest of Arden. But unlike Orlando, his every want has been provided for. In his greenwood, the icy fang and churlish chiding of the winter's wind constitute a stylized figure of inhospitality, the envious court from which he has been unkindly expelled no longer a peril, and hardly more personal than the light song on the summer lips of the professional singer, Amiens, who professes no enemy but winter and rough weather with which he has had no experience. It is a pretty fiction, a sweet use of adversity, for the duke and his comates and brothers in exile. Not only is he well fed; he luxuriates in every minute of his appointed role as outlaw. He is of course a primitivist, albeit somewhat Chesterfieldian both in scope and point of view. The Forest of Arden is for him an image of the sophisticated court, and he nourishes his wit by translating the whole natural landscape into the customary manners of civil life. In fact, he so revels in the pleasure dome he himself has built in the forest that he pointedly rejects returning to the society which banished him. And banishment makes its own sophistical compensations. He who would find sermons in stones and books in the running brooks could easily persuade himself that he was living, for the time being at least, "like the old Robin Hood of England," and that the impermanent and improbable society of young gentlemen who are purported to be flocking to him daily are indeed his merry men who "fleet the time carelessly as they did in the golden world." Unlike Valentine's band of outlaws, they require no discipline, content to share their captain's euphoric vision of social perfection as it existed in the prime of the world.

All but one. One among the duke's company, the cynical Jaques, stands apart from the rest, yet beloved of the duke for his caustic comments on civil and golden world alike. In his jaundiced view, all societies are equally derisible; his experience in the forest has merely enlarged the scope of his satire. What to the banished duke is an idealistic Garden of Eden, is to Jaques a dyspeptic image of court folly. Citizens are fools. But to meet a fool in the forest is proof positive that the simple life of the country is as rich a subject for ridicule as the city which he has hitherto found it his pleasure and made it his duty to anatomize. The duke sees good in everything. Jaques sees good in nothing; and from this vantage point he can now inveigh indifferently against country, city, and court. All human qualities, from the mewling and puking of the infant to the apoplectic second childishness of old age, are the subjects of his derisive laughter. No one is denied passage in his narrenshiff, even the duke, who though a victim of usurpation has himself established a society in the forest and thus usurped the kingdom of the beasts. In his inverted world, Jaques would be a fool himself in order to escape censure for his anatomy of folly, and it will do little good for the duke to remind him that he has once been "a libertine, / As sensual as the brutish sting itself." Thus the motley of the fool, together with the susceptibility of all humankind to his criticism, becomes the excuse for his antisocial conduct and an effective cloak for its essential brutality. Or so he reasons, and without reason, he avers he must die. As the duke's company sits down to a woodland feast, Jaques diverts them by translating the forest into an image of court incivility, turning outward the side of man's nature most subject to ridicule—most open, that is, to the incivilities that stock the quiver of the professional satirist.

It is of little point to argue that Jaques has almost no part in the movement of the play. In fact, his role as a static observer of the action not only defines by contrast Orlando's genuine civility; it may well be Shakespeare's response to the limitations of the satiric mood then current on the London stage.[31] He had acted in Ben Jonson's *Every Man in His Humor* where Jonson's declared intention was to sport with human follies, not with crimes; a merry play of knaves and fools, not yet crossed with the victimizations that cast

31. O. J. Campbell, *Shakespeare's Satire* (1943).

a somber shadow over the action of *Volpone*. Shakespeare may here have anticipated Jonson's tragicomic dilemma, and reaffirmed the course already evident in *Much Ado About Nothing*. In that play, it takes the very real plight of Hero's rejection at the church to dispel the affectation of Benedict and Beatrice and reduce them to a mutual confession of love; and the comic pattern there set is repeated in *As You Like It* and *Twelfth Night*. Thus, Jaques' casuistic indictment of human frailty is devastatingly refuted by Orlando's sudden intrusion into the duke's feast to demand food. In this, their first confrontation, human need sweeps aside affectation and exposes the inhumanity to which satire must ultimately be reduced. For the hungry Orlando, the Forest of Arden is no escape from court incivility; it is a forest of wild beasts from which subsistence must be wrested by force, even though, like Rosalind, he is "inland bred" and knows some nurture. To his utter surprise, instead of savagery, he encounters the Duke Senior's good manners and a proper reminder that he may be a despiser of them. So chastened, Orlando concedes that "the thorny point of bare distress" has taken from him "the show of smooth civility," but he insists nevertheless that "I and my affairs" be answered without revealing the humanitarian reason for his demand. The way is thus opened for the Duke Senior to anchor the root of civility in kindliness: "Your gentleness shall force / More than your force move us to gentleness" (2.7.102–03). Orlando is starving for food, but his own gentle background asserts itself, and he refuses to eat until Adam's needs are answered.

There can be no question that the Robin Hood motif has up to this point been near the surface of Shakespeare's mind. Orlando's flight to Arden from the repressive tactics of his brother, his precarious life in the woods as an outlaw, his care for the welfare of the starving Adam—these are sufficient reminders to an audience familiar since childhood with the legendary fugitive from justice who undertook the correction of local inequities in the administration of the law. But characteristically it is here supplemented and broadened to include all human kind by a current literary image of equal humanitarian value. Jaques' sardonic descant on the seven ages of man is dexterous but merely contrapuntal to Orlando's reentrance bearing old Adam on his shoulders. To Shakespeare's audience, Orlando is the figure of Aeneas bearing his father Anchises from burning Troy. For Shakespeare, it is invariably a humanitarian image,[32] though never more explicitly used than here. Without use of words, it becomes a symbolic confutation of Jaques' incivility. Presently it will become verbal in Orlando's gentle pulpiteering:

> Why should this a desert be,
> For it is unpeopled? No!
> Tongues I'll hang on every tree
> That shall civil sayings show.
>
> [3.2.133-36]

And when Jaques at their next meeting invites Orlando to join him in railing against "our mistress the world and all our misery," Orlando's retort confirms the humanitarian base on which civility rests: "I will chide no breather in the world but myself, against whom I know most faults" (3.2.294-98). This is more than a confutation; it is a foreshadowing of his decision to rescue his brother from the perils of gilded snake and hungry lioness, an exhibition of kindness nobler ever than revenge, of nature stronger than his just occasion (4.3.129-30). In Orlando's willing forgiveness of unnatural conduct, the nature of civility is conclusively defined. Whether in city, country, or court, it is a natural gentility, equally evident in the Forest of Arden and in the still-vex'd Bermoothes. It is no coincidence that in a similar situation in *The Tempest*, Prospero will use almost the same words. The grain of the wood is here for the first time exposed.

Flight from Reason

Bertram in *All's Well That Ends Well* sharpens that definition. For while Orlando's gentleness is never for a moment in doubt in spite of the test put upon it, Bertram's conduct brazenly and even willfully denies the gentility he was born to. Both Orlando and

---

32. 2 *Henry VI*, 5.2.62; *Julius Caesar*, 1.2.114; *Troilus and Cressida*, 4.1.21.

Bertram have lost courtly and highly respected fathers. But whereas Orlando, deprived of a courtly education by his brother exhibits the instincts of gentle behavior, Bertram, for all his courtly schooling, takes the opposite course. There is no escaping it—as a pure bounder, he has no equal in the entire canon, and few critics have had the temerity to defend him. Thrusting aside the name of his illustrious father, the hopes of his mother, and an offer of attendance on the king, he has taken up with the newer court fashion, betraying his noble birth in open violation of the courtier tradition.

The inexcusableness of Bertram's rebellion becomes even clearer as Shakespeare develops the story from his sources. One of the soundest guides to Shakespeare's thinking is that noble figure of his own invention, Bertram's mother, the Countess. Bereaved of her husband, she places all her expectations in this "unseason'd courtier," who should succeed his father "in manners, as in shape."

> Thy blood and virtue
> Contend for empire in thee, and thy goodness
> Share with thy birthright!
>
> [1.1.70–73]

The king, too, seeing that he bears his father's countenance, hopes that he has also inherited his father's moral integrity rather than adopted the fashion of the present generation of courtiers who are "mere fathers of their garments." So prepared for, Bertram's revolt from the courtier tradition can be expected as a dramatic necessity.

It is significant of this modern mode that Helena, the main structural counterpoint to Bertram, is associated on stage with the scurrilous Parolles, who undertakes to educate her to modern court manners and a newer kind of virtue. For her, as for Bertram, the court should be "a learning place." But under Parolles' extracurricular instruction, it becomes an academy where "virginity, like an old courtier, wears her cap out of fashion." As Bertram is expected to go to the wars, "nursery to our gentry," to prove his courtiership, so Helena according to her new instructor is expected to fight a defensive but losing battle to preserve her virginity, since virginity is "not politic in the commonwealth of nature." Furthermore, he arrogantly assures her that after the wars he will return "perfect courtier," "in the which my instruction shall serve to naturalize thee, so thou wilt be capable of a courtier's counsel and understand what advice shall thrust upon thee" (1.1.219–23).

Helena is as indifferent to these allurements as Bertram is indifferent to hers. The sum of Bertram's interest in Helena is in the performance of her duty as a waiting woman to his mother, the Countess; yet she entertains the unlikely but not wholly ingenuous belief that by curing the king's disease, her merit will win Bertram's love. Her problem, as she expresses it with astonishing clarity to her self-appointed mentor in courtly immorality, is not to preserve her chastity; that she would be glad to lose to a man of her own liking. But losing her chastity to a man who is bound for the wars and a thousand loves will hardly win him. Rather, she must overcome her inferiority in social rank as the daughter of a physician, and this could be done if in fact she had inherited her father's powers. Innate virtue, not educated vice, becomes quite literally not merely the chief hope for the king's recovery but her hope for a husband. Thus by an odd parallel circumstance at the beginning of the action, the fortunes at court of both Bertram and Helena seem to depend on the heritability of native qualities hitherto untested. They are yet to learn that neither the physician's art nor the art of war as practiced by their respective fathers will suffice in determining their own courtly qualifications, though Helena at least has great faith in the part that inherited powers must play:

> Our remedies oft in ourselves do lie,
> Which we ascribe to heaven. The fated sky
> Gives us free scope; only doth backward pull
> Our slow designs when we ourselves are dull.

[1.1.231–34]

But it is the Countess who understands that Helena "without other advantage may lawfully make title to as much love as she finds." Phrased in more muscular language than Castiglione's, she recognizes the surface distinctions of rank between Helena and her son, yet discerns the deeper natural affinity which might overcome the class barrier that separates them. In this understanding, the Countess offers to "mother" her, knowing that often "adoption strives with nature, and choice breeds / A native slip to us from foreign seeds." But Helena refuses, pleading her humble birth, even as she plays with the dilemma of becoming thereby a "sister" to the man she hopes to marry. Of one thing she is certain: she will not have him until she can find the way to deserve him (1.3.107–206). Answering the same natural instincts, Perdita in *A Winter's Tale* will reject the suggestion that she include pied flowers in her garden.

Now for Bertram, who has perennially called down the obloquy of critics, some defense seems called for. He is on trial as a courtier under the wardship of the king and the expectant eye of his mother. This would seem to be responsibility enough. But now he is suddenly confronted with a royal command to marry Helena. Surely we are to understand that his rejection of Helena, aside from his bad manners, is not wholly indefensible. He has in fact been trepanned. And allowing for W. W. Lawrence's views on this matter, one can hardly deny the validity of Bertram's manly and courageous plea: "In such a business give me leave to use / The help of mine own eyes" (2.3.114–15). His position in this respect is precisely like Helena's. The trouble is that Bertram's eyes haven't helped him to recognize her quality. He cannot abide a poor physician's daughter as a wife, even though the king offers to add title and wealth to her natural virtue. Thus, for quite different reasons, both Helena and Bertram reject the principle of innate virtue. It is the king's cogent argument at the organic center of the play which wholly confirms the Countess's judgments by negating rank-bound qualifications of nobility:

> Strange is it that our bloods,
> Of colour, weight, and heat, pour'd all together
> Would quite confound distinction, yet stand off
> In differences so mighty. If she be

> All that is virtuous—save what thou dislik'st,
> A poor physician's daughter—thou dislik'st
> Of virtue for the name . . . Good alone
> Is good without a name; vileness is so:
> The property by what it is should go,
> Not by the title. She is young, wise, fair,
> In these to nature she's immediate heir;
> And these breed honour.
>
> [2.3.125-40]

Helena's virtue is not merely an acquirement from her father's skill in medicine; it shines out in all she does. Nor can her low place blemish the honor she deserves but falsely rejects. Bertram, inheriting the tradition of court life and self-assured in the rank he inherits, has rendered himself incapable of recognizing her value. By his too rigid application of the courtier code, he has denied the claim of nature. Thus both have exhibited a form of unreason which Shakespeare had already satirized in the love patterns of the earlier comedies. When Helena "seeks not to find that her search implies, / But, riddle-like, lives sweetly where she dies!" (1.3.222-23) and Bertram rejects the proffer of Helena, "I cannot love her, nor will strive to do't," they echo Phebe's disdainful rejection of Silvius, "I shall not pity thee," and Olivia's rejection of Orsino, "I cannot love him," and both are answered by reason—by Rosalind's "Who might be your mother, / That you insult, exult, and all at once, / Over the wretched?" (*As You Like It*, 3.5.35-37) and by Viola's "In your denial I would find no sense" (*Twelfth Night*, 1.5.285).

But Bertram's unreason is more deeply seated and therefore harder to cure. Helena, already successful physician to the king, must now be physician to Bertram, a role in which she will act as both agent and beneficiary, in which the powers exercised are again inborn, and reason and nature are in involuntary but inviolable alliance. It is a pattern which is immediately recognizable as a major theme in *Cymbeline* and *A Winter's Tale*. For the moment, however, though the king forces their marriage, Helena presumes to be no more than his "most obedient servant" (2.5.77) and Bertram not only ungallantly refuses the service she offers but denies his own birthright in an orgy of uncourtly warring and wenching. A Beaumont and Fletcher audience would sympathize with Bertram as a hapless victim of conflicting loyalties: Let him stifle his personal feelings, and submit to the obvious injustice of the king's arbitrary command. But Bertram, of course, does nothing of the sort. With the encouragement of Parolles, another Falstaff to another Hal, he outwardly yields to the king's order to marry Helena, only to disobey it as soon as he is free of the court.

A proper alliance of reason and nature would have prevented such a course; but until that takes place, Bertram's shedding of natural ties amounts to an act of self-directed treason. The gravity of this act is indicated with the sharpest dramatic precision after he commands Helena to return to his mother's home, and then vows that he will never come there as long as there are battles to be fought. "Away, and for our flight!" he shouts to Parolles as they rush off to battle. To which his mentor in courtiership responds delightedly in his best Italianate manner, "Bravely, coragio!" (2.5.94–97). As Parolles well knows, his pupil has advanced far in courtly learning of the newer sort. The battlefield in Parolles' pragmatical ethic offers as convenient a means of escape from Helena as it does from the trivial sentimentality of Richard Lovelace: "I could not love thee, dear, so much, / Lov'd I not honor more." Helena accepts all responsibility for his flight from court; and since Bertram has vowed not to return while she remains there, she too steals away, leaving the Countess to lament that

> He cannot thrive
> Unless her prayers, whom heaven delights to hear
> And loves to grant, reprieve him from the wrath
> Of greatest justice.
>
> [3.4.26–29]

What neither tutor nor pupil understands is that Bertram's miseducation is in fact flight from himself. There are reports that he has flagrantly dishonored his inheritance by giving away his family ring to seduce a Florentine gentlewoman, an act correctly diagnosed as a revolt against his own nature. "Now God delay our rebellion!" is the reaction at court as it becomes clear not only that the noblest born carries within himself the seeds of his own corruption, but that he cannot save himself from his own corruptibility. "As we are ourselves, what things are we!" effectively anatomizes Bertram's defection. They at least in a moment of self-revelation sense its meaning: "Merely our own traitors." And while Bertram indulges his appetite for pleasure, they sense also that his escape is only self-delusion: "And as, in the common course of all treasons, we still see abhorr'd ends, so he that in this action contrives against his own nobility, in his proper stream o'erflows himself" (4.3.23–30).

So it is with Bertram, and so, it would seem to be with man in his unnatural condition. The course which Bertram adopted to become a courtier in le beau monde has led in headlong and irrational flight from self to rebellion and treason against the values he was born to and indeed cannot escape. Does *All's Well That Ends Well* reveal, in essence, the bankruptcy of the courtier tradition? Paris and Florence, hitherto accepted finishing schools for gentlemen, the battlefield, traditional "nursery to our gentry, who are sick / For breathing and exploit," have now produced—a Bertram. Spenser's grand design in *The Faerie Queene* "to fashion a gentleman or noble person in vertuous and gentle discipline" seems hopelessly passé in a world which has become traitor to its own heritage. Confronted with such incivility and moral profligacy as Bertram's, would it not be better to seek education in courtiership beyond the traditional centers in France and Italy? In some such quandary, the extraordinary alternative of untaught civility titillated Shakespeare's fancy just as it did Spenser's and Montaigne's.

Perhaps, it is reasonable to conjecture, as Shakespeare fingered through the mint pages of Florio's translation of Montaigne on the cannibals his mind flashed back to an outlandish tale of Cinthio's about an unsophisticated Moor, by European standards a barbarian. The resulting play carries an implicit cultural paradox in its title. Noble as Othello, the Moor of Venice, is, he never forgets that he is a servant to the city most renowned for government. In Lipsius's words, Venice was a city "lifted up with the stablenesse of a thousande yeares continueance." La Perrière states the point precisely: "Neither do the Venetians euen to this day admit strangers to any dignity in their commonweale, as we may see in their histories written by the learned and eloquent Antony Sabellius, and Gasper Contarene, yet notwithstanding, they execute both good and seuere iustice." [33] Othello was a hireling stranger to Venice; yet in present danger of Turkish invasion, he was cast to be its savior and preserver.

An Extravagant and Wheeling Stranger

Rosalind's arch chiding of Jaques for his affectations of Italian manners at the expense of his own country (4.1.33–38) is hardly more than any untraveled Englishman would have heard in the streets of London. But the purview of the Moor reaches far beyond the Venetian horizon, opening up broader vistas and stranger new lands than even Aaron or Portia's suitor, the flamboyant Prince of Morocco, had laid eyes on. No Italian city was by reputation more cosmopolitan than Venice, and Shakespeare's Venetian ladies could be expected to reflect their sophisticated environment. Portia, that widely sought-after golden fleece to other hopeful Jasons, is merely mildly amused by the scimitar that slew the conqueror of the Sultan. It can only be imagined what her response would have been to Othello who, according to his own unvarnished tale, had carved out much of his career beyond the margins of civil life. He had looked without fear upon the most barbarous races known to man—Anthropophagi and men with heads between their shoulders. Turks, the dread of Europe, were no more than a familiar and detested nuisance to him. Little wonder that Desdemona, no ingenue amidst the polished frivolities of the little world of Venice, should have been awed as much by the grave composure of the Moor as by his far-flung adventures. Whether Shakespeare discovered him in a map of Ortelius, in Raleigh's Guiana, or in the Africa of Leo,

33. *The Mirrour of Policie* (1598), sig. Lliiiᵛ. La Perrière endorses the Venetian custom of excluding all strangers from office.

or in all of these, is inconsequential. What is of the utmost consequence is his racial difference, his strangeness—which separates him from them as it does them from him. Not consciously stressed in Shakespeare's first deliberate stage representation of black and white in Moor and Roman, it becomes in *Othello* far more than a constant visual confrontation. Aaron is devilish, the Moroccan prince merely pompous. Othello is militarily indispensable, yet for all his prestige, in the closed society of Venice, he is nonetheless an intruder. Thus, the initial contrast of color is immensely amplified by social disparity, the more discomforting since a rigid Venetian code of manners is now a means of exhibiting in sharp relief an innate nobility easily exceeding the surface polish of civility which surrounds him. Artistically, the cultural ambivalence of Aaron which vitiated the emotional potential of Shakespeare's earlier Moor has now been surmounted, with the result that the whole range of ethnic values which his audience associated with the opposed images of sophistication and primitive life is now given free play: Venetians as the epitome of an Italian culture of which the Moor confesses his ignorance; the Moors as distant Africans, barbarous though capable of civility, but above all, strange—perhaps ineradicably —to Italian manners. In the sensitive dramatizing of these accepted incompatibilities lies the kinetics of love and fear, basic in the play. "To fall in love with what she fear'd to look upon" is as false as it is true.

One may measure the distance Shakespeare has traveled since writing *Titus Andronicus* by the fact that Aaron, with his strong admixture of Machiavellian deviltry, is inconceivable in Othello's place. Equally incongruous, for that matter, is Shakespeare's other Moor, the tawny Prince of Morocco, resplendent with a retinue and a hilariously self-conscious dignity, who prejudices his suit to Portia by first apologizing for his complexion, and once departed is "a gentle riddance." Othello at the beginning of the action is wholly confident of himself, not merely because of his royal blood but because of his earned reputation as a soldier. As a man, he appears and acts head and shoulders above his compeers in Venetian society. The senators seem like dwarfs by comparison with him. When he strikes his wife, they are shocked, not by the possible injustice of his act but by his bad manners: "My lord, this would not be believ'd in Venice, / Though I should swear I saw't" (4.1.253–54). In the presence of these marionettes, Othello is magistral. "Keep up your bright swords, for the dew will rust them," is spoken above the level of scorn. But he is totally unarmed against the real or imagined sophistications of the society he serves and to which he has committed his fortunes. For servant he is—universally respected, it is true, but still a servant. And so he describes himself at the end of the play. Hitherto eminently self-sufficient, he has now put his "unhoused free condition" into conscription for the love of Desdemona, daughter of one of the signory. He is a proud Moor, but by choice and profession, a Moor of Venice, and therein lies the tragedy and the pity of it.

In this state of social innocence, he is admirably conditioned to become the fascinated and fascinating prey of Iago, whose egocentered deviltry, unlike that of Aaron, springs only remotely from revenge, primarily from a sportive use of his talent to deceive. His victim is an alien, and Iago's aim is to make him conscious of it, to persuade him that his marriage is a mistake, and to suggest to him what in cool logic should follow from such a mésalliance. At the same time, he plays artfully on the subliminal suspicions of an alien race in Brabantio, Desdemona's father. His attacks are exquisitely tempered to the instincts and fears of both races. He is in turn the self-effacing yet knowing tutor of Venetian manners to Othello, of barbaric bestiality to Brabantio, of brute force to Roderigo; and all his victims become poisoned and presently wholly enmeshed in his elaborate web. The design, contemptuously improvised as he goes, is all. His mind dances. He is neither motiveless nor malign. He states his reasons, but they are palpably insufficient or insupportable by his conduct, and in effect they cancel out each other. His real reason he keeps to himself. He is evil only incidentally, moral considerations being irrelevant to his zest for the game. Roderigo, who regards him as a friend, and Emilia, who regards him as a husband, are both useful tools to conceal handkerchiefs or to

knock out brains—dispensable when they have served his purposes. Like Machiavelli himself, he is primarily, dispassionately,
an artist, and the fact that he causes tragedy is an incidental if
necessary consequence of the awesome success of his art.

The measure of Iago's success is Othello's reversion to his most
primitive instincts. Brabantio, casting desperately about to explain his daughter's infatuation with "the sooty bosom" when she
has "shunn'd / The wealthy curled darlings of our nation," can
only believe that Othello used charms to enchant her, "arts
inhibited and out of warrant" in a civil society, an imputation
which Othello amusedly denies. Yet Iago, who works by wit, not
witchery, picks up the point as he softens up Othello for the kill:
"He thought 'twas witchcraft." And presently, ironically, from
Othello's own lips, Desdemona learns with horror that magic
indeed inhabited the very threads of the handkerchief that she has
so inadvertently mislaid. Iago's potent medicine works, and before
he is done, Othello is persuaded that she has become a strumpet,
whose eyes, "those charms," must be blotted from his heart.

But it is in ethnic revulsions that Iago finds his most deadly
weapon. "To fall in love with what she feared to look on" is an
acceptable non sequitur in the social milieu of Venice, whether it
be keyed to inflating Roderigo's hopes: "A frail vow betwixt an
erring barbarian and a supersubtle Venetian," or to educating
Othello's ignorance of the Venetian haut monde. At one moment,
he affects the humor of the boudoir, at another, the voice of social
bias:

> I know our country disposition well:
> In Venice they do let heaven see the pranks
> They dare not show their husbands; their best conscience
> Is not to leav't undone, but keep't unknown. . . .
>
> [3.3.201–04]

> Not to affect many proposed matches
> Of her own clime, complexion, and degree,
> Whereto we see in all things nature tends.
>
> [3.3.229–31]

Brabantio is genuinely perplexed: "For nature so prepost'rously to err" (1.3.62). Even Emilia muses in the same vein: "Hath she forsook so many noble matches, / Her father and her country, all her friends" (4.2.125–26). We shall find the end of it in her later outburst: "O, the more angel she, / And you the blacker devil!" (5.2.130–31). But, by then, Othello has fulfilled his commitment to the social code of Venice ("else she'll betray more men"), and Iago's careful artistry of destruction is complete.

It is pertinent to this emergence of barbarity that the coarse sexual imagery with which Iago first describes the elopement to the sleepy Brabantio transfers to Othello as he becomes infected with Iago's poison; and that Roderigo's reference to "the gross clasps of a lascivious Moor" is twice picked up in Othello's language of savagery:

> I had rather be a toad
> And live upon the vapour of a dungeon
> Than keep a corner in the thing I love
> For others' uses.
>
> [3.3.270–73]

> to be discarded thence
> Or keep it as a cistern for foul toads
> To knot and gender in.
>
> [4.2.60–62]

In another mood, equally savage, he will "tear her all to pieces," thus reliving Thyestes' feast in imagination as Aaron did in practice.

But barbarity is not the character of the Moor. He is, of course, a Christian, like Desdemona, and it is significant that her miraculous landing on Cyprus during the storm is coincident with the withdrawal of the Turkish fleet, and coequal with the pictured adorations of the Virgin Mary.

> O behold!
> The riches of the ship is come on shore!
> Ye men of Cyprus, let her have your knees.

> Hail to thee, lady! and the grace of heaven
> Before, behind thee, and on every hand
> Enwheel thee round!
>
> [2.1.82–87]

Likewise, the storm of emotion in which Othello kills Desdemona is brought to a climax in a perverted "sacred vow," though in both instances ethnic, not religious considerations are paramount. In this context, Turks, not Moors, were the more effective symbol of barbarism to Shakespeare's audience, and the contrast between Turkish and Christian ethics is maintained throughout the action. Othello's own words in quelling the street fight carry their proper weight:

> Are we turn'd Turks, and to ourselves do that
> Which heaven hath forbid the Ottomites?
> For Christian shame, put by this barbarous brawl.
>
> [2.3.170–72]

Around this contrast Shakespeare builds his closing irony. At the beginning of the play, Othello is the preserver of that Venetian society which destroys him. Yet with the passing of the threat of war against the Turks—in Richard Knolles's phrase, those "barbarous" and "capitall enemies of the Christian commonwealth" [34]—the civil war of barbarism vs. civility within Othello has just begun. It is a war that he will now end with self-destruction as a fancied enemy to that same society, even as

> in Aleppo once
> Where a malignant and a turban'd Turk
> Beat a Venetian and traduc'd the state
> I took by th' throat the circumcised dog
> And smote him—thus.
>
> [5.2.352–56]

It is a last heroic gesture which dismisses not lightly the signal reputation he has gained as servant to the Venetian state to

---

34. *The Generall Historie of the Turkes*, 1603, dedication to King James.

identify himself with "the base Indian" who in failing to recognize
Venetian values "threw a pearl away / Richer than all his tribe,"
and with the Turk, who in beating a Venetian deserved the
ignominious death he now metes out to himself. To Emilia, who
in spite of her occasional obtuseness understands those values as
well as any in the world of Venice ("It is a great price for a small
vice"), the murderer of her mistress is a "most filthy bargain," his
deed no more worthy heaven than he was worthy her. He is a
dolt, "ignorant as dirt." Iago earlier speaks the same language to
the believing Moor: "Take note, take note, O world, / To be
direct and honest is not safe" (3.3.377). Now Othello's education
is complete.

Such worldly estimates prepare us for Othello's own self-ap-
praisal as loving not wisely, and in a world where honesty has
limits, too well. We as audience will recall Iago's remark to
Roderigo at the beginning of the play: "I am not what I am," as
Othello now insists, "Speak of me as I am." For what he is affirms,
even as Iago's civil barbarity denies—that civility in civil life is a
stranger.

A City of Beasts

Viewing civility in these terms, it is a brief journey from Venice
to Athens; on almost any other terms, it seems far removed, and
critics of *Timon*, seeing little to praise in either workmanship or
style, almost universally have not excused it without labor. To
Kittridge and many others, it is an obvious fact that Shakespeare
never really finished the play. But textual and structural frailties
notwithstanding, the central proposition in *Timon* is as clear as
that of *Othello*, and in fact follows upon it. Athenians, like the
Venetians in *Othello*, like the Romans in *Titus Andronicus*, represent
a high degree of culture; yet like other reputedly cultured nations,
they are capable of the utmost incivility. Unkindliness in friends,
a theme for which Shakespeare need not have gone beyond
Plutarch, associates the play with *Lear*. Both Lear and Timon fall
victims to flattery, the counterfeit currency of civil life; both
define the beastliness of mankind in terms of ingratitude. And
there are, of course, verbal likenesses: the same naked, houseless

wretches of *Lear* are still bare and unhoused in *Timon* (*Lear*, 3.4.26–32; *Timon*, 4.3.227–31).

But there are important differences, and they serve to underline the peculiar astringency of the later play. The sense of redemption in *Lear* disappears from *Timon*. Lear's exchange of kingdom for hovel is forced and presupposes a return; Timon's rejection of civil life in Athens for root-gnawing in the surrounding woods is of his own doing and remains irrevocable. Lear's anguish is given human dimensions throughout the action by the personal loyalties of Gloucester and Kent, and the inhumanity of Goneril and Regan is offset by the careful ministrations of Cordelia at the end. *Timon* is not without this warming element. Servants, especially Timon's steward (4.3), are embarrassed by his bankruptcy and show sympathy and loyalty to him in his distress. But he gains nothing in audience sympathy by comparison with Alcibiades who yields to entreaty on humanitarian grounds and gives up his plan to destroy Athens, whereas Timon not only remains obdurate to persuasion to return to civil life but continues to contaminate the Athenians with the gold that has brought about his alienation.

The net indictment of society must therefore be less clear in *Timon* than it is in *Othello*. It is indeed as much by its banishment of Alcibiades, its chief soldier, as by its incivility to Timon, its chief citizen, that it earns the diatribes at the play's center. Not for any love of beasts does Timon, like Coriolanus, banish the city that bred him. By any standard of civility, Athens has proved itself predatory by nature. In his over-violent revulsion at the unkindliness of Athenians, he renounces mankind, and in this respect the train of Shakespeare's thought moves more directly beyond Othello, who is perplexed in the extreme by a great world of Venice of which he knows nothing. Timon's experience with his fellow citizens has taught him only to hate them and by extension, to hate "all living men." Othello in killing Desdemona is still the Moor of Venice: "She must die, else she'll betray more men." Timon, consumed by hate, is no longer Timon of Athens but by his own choice, a citiless corpse, expecting only curses from those who survive him.

To this end Shakespeare seems to have deliberately depersonalized the Athenians. Lucius, Lucullus, Sempronius, Ventidius are simply Flatterers, inhabiting the same circle of Timon's purgatory. The insipid Ladies in the Masque of Amazons, though they represent the five best Senses, are paid for their dry entertainment with an "idle" banquet. Nameless senators use the law to "bruise" an erstwhile defender of Athens. A Poet and a Painter, having heard a rumor that Timon still has gold, pursue him to the woods hoping for reward in return for the mere promise of praise. They are faceless predators all, in a society of no moral values. Given a chance to be generous, they find "no power to be kind" (3.1.61) though Timon has previously loaded them with kindness. The most trenchant comment on the spiritual depravity of the city comes as a choral comment from a shocked Stranger: "O, see the monstrousness of man / When he looks out in an ungrateful shape!" (3.2.79–80). The civil world, observing the present state of Athens, can conclude only that men must now dispense with pity, "for policy sits above conscience."

As the mark of civility is kindness, so incivility exhibits itself in policy. Fortified by ingenious equivocation, each of the beneficiaries of Timon's generosity folds his conscience away and refuses under one pretext or another to help him, the latest of them lest his help "prove an argument of laughter / To the rest." One of Timon's loyal servants puts a timeserver's conduct in its proper context: "Excellent! Your lordship's a goodly villain. The devil knew not what he did when he made men politic" (3.4.28–29). Only his retainers in fact maintain the line of proper conduct against the "politic love" of the new possessors.

Timon's revulsion to the social turnabout is violent and excessive. Like Lear who tears off the hypocritical vestments of society and Coriolanus who rejects Rome for an alien city, Timon seeks the woods as a refuge from civil savagery. Like them, he expands his indictment to include all of mankind:

> Th' Athenians both within and out that wall!
> And grant, as Timon grows, his hate may grow
> To the whole race of mankind, high and low!
> Amen.

[4.1.38–41]

His servants still wear his livery in their hearts, but they realize that his "fierce wretchedness" cannot be stemmed. The misanthrope—now himself depersonalized—has turned away from "all feasts, societies, and throngs of men," quite willing to see Athens destroyed by its own captain, Alcibiades, a figure of military destruction of a city, itself an image to Shakespeare's audience of a once-living but now corroded culture.

This allegorical turn of the play is its distinguishing quality. Lear's anguish over the ingratitude of his daughters is a personal thing, finely balancing the moral blindness of habituated egoism and a growing sense of compassion, not to be cured until he has learned by suffering to strip himself of the garments of royalty in which he has hitherto presumed to judge his fellowmen and discovered the humility of nakedness. "Off, off, you lendings!" is an act instinct with human feeling on the part of a man who has felt himself—and justifiably—more sinned against than sinning. But Timon's similar claim against his fellow citizens is not so complicated by pity; it is reported impersonally by the Poet:

> I am rapt, and cannot cover
> The monstrous bulk of this ingratitude
> With any size of words
>
> [5.1.67–69]

And Timon's response is a desiccated aphorism: "Let it go naked; men may see't the better" (5.1.70).

No less contributory to the air of allegory in the play is the satirical extension of the mood of Timon in the churlish philosopher, Apemantus. To him, Athenians per se are knaves (1.1.182); to knock out an honest Athenian's brains would be doing nothing (196). Timon welcomes Apemantus to his table because he is an Athenian, but Apemantus refuses: he will not eat lords (207). In Athens, "the strain of man's bred out / Into baboon and monkey" (259–60). At the height of Timon's diatribe against flattery, he seeks him out to scoff at his hate for mankind. They are suitable companions, professional cynic and professed hater of men, at one in their rejection of the civil life. Athens has shown itself to be unkind, ungentle, and therefore by definition, uncivil. "What wouldst thou do with the world, Apemantus, if it lay in thy power?" asks its own answer: "Give it the beasts, to be rid of the men" (4.3.321–24). In the confusion of men and beasts, Apemantus would remain a beast with the beasts, for "the commonwealth of Athens is become a forest of beasts" (352–53). Timon, too, will leave Athens to the beasts that they "may have the world in empire" (392–93). Giving gold to the bandits is a natural consequence of this rejection, and the loyalty of his steward only accents by exception his universal hate.

It remains for Timon like Coriolanus to refuse to give up exile and return to Athens to protect it from Alcibiades who threatens the city. His only response to the delegation of Athenian senators is an offer of a tree to hang themselves on. As for himself, he has set up "his everlasting mansion / Upon the beached verge of the salt flood," where his last message to Athens is carved on his gravestone: "A plague consume you wicked caitiffs left!"

To Wales, Bohemia and Back

If the highest European culture can breed such creatures as Iago and Timon's flatterers, what hope is there for finding better elsewhere? Perhaps in Wales, breeder of kings? Or in pastoral Bohemia (presuming that Bohemia has pasture)? Or in Tunis, so far from Naples that it could not be reached till newborn chins be rough and razorable? Perhaps Shakespeare never asked the question. Nevertheless, the late romances suggest fleetingly, such possibilities, as if from the imagination of a man willing to persuade himself that it might be so. Looking at *Cymbeline* as a point of vantage gained, a voyager will find, I hope, no great difficulty in identifying past as prologue. For in that play the organizing symbols of civility and barbarism are explicit and dominant. A Jacobean audience no more than an Elizabethan would cavil at its casual blend of Roman and Italian culture. By comparison with the ethnic hodgepodge of *Titus Andronicus,* it is mild indeed. But whereas in *Titus,* the primitive elements that spring up within the ethnic norm of Roman culture are Goths and

Moors, the at-that-time sufficient symbols of savagery, in *Cymbeline*
they are early Britons, whose barbarous conduct springs paradoxi-
cally from innate nobility.

Initially, the cultural grouping is reminiscent of *Othello*. Imogen,
the king's daughter by a previous marriage, shows her good taste
by refusing to marry her step-brother, Cloten, a dull clod who
hires ballads sung to his mistress's eyebrow, taking up rather with
Posthumus Leonatus, "a poor but worthy gentleman" at court.
When her father, Cymbeline, protests, "Thou took'st a beggar,
wouldst have made my throne / A seat for baseness," she responds
with the confidence of Desdemona rejecting the social eligibles of
Venice, "Would I were / A neatherd's daughter, and my Leonatus / Our neighbor shepherd's son!" (1.1.141–50). Iachimo is a
replica of Iago for sophisticated court manners, and in the same
gamesome spirit, yet exceeding Iago in boldness, he succeeds in
convincing the credulous Posthumus of his wife's infidelity by
claiming that he himself is the correspondent. Early in the action
Posthumus is persuaded that he has been completely victimized
and breaks out in the same overblown rage as Othello, but
dissolves immediately into quasi-comic flaccidity:

> O that I had her here, to tear her limbmeal!
> I will go there and do't, i' th' court, before
> Her father. I'll do something—
>
> [2.4.147–49]

He is a man of words, not deeds. His "I'll do something" means
that he will do nothing at all. Like Othello, he talks of vengeance
and persecutes himself with similar sexual phantasms:

> O, all the devils!
> This yellow Iachimo in an hour—was't not?
> Like a full acorn'd boar, a German one.
> Cried 'O!' and mounted; found no opposition
> But what he look'd for should oppose and she
> Should from encounter guard.
>
> [2.5.13–19]

But he relapses into emasculated invectives against women and a peevish vow to "write against them / Detest them, curse them" (2.5.32–33).

This is Othello reorchestrated. Shakespeare not only shrinks the score but replays it in a changed key, stopping short of tragedy, and only narrowly skirting the familiar comic overtones of cuckoldry residual in the theme. Symphonically, the action of *Othello* is a single sustained downward movement; *Cymbeline*, in a mood of disengagement from reality, the new mood of the dramatic romances, looks toward resolution rather than tragic irony. It is a symphonic poem in two parts, the second half the complement and counterpoint to the first. The immediate service of the first movement is to establish the Italianate refinements of court life, the second to remove the action to the pastoral setting of Wales where natural instincts can operate. Here Shakespeare is following the pattern of *As You Like It*; but again with a difference measurable by Rosalind's coquetry and Imogen's composure under the insidious pressure of Iachimo's attack. Thus by stressing the imminence of tragedy, *Cymbeline* brings into larger focus the contrast tentatively presented in the earlier play between the incivilities of civil life and the validity of man's moral intuitions. This contrast is already clearly foreseen in the first part in Imogen's deliberate choice of innate worth in Posthumus, and in her equally resolute rejection of Iachimo's offer of sexual pleasure, insolently concealed under cover of revenge for "that runagate" Posthumus's alleged "vaulting variable ramps" in Rome. Coming as it does before Posthumus has swallowed Iachimo's bait, Imogen's integrity creates the thematic bridge to the action in Wales.

In that pastoral setting the theme is immensely strengthened by the two princes, diamonds in the rough, who show "the sparks of nature" but profess that since they have seen nothing of the art o' th' court they are beastly. They yearn for experience in the civil life to which they are destined by birth; but Belarius, the old courtier who kidnapped them in revenge for the loss of his lands, is in the meantime making an ineffectual effort to turn each act of

their day into an emblem of the comparative virtues of rustica-
tion. To them Imogen comes in search of her husband. Acting
very much like Orlando, she approaches their "savage hold" with
sword drawn, an empty stomach, and an expectation of inhospitality: "If anything that's civil, speak; if savage, / Take or lend."
Fortunately, the cave is empty, and by the time Belarius and the
boys appear with the day's kill, she has made herself at home
browsing on the cold meats. The situation is a bit awkward, but
she begs and receives entertainment; and in less time than it takes
to read the verses, she is singing like an angel as she fashions the
hors d'oeuvres, marveling at such "kind creatures" who belie the
accepted opinion that "all's savage but at court" (4.2.33).
Meanwhile, the supercilious Cloten, seeking the life of Posthumus,
is given a different reception. With his talk of "runagates" and
"villain mountainers" and "lawbreakers," he shows himself
unworthy of the princely birth he boasts of, and is shortly less a
head by the hand of Guiderius, who in spite of Belarius's fears has
no compunction in exercising west-of-the-Pecos justice:

> The law
> Protects not us. Then why should we be tender
> To let an arrogant piece of flesh threat us,
> Play judge and executioner all himself
> For we do fear the law?
>
> [4.2.125–29]

Quite unknowingly, the boys follow the law of their own instinct,
a law of nature engraved in their hearts, for which they could
easily have found authority, had their tutor Belarius read with
them in Tudor political theory. To insure, at any rate, that the
audience will not miss the implications, Shakespeare allows
Belarius a soliloquy on the paradox of natural civility:

> O thou goddess,
> Thou divine Nature, how thyself thou blazon'st
> In these two princely boys! They are as gentle
> As Zephyrs blowing below the violet,
> Not wagging his sweet head; and yet as rough

> (Their royal blood enchaf'd) as the rud'st wind
> That by the top doth take the mountain pine
> And make him stoop to th' vale. 'Tis wonder
> That an invisible instinct should frame them
> To royalty unlearn'd, honour untaught,
> Civility not seen from other, valour
> That wildly grows in them but yields a crop
> As if it had been sow'd.

> [4.2.169–81]

What Belarius wonders at would have been clear to Shakespeare's audience. It is this invisible inner compulsion which will move them to the valorous deeds in the narrow lane, restore them to their princely place, and bring the peace between Roman and Briton so loved of the gods. As Rome begat Britain, so a worthy father begat worthy sons, though like Spenser's Satyrane they are ignorant of their origin.

We shall find this same invisible instinct equally operative in Bohemia. In its two-part structure, *The Winter's Tale* corresponds closely to *Cymbeline*. Again the urbanities of the first part give way after a sixteen-year interval to the broadly pastoral atmosphere of the second, where nature works her own resolutions. There is one important difference: the deceits to which Posthumus falls victim with near-tragic consequences originate in the quick mind of another; Leontes' delusions are self-induced. It is an instance, the last, of Shakespeare's intense interest in the phenomenon of the divided mind, which in various contexts he had successively dramatized from Hamlet to Bertram to Troilus. This vast civil war in the microcosm, blown up out of the elaborately artful social amenities incident to the mere departure of a household guest, is an unallowable display of distempered irrationality, a divorce of the laws of reason and nature, which in Richard Hooker's hierarchy of laws are the same. There is a fundamental disruption here for which the term "dramatic romance" is inadequate.

Leontes' conduct publishes his lack of reason. Before the tongueless obsequiousness of his court, he condemns his wife and

proclaims his own child a bastard. Only the sane Paulina calls
these self-deceits by their right name, "unsafe lunes" (2.2.30). He
is traitor to himself in denying the visual evidence which "the
good goddess Nature" has imprinted in the child, the heritable
physical qualities of "eye, nose, lip, / The trick of's frown, his
forehead"

> nay, the valley
> The pretty dimples of his chin and cheek, his smiles;
> The very mould and frame of hand, nail, finger.
>
> [2.3.99–102]

His speech rings with the obsession: "the bastard brains" . . .
"Shall I live to see this bastard kneel / And call me father?" . . .
"this bastard's life—for 'tis a bastard, / So sure as this beard's
gray" . . . "Carry this female bastard thence." He repents his
foolishness only after the oracle has spoken; and then he is left to
repent at leisure. But in the meantime, reason and nature are
inviolably joined in the person of Perdita, the child whom he has
bastardized and thereby for the time being lost.

The sixteen-year gap in time is more than a convenience to
allow Perdita to grow up. It throws into immediate structural
contrast her father's act of barbarous irrationality and unnatural-
ness, and her own reliance on the gentility attainable in nature's
untampered process. By refusing to allow the bastard flowers a
place in her garden, she refuses the artificialities that man has
imposed on nature and that her father has in fact imposed on her.
Polyxenes reasons with her that "a gentler scion" may be wed to
"the wildest stock" and thus produce a "bud of nobler race." But
he is in Bohemia for just the opposite reason: to prevent such a
marriage. Thus in effect he rejects his own reasoning. Perdita, on
the other hand, unable to deny the enhanced beauty of the
flowers so produced, falls back on her instinctive distrust of
the seductive alliance of Nature and Art, and like Guyon in the
Bower of Bliss, refuses any part in it. For the springs of nobility
can only rise from the basic alliance of Reason and Nature,
unadorned, unsought, innate. Gentility is sometimes covered over
by rough justice as in *Cymbeline,* when Guiderius, following the law

of his own nature, decapitates Cloten, unconsciously identifying the barbarian in courtier's clothing, even though his victim is step-son of a king. More often, artifice can give the appearance of civility when too often it conceals barbarity, as in the Machiavellian tactics of Iago and Iachimo. Perdita's love for Florizel is free of such artifice, and hence in rejecting the bastard flowers, she unconsciously follows the rule of both reason and nature in not putting

> The dibble in earth to set one slip of them;
> No more than, were I painted, I would wish
> This youth should say 'twere well, and only therefore
> Desire to breed by me.
>
> [4.4.99–103][35]

The nice parallel is that both Perdita, a shepherdess so far as she knows, and Florizel, a prince now disinherited, by heeding only their natural attraction for each other, surmount the civilized barbarities imposed upon them. Perdita forthrightly rejects, though she does obey, Polyxenes' command that they separate. Her "philosophy" quietly annihilates social codes:

> The selfsame sun that shines upon his court
> Hides not his visage from our cottage, but
> Looks on alike.
>
> [4.4.455–57]

Free of court training, she is yet "the most peerless piece of earth . . . that e'er the sun shone bright upon" (5.1.94–95), and is destined to live in sunlight. Her courtly-educated counterpart, Florizel, by renouncing his inheritance to be heir to his "affection" (4.4.492), in the end gains both. Conversely, on a comic level, the clown, a thing of art in courtier's clothing, is a gentleman to the credulous shepherd—and has been, "any time these four hours" (5.2.147–48). Whether in Bohemia or in Wales, the pattern of Shakespeare's thought resolves into a rejection of the artificialities of civil life as inimical, if not destructive, to the

35. Cf. *Hamlet*, 3.1.51–53, 148–50.

reasonable though often unreasoning laws of our nature. Apparently, Shakespeare has not forgotten that the lion will not touch the true prince.

In what climate did these ideas breed? Not, it is safe to say, in Wales nor on a seacoast in Bohemia. And certainly not in Bermuda, to which Shakespeare's thoughts with all of London would presently be turned. Long before September 1610, when the news of the miraculous survival of the *Sea Adventure* became common property—even before Shakespeare wrote *The Winter's Tale*—he had cast his eyes westward through the perspective glass of Montaigne's voyaging mind. Montaigne too had looked through other people's eyes; indeed, he professed an aversion to coach, litter, or boat.[36] But like all stay-at-home voyagers, Montaigne's view was sharpened by distance. Curious as always of immediately observable human conduct, his historical perceptivity saw it against a background of cultures preceding those of Greece and Troy:

> Before great Agamemnon and the rest,
> Many liv'd valiant, yet are all supprest,
> Unmoan'd, unknowne, in darke oblivion's nest.

> Beside the Trojan warre, Troyes funerall night,
> Of other things did other Poets write.[37]

To Montaigne past cultures were proof of the perpetual rediscovery of forgotten arts. Contrary to the current belief that the world was at present in decline, new cultures could be confidently expected. The evidence presented itself daily: "Our world hath of late discovered another (and who can warrant us whether it be the last of his brethren, since both the Damons, the Sibylles, and all we, have hitherto been ignorant of this?) no lesse-large, fully-peopled, all-things—yeelding, and mighty in strength, than ours; nevertheless so new and infantine, that he is yet to learne his A.B.C." (*Of Coaches,* 3 : 141). Furthermore, it would seem to be

36. *Of Coaches,* 3 : 131.

37. Horace, *Odes,* 4.9.25–28; Lucretius, *De Rerum Natura,* 5.326–27. Florio's translation in *Of Coaches,* 3 : 140.

the order of the world that however "maimed or shrunken" one part of the universe, another will be "nimble and in good plight." Reports from the New World seem to indicate that "they were nothing short of us, nor beholding to us for any excellency of naturall wit or perspicuitie." Indeed, their cities were of "amazement-breeding magnificence," and Montaigne deplores—how rightly in a later day we have come to know—the subjugation of such innocent people by Old World policies and stratagems of war. Had such an alteration of empires and people occurred in the time of Alexander or of the ancient Greeks and Romans "such hands . . . would gently have polished, reformed and incivilized, [mains qui eussent doucement poly et defriché] what in them they deemed to be barbarous and rude; or would have nourished and fostered those good seedes, which nature had there brought foorth . . . therewithall joyning unto the originall vertues of the country, those of [their own]." Instead, we have taken advantage of their ignorance and drawn them into "treason, fraude, luxurie, avarice and all manner of inhumanity and cruelty" (3 : 142–44).

Sorry as Montaigne's picture of the present is—not least because of the accuracy of his humanitarian discernment of its failures—it has a special significance in the history of ideas. So far as I know, Montaigne is the first to put into words the concept of racial gentling, and Florio the first to put it into English. Now that the customs of hitherto unknown cultures were being daily reported, civil-izing as an idea was bound to be verbalized; and it is characteristic of Montaigne's speculative bent of mind that he should have looked at it as a matter of give and take: "The barbarous heathen are nothing more strange to us, than we are to them" (*Of Custom, and how a received law should not easily be changed,* 1 : 109).

There is much of *Othello* in this speculation, of course. It might even be said that until Shakespeare had grasped the implications of multiple cultures and their interaction, the tragedy of the Moor of Venice could not have been written. But I find *The Winter's Tale* a more particular and at times verbal response. Leontes' "bastardizing" of his own child is a rejection of those "true and most profitable vertues and naturall properties" which Paulina recognizes as "most lively and vigorous"; and conversely, Perdita's refusal to cultivate the bastard flowers is an unwitting acceptance of the laws of nature "which are but little bastardized by ours." Hence Montaigne's paradoxical conclusion: "We may then well call them barbarous in regard of reasons rules but not in respect of us that exceed them in all kinde of barbarisme" (*Of the Cannibals*, 1 : 219–26). This bland primitivism becomes for the first time a basic premise in *The Winter's Tale*. Civilized barbarism would continue to hold a persistent and conspicuous place in Shakespeare's thought. Aaron, Bertram, Iago, and Iachimo, each in his own way, plays to the popular image of Italian deceptiveness, and their likeness will appear again in *The Tempest*. Brabantio, a senator of Venice, is blinded by his own predispositions, as presently the innocent Ferdinand will be. But in *The Winter's Tale*, Machiavellianism ceases for the moment of the play to be a dramatic force. Leontes' violent, even barbarous revolt against his own nature leaves no room for an Iago whose art gains "the point of honour." In *The Winter's Tale*, as in no other of Shakespeare's plays, "great and puissant mother Nature"—I make no exception of Lear who apostrophizes her in vain—takes special watch over the action. And at the moment of crisis, despite the confinement Leontes has forced upon both Hermione and himself, Perdita, "by law and process of great Nature," is freed from the womb, and by the same law, from his unnatural tyrannies. The succeeding action comes very close to an unqualified affirmation of Montaigne's thesis of natural nobility. For though Perdita, like Guiderius and Arviragus, is not a primitive, her judgments like theirs are intuitively rational. As for Leontes, a benign Nature, by long process of time, has reasserted its alliance with Reason.

The Still-vex'd Bermoothes and Beyond

Even as Shakespeare pondered the implications of Montaigne's imaginary voyage to "Antartika France," the news of the safe return of a very real Virginia voyage broke in London, and forthwith Shakespeare set about writing *The Tempest*. A rash of pamphlets came off the press, and it is reasonable to assume that the theatre should also have made capital of the public stir. But if

among the adventurers America seemed to be the point of access
to a primitivistic paradise, Shakespeare did little to enhance the
image. The shipwrecked ones are astonished at their apparently
miraculous escape from drowning, but they do not know, as the
audience knows, that their fortunes and their very lives are wholly
at the disposal of Prospero. There are dangers on the island,
mainly in the person of the dispossessed Caliban, but they are
dangers which Prospero has under complete control. To some
modern critics, listening to Caliban's complaints of tyranny,
Prospero's rule is harsh. But in the early seventeenth century he
was everything to be admired in a colonial governor. He has
established and maintained order on the island, putting the
inhabitants under service according to their deserts, and educating them according to their abilities. He rewards good performance of duty by shortening terms of apprenticeship, and he holds
under tight reign those who are threats to the order he has
established and maintains. If his rule is tough on occasion, it is no
tougher than the occasion warrants. Caliban has proved that he
cannot be trusted with his liberty, and is quite properly reduced
to scullery duty in spite of his protests. Yet even these chores will
come to an end when Prospero leaves him, a lonely oaf, on the
island he once inherited. He will be seen in better perspective in
the general framework of the action in which Prospero is the
central figure. Ariel, too, by Jacobean standards, has very little to
complain about. Rescued from the cloven pine, his term of service
is near its end. He grudges, like all servants, but he will be
released after his present duties are over. Toward both the
natives, Prospero's civil conduct is exemplary.

If it be allowed that in *Cymbeline* and *The Winter's Tale*
Shakespeare was inclined to conceive of civility in terms of innate
nobility, and that in doing so, he was yielding to the enormous
persuasion of Montaigne's views, then I believe that in *The
Tempest* he will be seen to have found the grounds for regarding
that position from a public point of view as insufficient. To this
end, I should first like to be specific about Shakespeare's
architechtonics in this play, especially since, so far as we know, it
is wholly of his own contrivance.

As I have already emphasized, the fundamental condition of the action at the beginning of the play is that everything on the island, every person, every circumstance, is completely under Prospero's governance. The storm is of his making, the safe and calculated dispersal of the shipwrecked ones at separate stations on the island is his. By his magical powers and the help of Ariel, nothing they do is unknown to him, and he interrupts or continues their actions at will. It is a further necessary condition of the action that the survivors of the shipwreck believe that all the others have perished, and that they believe they are free—as up to a certain point they are indeed—to do as they wish. Under these conditions, the island becomes in effect Prospero's theatre for observing man's capabilities as a political animal. Presume Montaigne's hypothesis, Shakespeare seems to say. Let us create an island as removed from Old World civilization as, say, Bermuda. Let the climate be as gentle, the air as salubrious, its fruits as plentiful as the Golden Age. In this ideal setting for plantation, how valid will we find Montaigne's suave speculations on man's innate nobility? I think something like this must have passed through Shakespeare's mind between the writing of *The Winter's Tale* and *The Tempest*. Perhaps it was while the newly returned ships from the Virginia voyage rested at their anchors in the Thames that the idea took shape in his mind. For certainly by the time he wrote *The Tempest*, he had brought the whole primitive postulate under review.

Once before, Shakespeare had set up such a contrived freedom, and his purpose then was the same. When in *Measure for Measure*, the Duke Vincentio voluntarily surrenders the rule of Vienna to a deputy and retires into the role of disguised observer, the principals are allowed to act out their parts as their consciences direct them, not knowing that they are observed. Thus their inclinations to do good or evil are permitted free play. The duke's intention is not revealed until Angelo, his appointed deputy, has publicly incriminated himself, and Isabella, Angelo's intended victim, has publicly illustrated the extremity of human forgiveness. Of the role of the duke at the close of the action, I shall presently have more to say. For the moment, allowing for a social rather than a political context, Duke Vincentio's supervision of the action closely parallels Prospero's in *The Tempest* in that each is holding a close rein on the action and in fact manipulating it toward a moment of free choice.[38]

Prospero as governor has already established the cultural pattern on the island before the Old World meets the New. But in his role as civilizing agent for both the natives and his daughter, he has gone far beyond the demands of orderly government. Conscious of the fact that the island is no more than a place of sojourn, his main effort has been to educate his daughter in the humanities in active preparation for her future role as Duchess of Naples and Milan. She has been an apt pupil, though to say truth, occasionally bored by the lectures; and she is now ready for diploma. But like the two young princes in *Cymbeline,* she is still wholly ignorant of the ways of civil life. And this is one of the reasons for the tempest and its uncomprehending castaways. By comparison, Prospero's educational experiments with the native Caliban have been a dismal failure. I can say "native" only by the narrowest of margins, since his mother, the damned witch Sycorax, was close to littering when she was dumped on the island by Algerian sailors. This son of the devil, "a freckled whelp, hag-born, not honored with human shape" (*The Tempest,* 1.2.283–84), Prospero also undertook to raise to human station, lodging him in his own cell "with humane care," in the hope of teaching him language as a first step toward civilizing him. Frail hope! The gentling process, at first loved, was presently undone by his resentment at being kept from his inheritance; the language he was taught turned to cursing; and the freedom he was permitted turned to attempted violation of Miranda's chastity. He is, in brief, that phenomenon which our professional educators refuse to recognize, a nature on whom nurture never sticks. And this, by

38. Harold S. Wilson has noted the parallel between the two plays and anticipated some of the conclusions drawn here; and though I cannot condone his view of the moral stance of Isabella, his stress of the freedom of choice as a basic structural aim in both plays seems to me sound. See his article, "Action and Symbol in *Measure for Measure* and *The Tempest,*" *Shakespeare Quarterly* 4 (1953) : 375–84.

comparison with Montaigne's cannibals ("Caliban" invites the association), is Shakespeare's sole representation of the human population of the New World! Of course, it may be suggested that in a beastlike way he is not insensible to the sounds and sweet airs that surround him, but they fall on his ears as noises from twangling instruments, a useful inducement, like Bottom's, to sleep.

Into this pattern of primitive American culture, Prospero's manufactured tempest precipitates the flower of the civilized world, their clothing and opinions undamaged. Ferdinand, the king's son and his destined son-in-law, his arms in a sad knot, is left to cool his heels on a lonely bank, "weeping again the King [his] father's wrack." The rest of the company are collected in a council of despair, a rueful wedding party, to exchange recriminations over the just consummated marriage of Claribel, heir of Naples and Milan, to distant and alien Tunis, "ten leagues beyond man's life"—a marriage, as they remind Alonso,

> That would not bless our Europe with your daughter,
> But rather lose her to an African.
> . . . .
> You were kneel'd to and importun'd otherwise
> By all of us; and the fair soul herself
> Weigh'd, between loathness and obedience, at
> Which end o' th' beam should bow.
>
> [2.1.124–31]

Brabantio would have found a sympathetic hearing in their company, and though abhorrence of miscegenation in this action is peripheral by comparison, it hints broadly enough that the familiar cultural prejudices of the Old World would doubtless be perpetuated in the New.

Other survivors of a political sort also emerge, once it is clear to them that in spite of their losses, the means of continued survival lie at hand, and that their corporate destiny, for all they know, is their own to make. To set up some form of government would seem to be an immediate necessity. But even in this narrow company, it is evident that a consensus will be impossible.

Gonzalo, with the support of Adrian, is the literate idealist.
More's traveler, Hythlodaye, had set out on his last voyage with a
ballast of books rather than merchandise, intending to return
"rather never than shortly";[39] so Gonzalo at the time of Prospero's
banishment, anticipating that even a banished duke whose
absorption in learning had cost him his dukedom would still have
need of books, had stuffed them into the leaky vessel along with
the rich garments and Miranda, never guessing that Ficino might
prove to be as important as Aristotle. Now speculating on the
opportunity to found an ideal government, he begins plantation
as a literary man would do, by quoting Montaigne's *Of the
Cannibals.* So supported, he will "with such perfection govern,
sir, / T' excel the golden age" (2.1.167–68).

But such idealism is treated with contemptuous ridicule by the
political opportunist, Antonio, who does not need to know
Machiavelli to act upon his precepts. Like his brother, Prospero,
he is an educator; but his subject is power politics, not humane
letters, and his recipe for success is simple and efficient. He knows
that when a king is asleep, he may not be long a king. Three
inches of obedient steel will be enough to depose him, and forget
your conscience. The same treatment will be equally efficacious
for that innocuous reader of Montaigne, "Sir Prudence." And
with those two out of the way, the rest will "take suggestion as a
cat laps milk." Sebastian, like Macbeth, is at first too deeply
steeped in the conventional political moralities of Erasmus's
Christian prince to catch the nearest way, too full of the milk of
human kindness to take to this new diet. Yet once his obtuseness is
overcome by Antonio's demonstrated success, Sebastian joins the
cats. Macbeth's borrowed robes hung loose about him, like a
giant's robe upon a dwarfish thief; Antonio's by benefit of
Prospero hang much feater than before. Indeed, Sebastian
becomes so apt a pupil that double murder is prevented only by
the intervention of Prospero, who through his art has foreseen the
danger. Starting from opposite premises, Gonzalo and Antonio
have each imposed their own images of governance on the island,

39. *Utopia,* ed. Surtz, pp. 104–05.

and each has been stayed, the one by mockery, the other by force.

For Ferdinand, Prospero has provided a different destiny. The Prince of Naples has been isolated from his company and presumes that they have perished in the tempest and that he is the sole survivor on a desert island. He has no design for founding an ideal society like Gonzalo, no scheme for perpetuating the treacheries of the Old World like Antonio. His present concern is his father's wrack which makes him heir of Naples, a duke with no hope of realizing his inheritance. Yet so seductive is the music that creeps by him on the waters that at the appearance of Miranda his instant fancy, reverting no doubt to Odysseus's meeting with Calypso, translates her into a resident goddess, which she is not, and a wonder, which by her name she is. Even so enchanted, his education as a prince comes instantly to his aid:

> Most sure, the goddess
> On whom these airs attend! Vouchsafe my pray'r
> May know if you remain upon this island,
> And that you will some good instruction give
> How I may bear me here. My prime request,
> Which I do last pronounce, is (O you wonder!)
> If you be maid or no?
>
> [1.2.421–27]

Miranda, whose education in the politic arts has never exposed her to the arts of love, answers with innocent hauteur: "No wonder, sir, / But certainly a maid." On the basis of her experience—she has seen two human beings in her life—she responds to Ferdinand exactly as he has to her: "Lord, how it looks about! Believe me, sir, / It carries a brave form. But 'tis a spirit." He is "a thing divine; for nothing natural / I ever saw so noble" (1.2.410–28). Quite as much as Antonio, Miranda needs control; and as Prospero prevents Antonio's evil designs, he likewise intervenes to reduce her vision to human proportions: "No, wench. It eats, and sleeps, and hath such senses / As we have, such" (1.2.412–13).

On a parallel comic level, Trinculo and Stephano have come upon gullibility of a less innocent sort. Quite willing to exploit the commercial possibilities of the island, they first toy with the idea that if Caliban were exportable as a savage Indian, he could be a source of profit in Italy. Plied with liquor, he is tame enough, even obsequious. But these very qualities suggest to the besotted pair more grandiose possibilities. They have, like Gonzalo, an opportunity to set up their own government of the isle. Caliban is willing to swear allegiance to Stephano, indeed worship him as a god, and provide him as his new master with the best delicacies the island affords. Characteristically, by image as well as by action, Shakespeare drives home the parallel responses of the moon-calf and those of the best of Milan and Naples. To the drunken Caliban, Stephano is "thou wondrous man." And Trinculo supplies the proper gloss: "A most ridiculous monster, to make a wonder of a poor drunkard!" The travesty runs its course as Stephano takes possession: "The King and all our company else being drowned, we will inherit here," and as Caliban leads the way with cries of "Freedom, high-day! high-day, freedom!" they presently find themselves by Ariel's direction "i' th' filthy mantled pool . . . dancing up to th' chins, that the foul lake o'erstunk their feet" (2.2.168–91; 4.1.182–84).

Of course it is to be remembered that the dangers to Prospero's rule are not real as long as his magical powers prevail; neither the native Caliban nor the castaways from Italy have freedom of action except as Prospero allows. But it is equally clear that Prospero's magic has accomplished his purpose—to make them think they do what they like and consequently to follow their uninhibited impulses. In this respect, Antonio and Caliban prove to be shockingly alike. There is a deadly parallel between the civil barbarity of the one and the gross savagery of the other. What three inches of obedient steel will accomplish for Antonio, Caliban can do by battering Prospero's skull with a log, or paunching him with a stake, or cutting his wesand with a knife. Caliban's uneducatability, except for his course in drinking, might even be cited in his defense. In any case, he shares the same instincts, and harbors the same lethal intentions toward the social order. The fact that Caliban, given his freedom, is here revealed as an unregenerate savage does not categorically deny the

possibility of innate gentility in the New World. He is not without
certain rudimentary instincts toward the civil life, even though his
unreasoning passions lead him to seek a means to destroy it. Far
more abhorrent is the superficially civil Antonio whose damping
of his conscience is alarmingly simple once he supposes himself
free of social restraint. Prospero's intermediacy of magic to
prevent their converging and simultaneous attacks is therefore a
final and unequivocal rejection of the societal primitivism of
Montaigne's Antartika France; but it also demonstrates the
necessity for control of the much more insidious dangers of
incivility under the masque of the conventional civil order of the
Old World. In this respect, Shakespeare's thought leads inevitably
back to the pattern of schooled civility characteristic of Richard
Hooker. While Hooker is willing to allow that in the state of
nature men might have lived without any public controls, "the
corruption of our nature being presupposed, we may not deny but
that the Law of Nature doth now require of necessity some kind of
regiment; so that to bring things unto the first course they were in,
and utterly to take away all kind of public government in the
world, were apparently to overturn the whole world" (*LEP*, ɪ.x.4).

For this reason also, Miranda and Ferdinand in the very
innocence of their love must be restrained from their natural
impulses, and at the same time, looking forward to their future
role as rulers, be made aware of the political implications of the
postlapsarian state of man. It is in part for them that Antonio and
Caliban must be controlled. For shortly, as Prospero has planned
it, the young couple must return to the Old World, just as
Rosalind and Orlando returned from the Forest of Arden, and as
Guiderius and Arviragus returned from Wales, and as Perdita
and Florizel returned from the flowered simplicity of rural
Bohemia. They must still achieve political as well as personal
sophistication. Presently, the royal game of chess must be played
out among the stark realities of lying, falsehood, treason, dissimu-
lations, covetousness, envy, and detraction by which Montaigne
characterizes the civil society over which they are destined to rule.
Only after that education is accomplished can Prospero safely
retire to his Milan where every third thought will be his grave. At

present, Miranda, though she has had education befitting a Christian princess, is still in a state of dangerous naïveté:

> O wonder!
> How many goodly creatures are there here!
> How beauteous mankind is! O brave new world
> That has such people in it!
>
> [5.1.181–84]

Her admiration must be tempered by the hard fact that the human composite, as her father has so forcefully demonstrated, from one point of view so wonderful, is from another beastly. Prospero's response to Miranda's wonder is not lost on Shakespeare's audience: " 'Tis new to thee." For him, wonder is more than a metaphor, a dream of America like all Utopias, little more than a dream.

It is time to return to Prospero's moment of crisis. As Ferdinand observes, "He is in some passion / That works him strongly." And Miranda cannot remember when he was "touch'd with anger so distempered" (4.1.143–45). He is well aware that with the approach of Antonio and Caliban, his magical powers are fast coming to their term, and that all his artistry, both actors and the set they play in,

> The cloud-capp'd towers, the gorgeous palaces,
> The solemn temples, the great globe itself,
> Yea, all which it inherit, shall dissolve,
> And . . . leave not a rack behind.
>
> [4.1.152–56]

But until that time, Prospero's duty as governor still remains, and it can properly be completed only after he has abjured his magic, broken his staff, and drowned his book. Up to that moment, his acts will have been wholly arbitrary, as if he were God; and so long as that state continues, his rule in effect will have been absolute, and in Caliban's view a tyranny:

> A plague upon the tyrant that I serve.
> [2.2.166]

I am subject to a tyrant,
A sorceror, that by his cunning hath
Cheated me of the island.

[3.2.48–50]

This is the root of Caliban's complaint, and though the freedom
that he thinks he now possesses has only succeeded in binding him
in fealty to a drunken butler, who he fancies will execute his
revenge against Prospero, "for I know thou dar'st," he has the
mind and talents of a subject, and the imagination boggles at the
prospect of government under King Stephano, even after he has
drained his cask. In any eventuality, Prospero entertains no
thought of plantation. Inevitably, the island will revert to Caliban
with the departure of the sojourners on it, and Prospero's
"tyranny" will come to an end. The more serious cause for
Prospero's present distemper is the imminent appearance of
Antonio, who has been accused by Ariel as a "man of sin," and is
at the moment in a sufficiently desperate mood to fight legions of
fiends. Not, however, fear of a desperate man intent on murder
but of an evil man allowed his freedom is the real cause for
Prospero's strong passion. Up to this time he has exercised
magical powers to accomplish his purposes; but he is first and
foremost a human being with human passions, sorely tried by
those whom he has brought under his control. As for Lear, so for
Prospero: divesting himself of arbitrary power is the necessary
precondition to human judgment. But for Prospero, divestation
will be a deliberate choice, not the result of fellow suffering in an
inscrutable universe in which ignorant man is caught up in
apparently indiscriminate cruelty. The essence of the matter for
Prospero, as indeed it is for those upon whom he must pass
judgment, is the reestablishment of their power of free choice. In
spite of the dangers, his staff must be broken, his book drowned.

The structural pattern of *Measure for Measure* earlier led to the
same conclusion. Although at the moment when Lucio plucks off
his hood the Duke Vincentio is still in the plenitude of his power,
Shakespeare's whole purpose has been to deploy the characters
into positions for judgment. Lucio's act, by divesting the duke of

his anonymity, forces Angelo's confession and conviction; but it leaves the execution of judgment contingent on Isabella's freedom to choose the course of mercy. For, to turn to Hooker again, "What we do against our wills, or constrainedly, we are not properly said to do it, because the motive cause of doing it is not in ourselves, but carrieth us, as if the wind should drive a feather in the air, we no whit furthering that whereby we are driven" (*LEP*, i.ix.i). Just as the duke, by placing Isabella in a position of judgment on the life of Angelo in payment for his condemnation of her brother gives her freedom to choose whether he live or die, so beyond Prospero's allowance of free choice for his enemies when their repentance is manifest, is his own free choice to take the risks incident to forgiveness. Even Ariel, a spirit, appeals their plight, pleading that although he is not a human being, he would pity them if he were. Obviously, Prospero should do no less. As with Orlando, "kindness [is] nobler than revenge," so the case still stands with Prospero:

> Though with their high wrongs I am struck to th' quick,
> Yet with my nobler reason 'gainst my fury
> Do I take part. The rarer action is
> In virtue than in vengeance.

> [5.1.25–28]

Shakespeare's mind in this matter is of one piece from *As You Like It* to *The Tempest*. In spite of man's depravity, the Law of Nature remains the Law of Reason; the one is the necessary counterpart of the other. It is Prospero's personal triumph that before the rising senses of his erstwhile enemies have chased "the ignorant fumes that mantle / Their clearer reason," he has forgiven the unnatural treason of his brother. "Burn his books," Caliban repeatedly urges the ambitious would-be King Stephano. He cannot know that the real source of Prospero's power lies in his willingness to burn them himself. If gentleness is the quality of civility, acceptance of choice in the judge and allowance of choice in the judged is Shakespeare's ultimate measure of civil men.

POSTSCRIPTUM

No reader needs to be reminded of the elusiveness intrinsic to an historical approach to Shakespeare's plays. We are all too apt to be bemused by an "Elizabethan world picture," static and sacrosanct, willing ourselves to disregard the fact that the sixteenth century, like all centuries, was in constant flux. But constancy is a public myth, dearly cherished.

The foregoing pages recognize the currency of this myth as a necessary preliminary to the more delicate task of describing Shakespeare's "speciality." Thus, in the first chapter, I have dealt with the historical set of his mind in the closing years of the Tudor dynasty, in the second with political considerations as the first Stuart came into office, in the third with his judicial bent in the light of legal controversy (to which he was no stranger), and in the last with the subtle union of his private and public ethic. What emerges is something that might be called the temper of his thought.

Every critic can justifiably set up different criteria. But in the area of historical concern, I can testify to the genuineness of the image on the coin. It is still negotiable in that sternest of all artistic media, the theatre.

INDEX

DATE DUE